Fantasy and Reason

GERMAN POPULAR STORIES,

Translated from the

Kinder und Hans-Märchen,

COLLECTED BY

M. M. GRIMM,

From Oral Tradition.

Published by C. Baldwin, Newgate Street.

LONDON,

1823.

FANTASY AND REASON

Children's Literature
in the Eighteenth Century

GEOFFREY SUMMERFIELD

Methuen & Co. Ltd

First published in 1984 by
Methuen & Co. Ltd
11 New Fetter Lane, London EC4P 4EE

© 1984 Geoffrey Summerfield

Typeset by Servis Filmsetting Ltd, Manchester
Printed in Great Britain at
the University Press, Cambridge

British Library Cataloguing in Publication Data

Summerfield, Geoffrey
Fantasy and reason.
1. Children's literature, English – History and criticism
2. English literature – 18th century – History and criticism
I. Title
820'.9'9282   PR990

ISBN 0-416-35780-6

CONTENTS

ILLUSTRATIONS

ILLUSTRATIONS

ACKNOWLEDGEMENTS

For encouragement of various kinds offered over several years of work on this book, I wish to record my debts to Douglas Chambers, Dame Jean Conan Doyle, David Hammond, Hugh Haughton, Marie and Seamus Heaney, Dorothy Heathcote, Martin Lightfoot, Peter Miller, Joyce Oldmeadow, Morton Paley, Edward Phelps, Adam Phillips, Gordon Pradl and the late Sir Geoffrey Keynes.

My friend Lawrence Darton first sowed the seeds of my interest in this subject, and my Berkeley students forced me to read Wordsworth in a new way; the work of M.H. Abrams, David Erdman, Marc Soriano and Eric Rabkin has been a source of varied inspiration.

I owe thanks to the staff of the Victoria and Albert Museum Library, the British Library, and of the Osborne Collection, Toronto. Jane Armstrong, of Methuen, and her pertinacious copy-editors, went beyond the call of duty in their work on the text; for this I am grateful. Thanks are also due to Peter Stockham for help with picture research and for lending books from his own collection; to Messrs Sotheby & Co. for permission to reproduce the illustrations on pages 7, 37 and 85; and to the British Library for permission to reproduce the illustration on page 231.

Judith Pearl Fishman passed a sharp pencil over an earlier draft, and for this and for much else I am thankful: it is to her that I dedicate the book.

Lay error and infelicity at my door only.

GEOFFREY SUMMERFIELD

York 1974 – New York 1982

INTRODUCTION

Enchantment proceeds from nothing but the
Chit-Chat of an old Nurse, or the Maggots in a
Madman's Brain.
(Anon, *Round About Our Coal-Fire: or Christ-
mas Entertainments*, 1734)

1

In Fay Weldon's novel *Praxis* the heroine is married to a
sober, ambitious Junior Management Director, and they live
affluently in the largest house on a 'good' estate. But she
knows herself to be cut off from the life of the spirit, which is
symbolized by the remote pulsating light of the star,
Betelgeuse.

> On summer evenings, Praxis could look through the
> graceful folds of the net curtains which looped her wide
> drawing-room windows, and see the Red Dwarf Betel-
> geuse. But the affairs of heaven and the affairs of earth
> made no contact here. Little boxes of dwelling places
> covered the hill: stars, like ornaments devised by the
> estate agent, sprinkled the sky at night, and that was that.
> No one on the hill went to heaven or hell, Praxis thought.
> All dwelled in limbo. . . .

Her children go to a nice preparatory day-school, and
sometimes 'when she collected them, she found it hard to
distinguish them from the other children'. When she contrived to make playthings for them, out of egg-boxes, they

responded by simply telling her that she was making a mess. But she persevered:

> 'See,' said Praxis. 'It's a castle with a submarine moored in the moat.'
> 'How would a submarine get into a castle moat? You are silly, mummy.'[1]

The child's precocious rebuke is, alas, not playful. But what does it mean? It is possible that the child's conception of the fantasy-castle is so clearly focused as belonging to a remote past that the play-submarine, emphatically modern, is felt to be anachronistic, and therefore incongruous. But it is more likely that this child's view of the world is already so 'realistic' that the very idea of a submarine finding its way – actually – into a moat, has to be dismissed as absurd. The rules and constraints of reality are trespassed against when submarines trespass into moats. In Fay Weldon's fiction, there is an implicit and intimate connection between the 'limbo' of the impeccable estate, the homogenized anonymity of the children, and their precocious and relentless dismissal of fantasy as 'silly'; connections that the reader of Dickens will recognize as old friends.

Almost four centuries earlier, Cervantes explored these matters in *Don Quixote*: Sancho Panza, his sensible feet on the ground – almost *in* the ground – insisted, in effect, that to expect to find submarines in moats is indeed silly. Don Quixote committed his days to the defence of the view that submarines are indeed to be found lurking in moats, and that such a fact involves us in accepting certain moral obligations. In polarizing and separating out incredulity and credulity, scepticism and belief, reason and fantasy, and in lodging them respectively in the persons of Panza and Quixote, Cervantes established the mainspring for his narrative, and for its ironies, misunderstandings, absurdity and pathos.

The Worldly Wiseman of the eighteenth century, not to mention his wife, is poised in time between Cervantes' Panza and Fay Weldon's Junior Management Director; while conversely, the eighteenth-century child, surreptitiously devouring an old 'romance', is a link in a chain that connects Quixote and Praxis: those who concede that 'reality' is all very well, but insist that no one in their right mind would want to live there all the time.

2

In Western culture, childhood is said to be a relatively recent invention; and literature for children, therefore, even more recent. It's hardly surprising, then, that in the 'history of childhood' and the 'history of children's literature' we are still at the stage of inventing the wheel. But it is already clear that one of the most salient features of any such history will be the issue that informs the fiction of Cervantes: namely, the respective claims of the 'realist's' view of the world, and of the contrary view, that there is an alternative and equally legitimate 'model' of reality, which indeed, at certain stages in the child's development, must be sanctioned, however irrational it may appear to be to those of us with a severely scientific temper.

In pre-technological cultures, in societies without 'science', rites of passage clearly mark the individual's growth toward sexual and economic adulthood; but there is no crucial discontinuity between the ways in which the children of such societies perceive the world and the ways in which adults do so. In a word, the epistemology is seamless; there is no radical shift or discontinuity, for both child and adult see the same phenomena as real, and see them as being real in the same way. But we possess at least two complementary, and potentially conflicting, ways of knowing. One is the poetic, metaphorical, animistic, even magical – the 'useless' – way. The other is the empirical, scientific – the 'useful' – way. The relationship between these two epistemologies can, and does, generate tension, conflict, anxiety and jokes.

When, for example, Tolstoy wrote a series of readers or

primers for school children in 1870–2, P.M. Polevoy sternly rebuked him, arguing that

> it was criminal to affirm that a pupil who was sincerely convinced that the earth was held up by 'water and fish' showed sounder judgement than one who knew the earth turned on its axis but was incapable of understanding or explaining the phenomenon.[2]

Sixty-five years later, the same question cropped up in Alabama, where James Agee reported of Fred Ricketts, a poor tenant-farmer:

> Fred Ricketts learned quickly. . . . He got as far as the fifth grade and all ways was bright. When his teacher said the earth turned on a axle, he asked her was the axle set in posts, then. She said yes, she reckoned so. He said well, wasn't hell supposed to be under the earth, and if it was wouldn't they be all the time trying to chop the axle post out from under the earth? But here the earth still was, so what was all this talk about axles. 'Teacher never did bring up nothn bout no axles after that. No sir, she never did bring up nothin about no durn axles after that. No sirree, she shore never did brag up nufn baout no dad blame axles attah dayut.'[3]

3

In eighteenth-century England, as the scientific view of the world grew in influence and status, and was more widely dispersed, the old pre-empirical, pre-rational versions of 'reality' became more and more the preserve of uneducated 'superstitious' adults, and of children. Many rationally disposed adults came to hold the view that the sooner children could be educated out of poetic 'fairy' foolishness, the better for all concerned. In essence, we have inherited such views, and mostly subscribe to the view that intellectual and moral growth involves an increase in the capacity to construe the world in terms of the empirical sciences, and a complementary willingness to abandon the metaphors, the multivalences, the poetic resonances of the cosmic fictions that we call fantasy.

Empiricism and the protestant work-ethic have bitten deep into our collective psyche. Even when we agree to allow children to have a childhood, we still tend to assume that the sooner they abandon the modalities of fantasy, the sooner they will begin effectually to exercise and prove their intelligence in useful ways. Infants are allowed, even encouraged, to believe in Father Christmas, but any child who clings to the belief for a year longer than is felt to be appropriate will meet with some rather severe asperities.

Fantasy, in our culture, tends to be associated with the 'pleasure-principle', and with the self-indulgent gratification, albeit vicarious, of rather disreputable desires: the satisfaction of selfish wishes, rather than the answering to natural needs. Growing-up, conversely, seems to necessitate the increasing dominion of the 'reality-principle', of duly wincing, and being seen to wince, when we bruise our toes on stones too heavy for us to kick. It is also, of course, good for us to admit that such bruisings are good for us.

Since the purpose of growing-up is to grow out of childhood, it follows that the status of most children is one of powerlessness: the consolation for such impotence is that, when we leave behind the childlikeness and the childishness of the child, we can then inherit and enjoy adult power in our turn. With deferred maturation, and an extended adolescence, we have of course mutilated this natural justice. Unlike adulthood, childhood is inherently a state to be grown out of; it is always something that we must discard; not merely the androgynous body, and the unsexed voice, but also the licentious ways of knowing that constitute fantasy.

When, therefore, reasonable eighteenth-century minds conceived of education as an ascent toward rationality – *gradus ad mentem* – it followed that two forms of cultural subordination became closely associated. 'Foolish' pre-rational or sub-rational fantasies – folk-tales – were relegated to children and to those adults who persisted in remaining childish: the 'uneducated'. But the matter was not allowed to rest there. Since an attachment to fantasy came to be construed as vulgar, immoral, or mentally regressive – or all three compounded – it followed that many earnest minds were at pains to ensure that children's minds should be protected from pollution by fantasy.

In an era of upward social mobility, the growth of trade and commerce, the increasing power and influence of City as distinct from Court, and a general refinement of manners and appearances, certain limited forms of 'unreason' or 'primitivism' were allowed to slip through the *cordons sanitaires*: the polite, exquisite and mostly effete French 'fairy-tales', which had been very popular with the late seventeenth-century French court, for example; and some of the 'Eastern' tales, duly moralized, and sanctioned by sporadic fads for the exotic. But in general, the shaping minds of the age were committed to reason, prudence, a respectable and moderate religious observance, enlightenment, science and commerce: and, increasingly during the last four decades, to the growth of technology, industrialization and utility, not to mention a revitalized evangelicalism which responded to social and political unrest by invoking a more emphatic and authoritarian paternalism.

It may, then, come as something of a surprise to discover that, throughout the century, the claims of fantasy, of a pre-rational, pre-decorous, pre-Christian world, continued to prove irresistible. At a polite, adult level, this is evidenced by the fact that Shakespeare's reputation – the Shakespeare of *The Tempest, A Midsummer Night's Dream* and *Macbeth* – was never seriously threatened, even though Herder may have been right to claim that eighteenth-century literary–critical theory was never really comfortable with, or adequate to, the pre-conscious dynamics of such drama. At the lower, subordinate, level – of the semi-literate masses and of children – fantasy remained potent and unkillable: the 'vulgar' romances clearly satisfied a need that demanded satisfaction, that would not be denied. The 'folk' sub-culture persisted, sometimes with the antinomian energies of a counter-culture. And the chapmen, who kept up a lively nationwide trade in hawking the penny chap-books, found themselves sustained by a sustaining commerce that continued alongside the more respectable sectors of the book trade.

It is, then, a nice irony that while 'official' adult-sanctioned children's literature was striving tediously and even stridently to promote the orthodox mercantile values, children continued with great determination to devour the vulgar nonsense of the romances under the very noses of the didactic adults. Ironic, too, that in the 1750s and 1760s the 'polite' world began to rediscover the literature of romance that had in effect been relegated to children and the 'vulgar': a rediscovery, associated with urbane episcopal antiquarians such as the bishops, Percy and Hurd, that formed part of the larger shift in consciousness that also expressed itself in a sensitivity to the wilder aspects of landscape, to the paradisal ingenuousness of the 'noble savage', and to the claims of the imagination; all this at a time when the orthodox rational wisdoms of the first half of the century were displaying clear signs of wear and tear.

The rehabilitation of the imagination, especially in connection with childhood and the child's peculiar culture, did not in the event wait on Wordsworth, or his derivatives, Lamb, Coleridge, or De Quincey. It is abundantly and convincingly evident in the work of such relatively unknown late eighteenth-century writers as Morgan, Pott and Scolfield. But it is clear that this renovation of imagination and a growing recognition of its legitimate place in a child's life was relatively slow to take effect. The late eighteenth century offered children a literature that was quick to include science and, indeed, technology, but which on the whole continued to express the moral, social and psychological values of the mid-century. The hacks, and indeed the writers of genuine talent, were almost uniformly orthodox, conformist and conservative. The publication of Taylor's translation of Grimm in the

1820s – a point of no return – was the consummation of aspirations and intuitions that can be found, tucked away embryonically, in the 1760s and 1770s.

In general, the rehabilitation of fantasy was one way of recognizing that a culture that had been committed to the obliteration of vexatious mysteries, and to 'realism and rationalism, [as] basic ways of making discourse',[5] could no longer continue to frustrate, in Malcolm Bradbury's words, 'its desire for metaphor, its wish to transcend the environment which gives only a literal meaning, its search for density of being'.[6] In this respect, it is entirely appropriate that one of the unanswerable defences of fantasy, and specifically of fantasy in childhood, should be found in Wordsworth's *Prelude* which is itself, among many other things, an affirmation and a case of density of being. As with Taylor's Grimm, so with *The Prelude*, what is in fact offered is a point of no return, but one which was withheld for half a century.

4

It would have been neater to have followed a clear linear chronological path through the century, but the material insisted on being disposed otherwise. Chapter One is concerned with Locke's *Thoughts*, and Addison's essays on the imagination. Lawrence Stone's work has served to reinforce my own view, that these were the key works in forming the dominant values and attitudes of early eighteenth-century society. Locke and Addison offer us the civilized adult view of the need for, and the means to achieve, decent acculturation. Chapter Two attempts to follow the underground stream of 'vulgar' stories that continued to flow throughout the century. Chapter Three offers various examples of adults deliberately engaged in the making of a literature for children, from Isaac Watts at the beginning of the century to Dr Aikin and his sister towards the end. (Any reader with a wish to proceed chronologically should skip the later part of this chapter, pages 100–10, and return to it after reading Chapter Seven.)

Chapter Four offers the two major mid-century influences on education – Rousseauism and science; and Chapter Five pursues this further, with particular reference to Thomas Day and to Maria Edgeworth's various reactions to him; indeed, I pursue Maria well into the nineteenth century, to see her carrying orthodox eighteenth-century views almost to 1840. Chapter Six offers three cases of a shift in sensibility and in 'psychology'; responses to didacticism in children's literature; and the indefatigable Mrs Trimmer, exemplifying all the vices of her virtues, in the face of a national moral collapse. Chapter Seven attends to William Blake, both as a sublimely successful writer for children, and as rather problematical, while Chapter Eight examines Lamb and Godwin as manifestations of compromise and confusion. Chapter Nine examines book V of *The Prelude* as a poem responding to specific and representative aberrations in the acculturation of children in the late eighteenth century, and discovers in the process that it offers a uniquely powerful defence of freedom and of fantasy in the lives of children.

NOTES AND REFERENCES

1 Fay Weldon, *Praxis* (London: Hodder & Stoughton, 1978), pp. 176, 178.
2 Henri Troyat, *Tolstoy*, trans. Nancy Amphoux (Harmondsworth: Penguin Books, 1970), p. 460.
3 James Agee, *Let Us Now Praise Famous Men* (New York: Ballantine Books, 1966), p. 276.
4 See Johann Gottfried Herder, 'Shakespeare', in *Von der Urpoesie der Völker* (Stuttgart: Reclam, 1972). First published in 1772.
5 Malcolm Bradbury, *Possibilities* (London, Oxford and New York: Oxford University Press, 1973), p. 270.
6 ibid., p. 268. For current theoretical studies of fantasy, see W.R. Irwin, *The Game of the Impossible* (Urbana, Ill.: University of Illinois Press, 1976); Rosemary Jackson, *Fantasy* (London and New York: Methuen, 1981); C.N. Manlove, *Modern Fantasy: Five Studies* (Cambridge: Cambridge University Press, 1975); Eric S. Rabkin, *The Fantastic in Literature* (Princeton, NJ: Princeton University Press, 1976); and Tzvetan Todorov, *The Fantastic*, trans. Richard Howard (Ithaca, NY: Cornell University Press, 1973).

CHAPTER ONE

HIGH-RANGING SPANIELS AND PHILOSOPHICAL DISPOSITIONS

Pray, sir, in all the reading which you have ever
read, did you ever read such a book as Locke's
Essay upon the Human Understanding? Don't
answer me rashly, because many, I know, quote
the book, who have not read it.
(Lawrence Sterne, *Tristram Shandy*, 1760)

Youth and white paper take any impression.
(John Ray, *A Collection of English Proverbs*, 1670)

1

Raw-Head and Bloody Bones
Snatches naughty children from their homes,
Takes them to his dirty den
And they're never seen again.

If you use a traditional rhyme such as that to frighten a
naughty child into submission, then your 'Remedy is much
worse than the disease'. Such was the sensible, considered,
and experience-based opinion of the celebrated philosopher,
John Locke.

His book on the rearing of children and young people, *Some
Thoughts Concerning Education*,[1] with its characteristically
modest title, was published in 1693 as a result of urgent
persuasions from his friend, William Molyneux, whose own
son was reared on the lines recommended by Locke. The book
started life as a series of letters, which simply 'growed and

growed' both as a result of Locke's animated interest in his subject, and also from a growing conviction that there was a general need for such a book, at a time when 'the early Corruption of Youth' was 'so general a Complaint', and so many parents confessed that they were 'at a loss how to breed their children'.[2]

The task of breeding, or rearing, children, said Locke, required 'great Sobriety, Temperance, Tenderness, Diligence, and Discretion': and all of these could be numbered among the many virtues of Locke himself. His book is, in fact, a perfect realization of the very virtues that it commended: it is reasonable, tentative, moderate, generous, couth and continuously responsive to the checks of real experience. It is the admirable work of a scrupulously alert and perfectly disinterested enquirer, and the perfectly characteristic work of a virtuous man.

For three-quarters of a century, Locke's *Thoughts* was the most influential English book on child-rearing: in effect, *the* book. So extensive was its influence, so powerful and prestigious its reputation, that many of the landed gentry, the Roger de Coverleys, learned to take the education of their children as seriously as the breeding of their horses,[3] or the training of their hounds. They learned from Locke – or, rather, they paid others to learn – to care, and how to care, for their children; they paid them to supervise, to instruct, to supervene; and, indeed, to worry, especially about the depraving influence of servants. As for the 'Andrew Freeports' – the 'new men, the wealthy merchants, the moneyed interest, the Whigs' – they were even quicker to join the quest for a next generation with improved manners and useful learning.

The essential premise of Locke's argument was this: that 'of all the men we meet with, nine parts of ten are what they are, good and evil, useful or not, by their education. It is that which makes the great difference in mankind.'[4] Both manners and abilities owe more to education than to anything else. This conviction derived not from any *a priori* dogma or doctrine; it did not appeal to any higher authority, however august; Locke drew it from his own experiences as a tutor. By the time he came to write the *Thoughts* he had not only delivered babies and supervised their early nursing, but had tutored, observed, and gained the respect or affection of many children and young people, both in private households and at Oxford.

The *Thoughts* appeared in French translation in 1695, and were soon known throughout Europe. Needless to say, some of his disciples proved to be more insistently nurturist than Locke himself. Helvétius, for example, went on to argue that 'Man is, in fact, nothing more than the product of his education'. Drawing on a rather sinister metaphor, he insisted that 'to guide the motions of the human puppet, it is necessary to know the wires by which he is moved.'[5]

What, then, were the wires? How were they to be manipulated? In what order? To what end? Locke bases his answers to these questions on an appeal, not to prejudice, precedent, or inclination, but to reason: reason in the service of virtue. Just as the scientific revolution of the seventeenth century had shown that it was possible – and useful – to apply empirical method and inductive reasoning to the task of understanding the nature of the physical world, so it seemed equally feasible – and potentially efficacious – to apply such methods to the task of forming a child's mind.

The only legitimate appeal for Locke was to closely observed particular experience, and to the careful teasing out of general principles from a series of such observations. And over all, for Locke, was the inalienable general principle that the end of all learning was to grow in virtue, and in the virtuous exercise of reason.

Locke's *Thoughts* struck many of his contemporary readers as offering benign light in hitherto dark places. Here was a patient, urbane, intelligent, moderate, tentative mind writing – his tone was so informal, that I was tempted to write 'talking' – about matters that in most quarters had previously generated more heat than light. He spoke explicitly for possibility, and implicitly for pacification: the peaceableness of quiet reasonableness. His predecessors in this field had offered little more than the view that children were peculiarly vulnerable to the snares of the devil. Given a very low average life-expectancy, children had offered their parents the urgent task of pointing their tender young souls to heaven; the alternative being so dire as to be unthinkable. And it was not enough for parents only to take such questions seriously: the young, also, had to take due note of Hell:

> Every corner hath a Snake
> In the accursed Lake.
> Seas of Fire, Beds of Snow
> Are the best Delights below:
> A Viper from the Fire
> Is his Hire
> That knows not Moments from Eternity.

So warned the saintly Jeremy Taylor in his *Festival Hymns, for the use of the Devout, especially of younger persons,* in 1655. Thirty years later, John Bunyan, in his wretched *Book for Boys and Girls* (1686),[6] warned children that every silly plaything, every frivolous game, was a 'fingle-fangle,' that would 'their Souls entangle'. Such gloomy doggerel was, of course, written to prepare children, not for life, but for death.

Surprisingly for a man who characterized himself as 'bookish', Locke admitted that, in rearing children, books were among the least of his concerns. His first aim was to make a genuine contribution to the task of rearing 'vertuous, useful, and able Men'; to promote 'Virtue, Wisdom, Breeding, and Learning', in that order, which like everything else in Locke is not casual. He must have been an excellent tutor: testimony exists, of course; but *Thoughts* displays an unusually delicate and attentive awareness of development – of the way in which a child grows, both physically and mentally, and of what is apt to each stage of its growth. It is an insight of which Locke's appreciative and alert readers always took due note. Vicesimus Knox, for instance, wrote in *Winter Evenings*: 'If the bud, which would naturally expand in April or May, were rudely opened in March, what fruit could justly be expected in August or September?'[7] and Coleridge embellished the point by quoting from *Love's Labour's Lost*, in one of his 1811 lectures:

> At Christmas I no more desire a Rose,
> Than wish a Snow in May's new-fangled shows:
> But like of each thing that in season grows.[8]

Sensitivity to such appropriateness was one of Locke's subtler strengths. It allowed him to recommend that, with young children, 'all their innocent Folly, Playing, and Childish Actions, are to be left perfectly free and unrestrained, as far as they can consist with the Respect due to those that are present'.[9] But, since their Reason is as yet undeveloped,

> the *younger* they are, the less I think are their unruly and disorderly Appetites to be complied with; and the less Reason they have of their own, the more are they to be under the Absolute Power and Restraint of those, in whose Hands they are. From which, I confess, it will follow, that none but discreet People should be about them.

He continually stresses his belief that children must be reasoned with, in order that they shall exercise, develop, and refine their own powers of reasoning:

> It will perhaps be wondered that I mention *Reasoning* with Children. And yet I cannot but think that the true Way of Dealing with them. They understand it as early as they do Language; and, if I mis-observe not, they love to be treated as Rational Creatures sooner than is imagined. 'Tis a Pride should be cherished in them, and as much as can be, made the greatest instrument to turn them by. But when I talk of Reasoning, I do not intend any other but such as is suited to the Child's Capacity and Apprehension.

5

Unfortunately, as Locke's *Thoughts* were diffused and popularized in eighteenth-century society, the crucial caveats and conditionals that Locke was at pains to present were very often overlooked or denied, with unfortunate consequences. Locke's posthumous misfortune was that his views were misrepresented almost as often as they were invoked.

But what of learning? What should the child actually learn, in the narrower sense of curriculum? 'You will wonder, perhaps, that I put *Learning* last, especially if I tell you I think it is the least part.' Again he insists: first, good manners, virtuous inclinations, and proper habits; then, and only then, should we attend to learning. He argues benignly and convincingly that through a canny, thoughtful and subtle use of the child's delight in play, 'he may learn to Read, without knowing how he did so' – a fact that many readers will endorse – and he justifies this use of play on the grounds that 'Children should not have anything like Work, or serious, laid on them': if they do, especially in connection with books, the experience will be exactly as with food: a deplorable 'Surfeit, that leaves an Aversion behind, not to be removed' – a view that the Edgeworths were to repeat with great emphasis a century later. As a child acquires a capacity for reading, 'easy pleasant' books should be made available, so that 'the entertainment that he finds might draw him on, and reward his Pains in Reading, and yet not such as should fill his Head with perfectly useless trumpery, or lay the principles of Vice and Folly'.

The best of such 'easy, pleasant' books, he suggests, is *Aesop's Fables* for they are 'apt to delight and entertain a Child', and 'may yet afford useful Reflections to a grown Man'.[10] When the child grows up, if he still recalls them, 'he will not repent to find them there, amongst his manly Thoughts, and serious Business'. If an illustrated copy is used, 'it will entertain him much the better'.[11] Furthermore, it will also be more soundly educative, according to the principles of Locke's psychology, because the child will be able to attach the ideas in the words to 'visible Objects': for it

return to their labours with chearfulnefs, fo a little
holiday in our ftudies qualifies us to purfue them with
frefh affiduity, and greater probability of fuccefs.

FAB. CC.   *The* Fool *and the* Moon.

A Fool fitting one night by a river-fide, faw the
reflection of the Moon in the water, and immediately baited his hook with cream-cheefe, and
threw in his line to angle for it. After he had
fat for fome time, and wondered that the Moon
did not bite, the Man in the Moon cried out to him
with an hollow voice, and faid thus : Fool that thou
art ! to fifh for the fhadow of the moon in the river !
thou hadft better put a worm upon thy hook, and
angle for barbel and gudgeons.

M O R A L.

Smit with the dazzling glare of empty fhew,
The fimple maid thus angles for a beau :
The wifer fair with fcorn the bauble views,
And men of fenfe, a nobler game, perfues.

P 6   APPLI

must be rememberd that 'Ideas are not to be had from Sounds; but from the Things themselves, or their Pictures'. In addition to Aesop, Locke recommends *Reynard the Fox*, which had first been published in English by Caxton in 1481. He merely mentions it, without comment, for he is more interested in the ways in which such books can be made more useful by informing the child's conversations: 'those about him should talk to him often about the Stories he has read, and hear him tell them', for this will add 'Incouragement and delight' to his reading: he will thus discover that 'there is some use and pleasure in it'.

With disarming honesty, Locke confesses: 'What other Books there are in English of the kind of those above-mentioned, fit to engage the liking of Children, and tempt them to read, I do not know.'[12] and it is one incidental measure of Locke's influence that, when Hawkesworth came to write his essay on fables for the *Adventurer* in 1753,[13] he focused on the fables of Aesop and on the stories of Reynard, and remarked that it was the fables of Aesop that 'are often first exhibited to youth, as examples of the manner in which their native language is written'. But he also remarked that when children read fables which intend to illustrate virtue and vice in action, they have a contrary habit of identifying or sympathizing with the wrong party. Reynard may be a cunning villain, but he is also irresistibly attractive: 'In the fox there appears a superiority which not only preserves him from scorn, but even from indignation: and indeed the general character of Reynard is by no means fit for imitation'![14] It was a moral and emotional irony that the didactic writers have never been able to avoid, and Rousseau characteristically made great play with it, as we shall see. Hazlitt's is, perhaps, the clearest recognition of the problem; in his 'Letter to William Gifford', he wrote: 'it is the same principle that makes us read with admiration and reconciles us in fact to the triumphant progress of the conquerors and mighty hunters of mankind, who come to stop the shepherd's pipe upon the mountains, and sweep away his listening flock' – we are aroused, excited, enlivened by 'the sense of power abstracted from the sense of good'.[15]

But Locke did not stay long enough with books to allow himself to consider such questions; for him, virtuous and civilizing socialization was more important in childhood than were literature and its attendant ironies. In his view, the most serious obstacle to the formation of a virtuous and rational character was to be found below stairs, in the 'taint of servants' – girls and young women, in the main, of very meagre education, if indeed any at all.

It is for servants that Locke reserves his most severe mistrust and disapproval, not to say contempt: the tutor must be vigilant to keep the child protected from 'the Influence of ill Precedents, especially the most dangerous of all, the Examples of the Servants.'[16] He raises the issue, as one calling for extreme care, on at least a dozen occasions, and always the burden is the same: servants are a menace, for within the household they actually constitute a pernicious sub-culture. Above stairs, all efforts are devoted to the child's progress toward virtue and reason; but below stairs lurk the counter-vailing influences of foolishness, unreason, and even wickedness.

Locke argues that servants work to create moral confusion and contradiction: when the child is justly rebuked by parent, tutor or governess, he runs for indulgent solace to the servants. And, of course, the silly wenches – the 'clownish or vicious' wenches – are only too willing to oblige, and so subvert the good work done upstairs. But his most severe disapproval is reserved for the 'culture' with which they can so readily pollute the child's mind – an unredeemed, primitive and barbarous culture. If not prevented, the servants will 'awe children, and keep them in subjection, by telling them of *Raw-Head* and *Bloody Bones*, and such other Names, as carry with them the Ideas of some thing terrible and hurtful, which they have reason to be afraid of, when alone, especially in the dark'. Once the fear of Goblings and Bug-bears is lodged in the mind of a child, it is extremely difficult to dislodge it.

Locke here warms to his subject, for it provides a vivid example of his theory of the association of ideas: these are formed most strongly when the child's mind, like soft wax, is still very impressionable. Once the child has come to associate Bug-bears[17] and other terrors with the dark, then night-time, however circumstantially innocuous it may be, will tend to arouse such terrors. Indeed, this re-awakening of night-fears offers so vivid and dramatic an illustration of the theory, that Locke returned to it again in the expanded fourth edition of his *Essay Concerning Human Understanding* (1700), and again seized the opportunity to chastise 'foolish Maids'.

But how closely related are the fear that is aroused by talk of Goblings and the fear inspired by homilies on Hell and the Devil? It was a delicate question for scrupulous minds such as Locke's, though less rational, more enthusiastic minds were not slow to rush in: early Methodism was warmly committed to a belief in witches. Locke handled the matter circumspectly, almost moving on tip-toe: 'of Evil Spirits, 'twill be well if you can keep a child from wrong Fancies about them, till he is ripe for that sort of Knowledge.'[18] In general he would 'not have Children troubled whilst young with Notions of Spirits'.[19] Those who have been unfortunate enough to suffer from terror of Goblings and Bug-bears in childhood, often strive so intently, later in life, to exorcise them, that they 'throw away the thoughts of all Spirits together, and so run into the other but worse extream',[20] i.e. a thoroughgoing scepticism. Where, then, does this leave Locke's reader, *vis-à-vis* the world of spirits, the realm of fantasy, the domain of fairies and goblins?

Discussion of spirits, especially the evil ones, is to be reserved for later years, when the young person will be 'ripe' for such matters; meanwhile, all the vulgar, superstitious nonsense that servants indulge in below stairs must be kept at bay; ideally, the child will learn nothing of such matters. In Locke's psychology, learning is clear, or it is nothing: 'The sure and only way to get true knowledge is to form in our minds clear settled notions of things, with names annexed to those determined ideas'.[21] Such a proposition, if it gains prestige and influence, augurs well for science and empiricism, but bodes ill for the indeterminate world of the spirit, of poetry, and of fancy.

2

It was left to Joseph Addison, the journalist and politician, to initiate the dilution and diffusion of Locke's ideas, mediated through the persuasive urbanity of his own irresistibly charming prose. Most relevant to my present purposes are Addison's essays on 'Taste and the Pleasures of the Imagination', which appeared in the *Spectator* in June and July of 1712.[22]

In an age eager to espouse toleration, compromise and reasonableness, Addison set himself the task of adjusting his readers' conception of the imagination, so as to effect an agreeable reconciliation of the claims of reason and judgement, on the one hand, and a breathing space for imagination, or fancy, on the other. To find a place for imaginative pleasures in the life of the reasonable man, and a place for the sobrieties of judgement in the psychological economy of those addicted to fancy: such an effort at fusion was part of the *Spectator*'s larger enterprise of civilizing its readers, improving their minds and their manners, showing them 'when to speak, or to be silent; how to refuse, or how to comply', as Dr Johnson characterized the role of the magazine as *arbiter elegantiae*, 'a judge of propriety, who should survey the track of daily conversation, and free it from thorns and prickles, which teaze the passer, though they do not wound him'.[23]

The pleasures of the understanding Addison preferred to the 'pleasures of the imagination', since the former were 'founded on some new knowledge or improvement in the mind of man'. Even so, he had to confess that the pleasures of the imagination were just 'as great and as transporting'. To possess 'a polite imagination' was to enlarge life, for it admitted one to 'a great many pleasures that the vulgar are not capable of receiving': aesthetic or imaginative pleasure thus became an element in – indeed, a sign, a mark of – refinement, of decently equipped politeness; this is, of course, an association that continues to plague us in a variety of ways. Addison in this respect, was both a portent and a lever, of social change, of an amelioration of manners, and of certain notions of cultural subordination that are so deeply embedded in our society as to pass largely unquestioned.

Imagination: image: something seen: the eye: so Addison comes to consider what it is that happens when we look at 'outward objects' such as comprise a landscape, for example. The pleasure, he suggests, springs from one or more of three sources: namely, what is great, what is uncommon, and what is beautiful. When we enjoy the vastness of a prospect, we 'are flung into a pleasing astonishment at such unbounded views, and feel a delightful stillness and amazement in the soul at the apprehension of them'. The human mind, he argues, hates confinement and constraints, and it is for this reason that a spacious horizon is perceived as a blessing. It offers 'an image of liberty, where the eye has room to range abroad, to expatiate at large . . . to lose itself. . . . Such wide and undetermined prospects are as pleasing to the fancy, as the speculations of eternity or infinitude are to the understanding.'

Our first encounter with what is 'new or uncommon', in its turn, 'fills the soul with an agreeable surprise, gratifies its curiosity, and gives it an idea of which it was not before possessed'. The uncommon cannot help but contribute to the variety of life; it offers forms of refreshment, and 'bestows charms on a monster, and makes even the imperfections of nature please us.' As for beauty, it 'diffuses a secret satisfaction and complacency[24] through the imagination, and gives a finishing to anything that is great or uncommon'. He remarks beauty in the inherent variety of nature and in the varieties of natural colour, adducing sunrise and sunset as perfect examples of a 'glorious and pleasing show'. As Addison's use of the word 'secret' – 'secret satisfaction' – adumbrates, he has the tact to stop short of a psychological reductivism: these causes of pleasure are not to be explained away, he insists. We simply do not know enough about the how and why, the covert correspondence between Nature on the one hand and 'the substance of a human soul' on the other. But he nevertheless detects the hand of the 'Supreme Author', the 'First Contriver' in all this: 'He has annexed a secret pleasure to the idea of anything that is new or uncommon, that he might encourage us in the pursuit after knowledge, and engage us to search into the wonders of his Creation'. The 'pursuit' and the 'search' – the terms look back to the scientific revolution of the seventeenth century and forward to the eighteenth century's growing commitment to 'useful knowledge'; knowledge of the natural world, and the pursuit of that knowledge are offered a divine sanction. In such ways, Addison speaks for his age, with a representative voice.

In canvassing and endorsing – promoting, indeed – the legitimacy of the imagination's pleasures, Addison was unwittingly offering a coherent and persuasive legitimation of the child's delight in fantasy.[25] Addison's argument, if that is not too strong a word for a performance that is so urbane and reassuring, can indeed be read as an analogy, and an apologue, of such childhood pleasures. A century later Wordsworth was to establish a very close equivalence between the joy of wandering in 'vales' and the joy of losing oneself in 'tales';[26] likewise, Addison's appreciation of the grand, or the 'Vast', (which is both his and Coleridge's word),[27] the uncommon and the beautiful, in nature, art and literature, may be seen as an entirely apt account of the powerful and compelling delights that children were then finding in the newly translated *Thousand and One Nights*, in Perrault's *Tales of Mother Goose*, and in the 'vulgar' romances that circulated below stairs in the penny chap-books. Addison's readers, for the most part, did not in the event apprise or avail themselves of such an urbane and reasonable rationale for a childhood love of fantasy; but it was undoubtedly there, for the taking. As it was, most of Addison's contemporaries made do with Locke's rather limited view of literature for children, and indeed with his marked distaste for the aberrations of the fantasies of 'vulgar wenches'.[28]

Addison accepts Locke's view that *colour* is a 'secondary quality' of the physical world, not found objectively to inhere in things themselves, but, rather, 'apprehended by the imagination' and not having any existence in matter. But he turns this cool empirical fact to good account, by a very deft sleight of quill. 'Colour', a secondary quality, is illusory, says science: hey presto, Addison neatly converts 'illusions' into 'pleasing shows and apparitions', 'imaginary glories' and 'visionary beauty'. To manage to derive such 'visionary beauty' from perceptual fallacy or optical illusion is a perfect measure of Addison's rhetorical cunning. But there is more to come, for the very fact that science cries 'Illusion!' allows him to indulge in a gothic fantasy. The very admission of illusion, an admission that is logically a negative – and for the lay reader, newly introduced to the idea, unsettling, even demoralizing – this very admission is *felt* as positively rhapsodic. It is one of Addison's neatest tricks:

> Things would make but a poor appearance to the eye, if we saw them only in their proper figures and motions: and what reason can we assign for their exciting in us many of those ideas which are different from anything that exists in the objects themselves (for such are light and colours) were it not to add supernumerary ornaments to the universe, and make it more agreeable to the imagination? We are every where entertained with pleasing shows and apparitions: we discover imaginary glories in the heavens and in the earth, and see some of this visionary beauty poured out upon the whole Creation; but what a rough unsightly sketch of Nature should we be entertained with, did all her colouring disappear, and the several distinctions of light and shade vanish? In short, our souls are at present delightfully lost

and bewildered in a pleasing delusion, and we walk about like the enchanted hero of a romance, who sees beautiful castles, woods and meadows . . . but upon the finishing of some secret spell, the fantastic scene breaks up, and the disconsolate knight finds himself on a barren heath, or in a solitary desert.

As if Addison realizes that his rhapsodic praise of illusion and enchantment has gone too far, Richard Steele is pressed into service at this point, to express some moderating reservations:

> The pleasures of the imagination are what bewilder life, when reason and judgement do not interpose; it is therefore a worthy action in you to look carefully into the powers of fancy, that other men, from the knowledge of them, may improve their joys, and allay their griefs, by a just use of that faculty.

The tactical intention of this interpolation is not, of course, made explicit. But it serves to reassure Addison's readers that a place could indeed be found in polite life for the irrational pleasures of the imagination, and that such an inclusion, such an admission, need not provoke gross perturbations, either psychological or social, need not disturb stability, ruffle amenity, or subvert manners.

Turning to art, Addison attends first to architecture and offers plausible reasons for preferring the classical to the gothic: in language that anticipates Coleridge, he argues that a great temple 'opens the mind to vast conceptions, and fits it to converse with the divinity of the place'. In literature, he has no difficulty in matching his three modes of imaginative pleasure – the great, uncommon and beautiful – to three poets: Homer, for the great; Virgil, for the beautiful; and Ovid, for the new and uncommon. He is especially eloquent in his praise of Ovid; while he relishes Homer for his 'thousand savage prospects of vast deserts, wide uncultivated marshes, huge forests, misshapen rocks and precipices', when we come to

Ovid's *Metamorphoses*, he finds that 'we are walking on enchanted ground, and see nothing but scenes of magic lying round us'. Ovid 'describes a miracle in every story' and he 'everywhere entertains us with something we never saw before, and shews us monster after monster.' Monsters that we delight in!

This is where we recognize the great advantage of art over nature, or 'real life'. Things that are actually disagreeable can give pleasure when we encounter them in fiction.[29] There are things in life that are only too 'apt to raise a secret ferment in the mind of the reader, and to work with violence, upon his passions', and these again, when mediated by art, afford pleasure. Serious poetry stirs up 'terror and pity' in us, and it seems strange that we 'should take delight in being terrified' when, if we were to meet the same experience in real life, we would feel a sense of unease, or worse. Addison's explanation of this deep paradox is that it is akin to the curiosity and satisfaction that we feel when we look on a dead monster or other such 'hideous objects': 'the more frightful appearance they make, the greater is the pleasure we receive from the sense of our own safety'. He seems to suggest that the terror and the sense of relief are simultaneous; but is this, in fact, possible? The clue may be found in the epicurean bias of Addison's own temper, or it may be that his 'reason or judgement' was continuously at hand, to hold terrors at arm's length or to defuse them. Certainly, the dark mystery of pleasurable terror continued to tease the eighteenth century mind. But the subordination of children and of the 'vulgar' is clearly evident in the recurrent attacks on *their* enjoying such dubious pleasure, a pleasure that proved resistant to any totally coherent rationale, and that carried within it some deeply problematic moral ironies.

As for Addison, the magical precedent of Ovid allowed him to turn his attention to the literature of 'fairies, witches, magicians, demons, and departed spirits', the literature, to use Locke's terms, of goblings and bug-bears. Addison observes that this 'fairy way of writing' – Dryden's phrase – is 'more difficult than any other that depends on the poet's fancy, because he . . . must work altogether out of his own invention'; moreover, if he is to succeed, the poet must possess an imagination that is 'naturally fruitful and superstitious'. Again, he must be 'very well versed in legends and fables, antiquated romances, and the traditions of nurses and old women, that he may fall in with our natural prejudices, and humour those notions which we have imbibed in our infancy.'

In acknowledging the vast reserves of source-material available in legend, romance and folk-lore, Addison seems unwittingly to contradict his earlier contention that the poet must 'work altogether out of his own invention', but in effect he is recognizing that these sources are no longer sustainingly and authentically available to him: that even were he so inclined, he himself could not tap them. Fifty years later, Dr Johnson drily consigned such matters to the remote pre-Augustan past: commenting on Shakespeare's *A Midsummer Night's Dream*, he observed, 'Fairies in his time were very much in fashion; common tradition had made them familiar, and Spenser's poem had made them great.'[30]

Francis Grose, trying to account for the distinctive power of Shakespeare, argued that it was to be explained in terms of the 'association of ideas':

> Shakespeare . . . drew his inimitable scenes of magic from that source [i.e. Popular Superstitions]. . . . Indeed, one cause of these scenes having so great effect on us, is their calling back to our fancies the tales and terrors of the nursery, which are so strongly stamped on our tender minds, as rarely, if ever, to be totally effaced; and of these tales, spite of the precaution of parents, every child has heard something, more or less.[31]

Again, he insists,

> we need only turn our recollection towards what passed in our childhood, and reflect on the avidity and pleasure with which we listened to stories of ghosts, witches, and

fairies, told us by our maids and nurses: and even among those whose parents had the good sense to prohibit such relations, there is scarce one in a thousand but may remember to have heard [them].[32]

Addison genially acknowledges his own recognition of a 'pleasing kind of horror', and the sheer amusement to be derived from the experience of 'strangeness and novelty' – just as we take pleasure in travel to foreign parts, and in observing foreign customs, so we may derive delight and pleasurable surprise when we are led into a fantastic fictive 'country', to observe the 'persons and manners of another species'. All such extravagant fantasies remind us of stories that we have heard in childhood, and 'favour those secret terrors and apprehensions to which the mind of man is naturally subject'. In deftly disposing that word – 'secret' – Addison both builds up a tacit sense of rapport and community with his reader, rendering the private public, and also achieves a delicate pre-emptive stroke: we too will admit this to be so, will we not? Addison, like Grose, had known such ambivalent *frissons* in childhood, even though he could no longer draw on them. There is a sense here of Addison's own personal growing away from such vestigial traces, as corresponding to, reflecting, the same shift writ large in the spirit of the age.

In Addison's view, the crucial contention is between 'Men of cold fancies, and philosophical dispositions', men who 'object to this kind of poetry, that it has not probability enough to affect the imagination'; and, on the other side, those who are prepossessed with the false opinion that 'there are many intellectual beings in the world beside ourselves, and several species of spirits'! Rather disingenuously, Addison tiptoes neatly between Scylla and Charybdis, not breathing a word about where his own allegiances lie, but moving nimbly into a tacit appeal to his sympathetic readers: for 'we have all heard so many pleasing relations in favour of them [the spirits], that we do not care for seeing through the falsehood, and willingly give ourselves up to so agreeable an imposture.'

Addison was a great walker of tightropes, a kind of philosophical Blondin, and he here leaves us with a neatly unresolving kind of resolution which enlists our support, not by any explicit philosophical alignment or commitment, but by appealing to a presumed, and presumedly good-tempered, well-mannered, consensus. We agree, do we not, to be imposed on, because the result of so being imposed on, is very agreeable. Nowhere else is Addison's 'political' intention clearer than it is here: the most delicate, the trickiest, the most potentially fraught, passage in the whole essay, ends in a quietly and cunningly managed compromise. It is a nice demonstration of Addison's famous politeness of touch, a deft settling of differences, a consummate papering-over of cracks.

As for the repertoire of the 'fairy kind of writing' it almost all came out of the dark ages. Ovid does not belong under this head, however much he may deal in the magical, the super-rational, for fairy-tales grew out of the dark ages, when 'pious frauds were made use of to amuse mankind, and frighten them into a sense of their duty'.[33] But, fortunately, all that took place before the world was 'enlightened by learning and philosophy'. Being a good patriot, as well as an enlightened man, he concedes that it was the English who wove such spells best; probably because, as a race, they are 'naturally fanciful' – no explanation at all! – and predisposed, on account of their gloomy and melancholy temper, to harbour 'many wild notions and visions'. And, of course, it cannot be denied that Shakespeare wove the best spells, and saw into the best fairy-lands, for he was gifted with a 'noble extravagance of fancy', which enabled him to touch this 'weak superstitious part of his reader's imagination'; his ghosts, fairies and witches are given speeches which are at once 'so wild' and 'so solemn' that we cannot help but think them natural: 'if there are such beings in the world, it looks highly probably they should talk and act as he has represented them.'

It is an astute, urbane and light-footed performance that Addison offers his readers; and it is indeed a performance: it is

FANTASY AND REASON

as if we are being invited to admire his footwork, his balance, his sheer dexterity. But it cannot be denied that, momentarily, he holds a finely judged balance between the claims of imagination and those of judgement. Such poise was a gift of the moment. His era henceforth will be irreversibly 'enlightened by learning and philosophy', and one begins to hear a faint but increasing snip, snip, as 'philosophy' proceeds to clip the wings of poetry. As the century wore on, such trimming was to become more ruthless, in the service of both a severer reason, and a narrower, more nay-saying, less benign morality. Many of those who would claim debts to Locke and Addison would wield heavier, blunter scissors, and use them more ruthlessly and more extensively, in rooting out error.

In 1664, Dryden wrote, 'Imagination is a faculty so wild and lawless that like a high-ranging spaniel, it must have clogs tied to it, lest it outrun judgment'.[34] Locke was disposed to turn the spaniel out to its kennel, to keep the servants company; Addison washed and trimmed it, and domesticated it. Before the century was out, some high-minded, tidy-minded individuals would try to have it put down altogether.

NOTES AND REFERENCES

1 The best modern edition of Locke's *Some Thoughts Concerning Education* is that of James L. Axtell (Cambridge: Cambridge University Press, 1968). All quotations are from this edition.
2 ibid., prefatory letter to Sir Edward Clarke.
3 A point made by Richard Steele, *Guardian*, no.94; by Blake, *Tiriel*, sect.8; and by Jane Austen: 'Lady Bertram thought more of her pug than her children' (*Mansfield Park*, ch.2).
4 Locke, *Thoughts*, p.60. Cf. Helvétius, *A Treatise on Man, His Intellectual Faculties and his Education*, Eng. trans. (London, 1777).
5 Helvétius, op.cit., vol.1, p.4.
6 The 9th edition (1724) was retitled *Divine Emblems*. Cf. Keats, who offered his brother George a page of ostensibly trivial anecdotes and jokes, all entertaining, and concluded: 'There's a page of Wit for you – to put John Bunyan's emblems out of

countenance' (Letters, ed. Robert Gittings, London: Oxford University Press, 1970, p. 321).

7 In *Winter Evenings; or, Lucubrations on Life and Letters*, 3 vols (London: Charles Dilly, 1788), vol. III, p. 157. There is a facsimile reprint of this edition (New York: Garland, 1972).

8 The fifth lecture on Shakespeare and Milton. The quotation is from *Love's Labour's Lost*, I.i.

9 Locke, *Thoughts*, p. 156. Such insistences on Locke's part may help to explain the inclination of some critics to see Locke as a decisive influence on Wordsworth. They also serve to blur any categorical opposition of Locke and Blake.

10 The view that good literature for children is also satisfying food for adult thought is one that runs through Philip Sidney, Steele, Locke and Wordsworth, among others. See Eric Rabkin, *Fantastic Worlds* (New York: Oxford University Press, 1979), p. 167.

11 One of Wordsworth's most vivid memories of the chap-books of his childhood is of the illustrative woodcuts. See *The Excursion*, bk 1, ll. 177 ff.

12 Locke, *Thoughts*, p. 260. Locke goes out of his way to insist: 'As for the Bible . . . I think that perhaps a worse could not be found.'

13 Reprinted in *The British Essayists* 45 vols (London: T. & J. Allman, 1823), vol. 23, no. 18.

14 Cf. Rousseau on La Fontaine, below, p. 116.

15 Hazlitt, *Works*, ed. P.P. Howe (London and Toronto: Dent, 1930–4), vol. 9, p. 37.

16 Locke, *Thoughts*, p. 187.

17 By the mid-eighteenth century, the word was well on its way to acquiring the lesser force of a mere nuisance or burden.

18 Locke, *Thoughts*, p. 244.

19 ibid., p. 303.

20 ibid.

21 See Locke, *The Conduct of the Understanding*, sect. XV.

22 See *Critical Essays from the 'Spectator' by Joseph Addison*, ed. Donald F. Bond (Oxford: Clarendon Press, 1970). All of the following quotations fall between pp. 176 and 201.

23 Johnson, 'Joseph Addison', in *Lives of the Poets*, 2 vols (London: Oxford University Press, 1961), vol. 1.

24 'complacency': pleasure.

25 Cf. Pott's argument, below, Chapter Six.

26 See below, p. 272.

27 Coleridge: 'from my early reading of Faery Tales, & Genii &c &c

– my mind had been habituated to *the Vast*. . . .' (letter of 16 October 1797, in *Collected Letters of Samuel Taylor Coleridge*, ed. E.L. Griggs, 6 vols, Oxford: Clarendon Press, 1956 – vol. 1, p. 354).

28 See the *Essay Concerning Human Understanding*, ch.8.

29 Two of the best-known cases of this argument are to be found in Wordsworth and Keats. See below, Chapter Nine, p. 284.

30 *The Works of Samuel Johnson*, vol. 7: *Johnson on Shakespeare*, ed. A. Sherbo (New Haven, Conn., and London: Yale University Press, 1968), p. 160.

31 Francis Grose, *A Provincial Glossary* . . ., 2nd edn (London: S. Hooper, 1790), p. vi. Cf. Addison in the *Spectator*, 1 July 1712: op.cit., vol. 3, p. 570.

32 'Popular Superstitions' (appended to *Provincial Glossary*) pp. 1–2.

33 This is a recurrent theme in the writings of Jeremy Bentham, and may be traced in part to his own childhood terrors.

34 Epistle of *The Rival Ladies* (1664).

CHAPTER TWO

'MAGGOTS IN
A MADMAN'S BRAIN'

Meantime the village rouses up the fire:
While, well attested and as well believed,
Heard solemn, goes the goblin-story round,
Till superstitious horror creeps o'er all.

(James Thomson, 'Winter', 1726)

1

In the 1790s, Tom Wedgwood,[1] son of the great Josiah, decided to establish a lending library for the pottery's workers. In 1808, Archdeacon Wrangham,[2] responsible for the spiritual succour of the people of the East Riding of Yorkshire, set up a library for their use. Both libraries had this in common: that they were aimed primarily at the moral improvement of their readers. How, then, did these philanthropists, motivated by a spirit of benevolence, choose the books for the library shelves?

In 1856, George Eliot, in her essay, 'The Natural History of German Life: Riehl', wrote that 'the dream that the uncultured classes are prepared for a condition which appeals principally to their moral sensibilities' was an illusion. An illusion, moreover, that could not 'co-exist with a real knowledge of the People, with a thorough study of their habits, their ideas, their motives'. And such a study, to be of any use, required an observer of 'sufficient moral and intellectual breadth, whose observations would not be vitiated by a foregone conclusion, or by a professional point of view'.[3]

Neither Wedgwood nor Wrangham satisfied any of these

conditions. Whatever their intellectual breadth, they were both, in their several ways, morally narrow. They certainly entertained foregone conclusions – at least two: that the books they provided would be acceptable, and of benefit, to their readers. And they both held a 'professional' point of view: Wedgwood's derived from his interest in the continuing success of the business, and the betterment of the 'labouring poor'. Wrangham's was inherent in his duties as an Anglican priest, his *Cura Pastoralis*.

Wedgwood was advised by a local bookseller, a Quaker, Samuel Phillips, and accepted his advice, that the library should contain no novels. Phillips's reason was that people whose lot it was to submit to the daily round and common task must not read fictions that might offer them representations of ways of life to which they could never aspire. 'Let them read *none*,' said Phillips. 'Few of them are true pictures of life. The best of them fill the mind with dreams of happiness not to be enjoyed in this life.'[4] A similar observation occurs in George Hadley's *History of Hull* (1788): 'What ploughman who could read the renowned history of Tom Hickathrift, Jack the Giant-Killer, or the Seven Wise Men, would be content to whistle up one furrow and down another, from dawn in the morning, to the setting of the sun?'

Wrangham, for his part, became actively interested in education in 1800. In 1802 he preached a sermon on 'the Advantages of Diffused Knowledge'. And in 1808 he preached the Assize Sermon in York Minster, 'The Gospel Best Promulgated by National Schools', in which he argued that the spread of education and the incidence of crime were inversely proportional: more schools, less crime; and produced statistics to support his case. He sent a copy of this sermon to his friend, Wordsworth, together with an Appendix – an essay, 'On Village Libraries'. The Society for the Promotion of Christian Knowledge, founded in 1699, had been publishing dreary tracts for over a century, for the benefit of readers from the lower orders; a village library could obviously be built round a collection of such tracts, which were very numerous and very cheap.

The most popular and beneficial books [wrote Wrangham], next to the word of God, would be tracts which should neither perplex by their abstruseness, harass by their diffusion [i.e. diffuseness] nor fatigue by their prolixity; which should be, in three words, Perspicuous, Interesting, and Short. If in these were combined the essential qualities of Piety, Fulness of ideas, and an Accommodation to the various situations and contingencies of humbler society, there would be little wanting, with the Divine Blessing, to excite attention or to reward it.[5]

Wrangham was careful to point out that the purpose of such a library would *not* be to 'polish the peasant's taste, to stimulate his feelings, or to gratify his curiosity by periodical essays and sentimental or satirical novels', but he went so far as to suggest that the tracts 'should be rendered Interesting in particular by incident, or dialogue, or general vivacity of composition' – this last he recognized as 'an indispensable requisite'.

But why should the tracts be so rendered interesting? Why put sugar-coating on the improving pill? Wrangham answered: because

it has long and justly been complained, that 'Sermons are less read than Tales.' The chief attention, therefore, upon this occasion should be to select Books, where narrative and precept are so intimately blended, that in seizing the first, even gross apprehensions may imperceptibly lay hold on the latter.

Or, as Philip Sidney, whom Wrangham seems unwittingly to echo, had remarked,

So it is in men (most of which are childish in the best things, till they be cradled in their graves): glad they will be to hear the tales of Hercules, Achilles, Cyrus, Aeneas; and, hearing them, must needs hear the right description of wisdom, valour, and justice, which, if it had been barely, that is to say philosophically, set out, they would swear they be brought to school again.[6]

What, then, did Wrangham offer as his equivalents of the great humanist's Hercules and Achilles? Mrs Taylor's *Lessons to Servants*; *Memoirs of Experimental Religion Delineated*; Secker's *Lectures on the Catechism*; Melmoth's *Great Importance of a Religious Life*; and *An Essay on the Happiness of a well-ordered Family* – these are representative titles, alas; and they speak for themselves. The hungry sheep looked up and were fed on juiceless chaff! Yet Wrangham's vision of what such titles would accomplish is this:

> It is by such books alone, that the cottager can be lured back from the alehouse-corner, and the boon-companion to his family and his own fireside. He will read them to his children, or his children will read them to him, with equal instruction and entertainment; and amidst their innocent Questions, and his own simple replies, the evening will glide more happily by, than if spent in the torpor of dozing or the tumult of a debauch.

It all speaks of a decent enough vision betrayed by the desiccation of the carrot. And it encapsulates, of course, something of the profound failure of sympathetic imagination that lay at the root of the church's almost universal failure to capture the respect, let alone the allegiance, of the labouring class. Where, indeed, is there any evidence of the moral and intellectual breadth that George Eliot was later to propose as the first requisite?

To his credit, Wordsworth gave his friend Wrangham a rather dusty answer. In the first place he pointed out that sectarians and evangelical enthusiasts failed to recognize that the life of such gross peasants as his own neighbours was in its own distinctively unshowy fashion genuinely religious. Those committed to religious observances were of course misled because the lives of such naturally religious people carried no obvious impression of the sectarians' particular modes of faith, and because they were not given to making a display of 'fervent piety and habitual godliness'. Such a life, Wordsworth urged, was 'as innocent as we have a right to expect'. And, moreover, he considered it to be 'much more intellectual than a careless observer would suppose'.[7] As for the kind of library that Wrangham was concerned to promote, it 'would not be of much direct use in any of the districts with which I am acquainted, though almost every person can read: I mean, of *general* use as to morals or behaviour', even though he was prepared to concede that 'it might with individuals do much in awakening enterprize, calling forth ingenuity, and fostering genius. I have known several Persons who would eagerly have sought, not after these Books merely, but *any* Books, and would have been most happy in having such a collection to repair to.' And the benefits would have been diffused more widely, too, through conversations 'at the door, or by the fireside'.[8]

What, then, were Wordsworth's neighbours, the 'vulgar' readers of the Lake District, actually reading? According to Wordsworth, they were reading, not tracts, but chap-books.

> I find, among the people I am speaking of, half-penny Ballads, and penny and twopenny histories, in great abundance; these are often bought as charitable tributes to the poor Persons who hawk them about (and it is the best way of procuring them); they are frequently stitched together in tolerably thick volumes, and such I have read; some of the contents, though not often religious, very good; others objectionable, either for the superstition in them (such as prophecies, fortune-telling, etc.) or more frequently for indelicacy.[9]

The chap-books were abundant and, as Wordsworth remarked, they were 'influential'; indeed, he confessed to Wrangham that he had earlier composed some of his own poems with the hope that they might circulate in chap-book form, and so avail themselves of such influence: 'I have many times wished that I had talents to produce songs, poems, and little histories, that might circulate among other good things in this way.' There is no evidence, one way or the other, to tell us whether Wrangham might subsequently have walked the

I met a little cottage girl,
  She was eight years old she said ;
Her hair was thick with many a curl
  That cluster'd round her head.

She had a rustic woodland air,
  And she was wildly clad ;
Her eyes were fair, and very fair,
  Her beauty made me glad.

" Sisters and brothers, little maid,
  " How many may you be ;"
" How many ; seven in all," she said,
  And wond'ring look'd at me.

" And where are they, I pray you tell,
  She answered " seven are we,
" And two of us at Conway dwell,
  ' And two are gone to sea.

'We are Seven'

short distance from York Minster into Colliergate, where since 1803 James Kendrew had been running his press and shop, with its large and varied stock of small, beautifully printed chap-books; nor indeed whether it was Wrangham who nudged Kendrew into publishing Wordsworth's 'We are Seven' as a chap-book. Certainly the chap-book exists – it is one of Kendrew's most handsome (see the illustration above) – but Wrangham's complicity in its publication remains merely a tantalizing possibility.[10]

2

What, then, did this great abundance of tales offer? In general terms they have been expressively characterized in the words of Ernst Bloch:

> They are little traits from life and other things which were somehow not forgotten . . . that older impulse was there, too, to listen to stories, good and inconsequential alike, stories of different sorts and from different times,

9

was of great service. I had difficulty
in getting in my harvest. After this, I
burned my clay-made articles, earthen
pipkins, &c.,and could dress my dinner
tolerably well. My next harvest yielded
20 bushels of barley and 20 of rice. I
made a rough boat out of a large tree,
which I could not take to the sea;
afterwards a smaller one, with which I
had better success, or rather worse, for
in it I was taken by the current farther

Robinson Crusoe

noteworthy stories, which, if they come to their end, have
to end by touching us. It's a reading of traces everywhere,
in all directions, in bits and pieces variously divided.[11]

They were 'bits and pieces' of the great repertoire of tales,
romances, epics, that also surfaced in such collections as
Basile's *Pentamerone* and Boccaccio's *Decameron*: some of
them were native, but mostly they had come to England in a
variety of forms, along the trade-routes, from Venice, Arabia
and other exotic places. Some had been in print in England
since the time of Caxton and Wynkyn de Worde;[12] others had
moved into print more recently from the oral tradition; and in
the early eighteenth century, their range had been vastly
extended by the arrival of translations of Perrault and of
Galland's version of the *Thousand and One Nights*,[13] soon to
be followed by versions of *Robinson Crusoe* and the Lilliputian
episodes of *Gulliver's Travels*.

By the late eighteenth century, before their decline, these 'stories of different sorts and of different times' had, in their chap-book form, reached their bare bones: they had been pared down to their essential, irreducible, active elements: their frequently exotic heroes had mostly been shaken down into a state of homely naturalization; reduced to a sheer primal kind of narrative, the narrations 'pass at once into action,'[14] and allow their events to speak wondrously for themselves. One finds a minimal kind of characterization, an economy of type, for here people *are* what they do, or *are* what some mysterious powers enact through the agency of their acts: they are typed sufficiently by their various salient functions[15] – of loyal friend, traitor, enemy, villain, wanderer, searcher, simpleton, wild man and so on.[16]

How then did such persistent and uniform fictive conventions arise? One is tempted to answer, by accident; for, in Wordsworth's phrase, the tellers of these tales 'care not, know not, think not what they do'.[17] But the exigencies of commerce provide a more matter-of-fact answer. For convenience and economy of printing, the tale was best told within the scope of twenty-four small pages,[18] the text affording a little elbow-room for a few enticing wood-cuts, such as Wordsworth recalled so vividly:

> Profuse in garniture of wooden cuts
> Strange and uncouth; dire faces, figures dire,
> Sharp-knee'd, sharp-elbowed, and lean-ankled too,
> With long and ghostly shanks – forms which once seen
> Could never be forgotten![19]

Given severe confines of space, the rich leisurely and rambling romances had to shed their glamorous detail of person, setting, scene, in order that the essential story might just be squeezed in. It is likely also that the dynamics of the oral tradition – the narrative economy of the story-teller – also played its part: 'text' would be a pared-down skeleton, easily retained in memory, and allowing for extempore improvised elaboration: as Walter Scott put it, the story-tellers were 'permitted to use freedom of compression or dilatation as best suited their purpose . . . proportioned to the time and patience of their audience.'[20] When Gomme wrote his preface to the Villon Society's edition of the chap-book tale of Hickathrift he observed: 'Let any one take the trouble to read [the story] aloud, and he will at once perceive that there is a ring and a cadence given to the voice by the wording of the story, and particularly by the curious punctuation, which at once reminds us of a narrative from word of mouth.'[21] Whatever the precise validity of this particular case, it is clear that the 'idiolect' of the chap-books is closer to that of the story-teller than it is to that of the writer: it is a voice reaching out to take its listeners by the ear and lead them willy-nilly into the eventful activeness of its beginning. And since this is intended for the ear, rather than for the eye, the story can indulge itself in none of the luxuries that the eye can afford – reading again, recapitulating, slowing the pace, and so on. The story must 'tell' first time round, must realize itself as directly and as clearly as possible. So its syntax is, not surprisingly, almost entirely paratactic:[22] it is the syntax of a story-teller who tells you one thing, and then another, and then another, and then. . . . There is no occasion for great subtlety or complexity of effect, no place for many-layered subordinate clauses, no time for complex embedding.[23] The stories proceed, indeed, like one of their recurrent subjects – someone going on a journey with an urgent purpose: they 'get a move on', as do the ballads.

These narrative conventions are, of course, ideally suited to unsophisticated listeners and readers, young and old alike; and their reactions, over many generations, must have played some part in the evolution of the narrative manner. But there were deeper reasons for their popularity, especially among powerless, subordinated audiences – children, women, the poor – for many of the tales express fantasies of power and wealth, achieved either through the operations of Fortune (a pagan and arbitrary alternative to the churches' Providence), through magic, or through feats of courage, cunning, strength, or endurance. The small hero, usually of modest or even mean birth, defeats the larger, richer, more politically and socially powerful foe. The odds are all stacked against the puny, insignificant, ostensibly ignominious hero, but he not only endures, he prevails. The author of *1984* once remarked: 'Perhaps the basic myth of the Western World is Jack the Giant-Killer',[24] thinking, presumably, of the antinomian, protestant strand in Western mythologies and fantasies: Milton, of course, was of Jack's party, without realizing it; and so was Blake. But even more distinctly, it is the essential myth of the insubordinate spirit discreetly locked away inside those who were treated without question as naturally subordinate: children and the poor. In 1901, G.K. Chesterton also identified something of the political resonance of Jack the Giant-Killer:

> all the massive fragments of primitive morality are secondary to the great moral spirit which is the very heart of the fairy tales. That spirit is the principle . . . that nothing can do a man harm unless he fears it. At no time in the history of civilization, perhaps, has there been so much need to recall the ethics of the ancient warfare of Jack against the Giant, of the small against the gigantic. Those who in our own day express a peculiar sympathy with the weak in their struggle against the strong are often accused of indulging in hypersensitive humanitarianism unknown to the robuster ages of the world. The thing is a delusion. The sympathy for the weak against the strong speaks out of the oldest twilight. . . .[25]

It is hardly surprising that the most eloquent tributes to the chap-book repertoire came from those who had a vivid memory of their spirited childhood selves, as they had been: and the tributes also testify to the fact that an abiding passion for literature was often found to have been sown by these small, crude, 'amoral' prototypes.[26]

3

We can trace the beginning of the accelerated proliferation of the chap-book to the same year as saw the publication of Locke's *Thoughts*. It is a nice coincidence that in 1693 the Act of 1662, which had set a strict limit on printing, should have been repealed. Within a few years, in the early 1700s, we can find the chap-book receiving its due meed of recognition and gratitude. That the penny histories were very soon in good supply may be deduced from the miserable strictures of the anonymous author of *The History of Genesis* (1708):

> It is indeed a great Blessing of God, that Children in England have liberty to read the holy Scriptures, when others abroad are denied it. And yet alas! how often do we see Parents prefer 'Tom Thumb', 'Guy of Warwick', or some such foolish Book, before the Book of Life! Let not our Children read these vain Books, profane Ballads, and filthy songs.[27] Throw away all fond amorous Romances, and fabulous Histories of Giants, the bombast Atchievements of Knight Errantry, and the like; for these fill the Heads of Children with vain, silly and idle imaginations.[28]

Such negative sentiments have risen relentlessly like a sporadic wave of righteous indignation or hysteria ever since – now powerfully, now feebly; often strident, even alarmist – from rationalists, moralists, and those who would improve the world's manners. But, conversely, the friends of the 'vain, silly, and idle imaginations' have offered many spirited and persuasive defences of such imaginations.

Consider, for example, Richard Steele, writing in the *Tatler* in 1709 of a child's delight in such tales.[29] The account is familiar enough in the histories of children's literature; but commentators have consistently overlooked the crucial drift of the context within which Steele pointedly places the child and its enthusiasm. And Steele is clearly at pains to create a full, rich sense of the context. It is the civilised household of old friends of the writer; he is not only very fond of them, but respects them for their intelligence, their generosity, and their good sense. Steele creates a convincing picture of a family in which affection runs deep, is genuine, warmly felt, and perfectly unaffected. It is in this setting of generous sanity, of benign warmth, of couth amenity, that he presents the child and his chap-books, and not without a neat glancing dig at Locke's Aesop:

> I found upon conversation with him, though he was a little noisy in his mirth, that the child had excellent parts, and was a great master of all the learning on the other side eight years old. I perceived him a very great historian in Aesop's Fables: but he frankly declared to me his mind, 'that he did not delight in that learning, because he did not believe they were true:' for which reason I found he had very much *turned* his studies, for about a twelve-month past, into the lives and adventures of Don Bellianis of Greece, Guy of Warwick, the Seven Champions, and other historians of that age. . . . I found the boy had made remarks which might be of service to him during the course of his whole life. He would tell you the mismanagements of John Hickathrift, find fault with the passionate temper in Bevis of Southampton, and loved Saint George for being the champion of England; and by this means had his thoughts insensibly moulded into the notions of discretion, virtue, and honour. I was extolling his accomplishments, when the mother told me, 'that the little girl who led me in this morning was in her way a better scholar than he. Betty deals chiefly in fairies and sprites; and sometimes in a winter night will terrify the maids with her accounts, until they are afraid to go up to bed.'[30]

It is worth noting here that, in recognizing that the child was capable of making 'remarks, which might be of service to him during the course of his whole life' – again one detects an echo of Locke – Steele is not here praising precocity or pertness, but is alert to the fact that the child remains unconscious that he has learned anything at all. For, just as the Elizabethans who heard the tales of Hercules and Achilles 'must needs [have heard] the right description of wisdom, valour, and justice,' so the child's 'Thoughts' had been '*insensibly* moulded into the notions of discretion, virtue and honour.'[31]

Steele's recognition of the unconscious nature of this influence became rarer as the century wore on and a kind of Lilliputian knowingness became the norm under the influence of a vulgarized psychology of reason and judgement. But did such tales not sit uncomfortably, incongruously, with the growing refinement of early eighteenth-century society? In 1711, Addison discovered a 'despicable simplicity'[32] in the old ballad of 'The Two Children in the Wood', a popular part of the chap-book repertoire in both its verse and prose versions.[33] Addison noticed the 'abject phrase and poorness of expression' and said that he refrained from quoting it, because if he did quote, he might appear to be holding it up to ridicule. 'The language is mean,' he thought, and he suspected that his reader would think him 'not serious' for mentioning such a rude and paltry thing. And yet . . . he sets all this play with stylistic niceties against the disarming admission that he is moved by it, very moved, with 'inward meltings of humanity and compassion'; the fastidious critic is displaced by the Man of Feeling. The ballad, therefore, 'cannot fail to please those who . . . have a true and unprejudiced taste of nature.' Three-quarters of a century later, Horace Walpole offered a parallel case in his comments on Bannister's performance in a theatrical version of 'The Children in the Wood': 'He made me shed as many tears as the original ballad did when I was six years old.'[34] As for the introduction of 'the circumstance of the robin-redbreast', the only just comparison for Addison is with Horace: 'that passage in Horace, where he describes himself when he was a child, fallen asleep in a desert wood, and covered with leaves by the turtles [i.e. doves] that took pity on him.' Addison's conclusion is that the capacity to appreciate such 'productions, which have nothing to recommend them but the beauties of nature' is one way of distinguishing between those who are 'endowed with a true greatness of soul and genius', on the one hand, and the 'little conceited wits of the age' on the other.[35]

Young Samuel Johnson was being introduced to the tales of romance – which were to remain a lifelong passion – just about when Addison's essay appeared. His mother and her old maid, Catherine, sat him in their laps and gave him prodigal supply of them. They stirred his imagination powerfully, and he never forgot the way that the story of St George and the dragon had stirred and stimulated his mind. 'The recollection of such reading', Mrs Thrale wrote, 'as had delighted him in his infancy, made him always persist in fancying that it was the only reading which could please an infant; and he used to condemn me for putting Newbery's books into their hands as too trifling to engage their attention.'[36] Characteristically he insisted, 'Babies do not want to hear about babies; they like to be told of giants and castles, and of somewhat which can stretch and stimulate their little minds.'[37]

Mrs Thrale countered by urging the 'numerous editions and quick sale of *Tommy Prudent* or *Goody Two-Shoes*', but his answer was decisive: 'Remember always that the parents *buy* the books, and that the children never read them.'[38] By the time that she came to record this exchange, Mrs Thrale had made a disaster of educating her own children. In accordance with the conventional wisdom of her time she never entrusted her children to the servants except when asleep, and therefore beyond the harm of contamination, and she dutifully stuffed their heads with 'useful knowledge'. Johnson's candid response was hardly more than she was entitled to expect: 'You teach your daughters the diameters of the planets, and wonder, when you have done, that they do not delight in your company.'[39]

St George, whose exploits so excited young Samuel, was of course one of the Seven Champions of Christendom, and as

CHAP. I.

How and about Little Margery and her Brother.

CARE and difcontent fhortened the days of Little Margery's father.—He was forced from his family, and feized with a violent fever, in a place where Dr. James's Powder was not to be had, and where he died miferably. Margery's poor mother furvived the lofs of her hufband but a few days, and died of a broken heart, leaving Margery and her little brother to the wide world; but, poor woman, it would have melted your heart to have feen how frequently fhe heaved up her head, while fhe lay fpeechlefs, to furvey with languifhing looks her little orphans, as much as to fay, *Do Tommy, do Margery, come with me*.— They cried, poor things, and fhe fighed away her foul; and I hope is happy.

It would both have excited your pity and have done your heart good, to have feen how fond thefe two little ones were of each other, and how, hand in hand, they trotted about. Pray fee them.

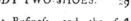

It

I once went e Ro nds with her, and was high'ly diverted, as you may be, if you pleafe to look into the next Chapter.

CHAP. V.

How Little Two-Shoes *became a trotting Tutorefs, and how fhe taught her young Pupils.*

IT was about feven o'Clock in the Morning when we fet out on this important

important Bufinefs, and the firft Houfe we came to was Farmer *Wilfon's*. See here it is.

Here *Margery* ftopped, and ran up to the Door, *Tap, tap, tap.* Who's there? Only little Goody *Two-Shoes*, anfwered *Margery*, come to teach *Billy*. Oh! little *Goody*, fays Mrs. *Wilfon*, with Pleafure in her Face, I am glad to fee you. *Billy* wants you

Walter Scott observed, in 1806, these were 'long known among the school-boys of this country'[40] – boys such as Laurence Sterne, whose novel, *Tristram Shandy*, touches in its own apparently inconsequential way on most of the issues felt to be of any consequence in the eighteenth century's rearing of children. In it, Uncle Toby offers a vivacious piece of reminiscence: 'When Guy, Earl of Warwick, and Parismus and Parismenus, and Valentine and Orson, and the Seven Champions of England [*sic*] were handed round the school, were they not all purchased with my own pocket money?' With a characteristic joke, directed both at himself and at his perplexed–delighted reader, Sterne observes that

> when a man sits down to write a history, – tho' it be but the history of *Jack* [*sic*] *Hickathrift* or *Tom Thumb*, he knows no more than his heels what lets and confounded hinderances he is to meet with in his way, – or what a dance he may be led, by one excursion or another, before all is over.[41]

In an unconscious echo, Walter Scott remarked of Thomas Warton's *History of Poetry* that

> whenever he has occasion to mention a tale of chivalry, it seems to operate like a spell, and he feels it impossible to proceed with the more immediate subject of his disquisition, until he has paced through the whole enchanted maze.[42]

It was in an 'enchanted maze' that Mark Akenside placed his 'virgin' reader in 1744; at the age of twenty-three, Akenside, a medical student, published his didactic poem, 'The Pleasures of the Imagination', a versifying of Addison's essays on the same subject. The poem is hardly likely to strike the modern reader as in any way 'enchanted' for the versifying involved him in convoluted excursions which effectively stifled whatever poetic talent he possessed. Addison's trinity of 'vast, novel, and beautiful' is translated into 'the sublime, the wonderful, and the fair', and it is in the second of these that what he has to say is to our present purpose. He celebrates 'the sprightly joy when aught unknown/Strikes the quick sense, and wakes each active power/To brisker measures', and 'the fond attentive gaze/Of young astonishment'. All human beings, he argues, feel a desire of 'objects new and strange': it is a gift of God, this craving, and if we obey it, it leads us to discover 'those sacred stores' that await us in 'Truth's exhaustless bosom'. It leads young men to leave home, to rove 'in foreign climes'; it keeps old men reading far into the night; it leads the virgin to follow 'with inchanted step/The mazes of some wild and wondrous tale,/From morn to eve'; and it also grips the juvenile audience of the village-matron:

> Hence, finally, by night
> The village-matron, round the blazing hearth,
> Suspends the infant-audience with her tales.
> Breathing astonishment! of witching rhymes,
> And evil spirits . . . of unquiet souls
> Risen from the grave to ease the heavy guilt
> Of deeds in life conceal'd; of shapes that walk
> At dead of night, and clank their chains, and wave
> The torch of hell around the murderer's bed.
> At every solemn pause the crowd recoil
> Gazing each other speechless, and congeal'd
> With shivering sighs: till eager for the event,
> Around the beldame all erect they hang,
> Each trembling heart with grateful terrors quell'd.[43]

Thomson, in 1726, had chosen to observe only 'superstitious horror' in such a scene; but Akenside, despite the conventional apparatus of gothic horrors, does recognize the emotional complexity and richness of 'grateful terror' – the paradoxical co-existence of fear and delight, and of the mysterious intertwining of these two emotions. It was a rich paradox, which was to receive due recognition in the remembrances of many writers fifty years later – Crabbe, Clare, Coleridge and Wordsworth among them. At an adult level it was to inform and energize one of the masterpieces of romantic drama – Goethe's *Faust*.

Like Uncle Toby in Shandyland, Goethe in Germany

recalled having spent his precious pocket-money on chap-books; so it was that he came to read a crude version of the *Faustbook*, a 'precious survival', and also discovered that grim actualities have a habit of breaking in on pleasurable fantasy:

> The publication, or rather the manufacture, of those books which at a later day became so well known under the name of *Volkschriften*, *Volksbücher*, was carried on in Frankfort itself. The immense demand for them led to their being printed from stereotypes on the most hideous absorbent paper, so that they were barely legible. We children were lucky to find these precious survivals from the Middle Ages every day on a little table at the door of a vendor of old books, and to make them our own for a few *kreutzer*. Eulenspiegel, the Four Sons of Aymon, the Fair Melusina, the Emperor Octavian, the Beautiful Magelone, Fortunatus, and all the rest of them . . . were at our service. . . . One great advantage was that, when we had read, worn out, or otherwise damaged one, it could easily be procured again, and devoured anew . . . childish ailments break in unexpectedly upon the most beautiful season of early life. Nor was it otherwise with me. I had just purchased Fortunatus with his Purse and Wishing-Cap, when I was attacked by discomfort and feverishness, the forerunners of small-pox.[44]

Carlyle, Goethe's greatest British disciple, wove a similar episode into *Sartor Resartus*:

> Meanwhile, what printed thing soever I could meet with I read. My very pocket-money I laid out on stall-literature; which, as it accumulated, I with my own hands sewed into volumes. By this means was the young head furnished with a considerable miscellany of things and shadows of things: History in authentic fragments lay mingled with fabulous chimeras, wherein also was reality; and the whole not as dead stuff, but as living pabulum, tolerably nutritive for a mind as yet so peptic.[45]

Despite the *cordon sanitaire* that separated many children from the grosser influences of servants – or perhaps because of it – it is clear that as soon as a boy had a spare penny in his pocket he thereby enjoyed access to a rich counter-culture, an alternative world, full of marvels and wonders, many leagues from the cold overview of adult rational supervision. At the same time as Goethe, in the 1750s and early 1760s, George Crabbe fell deeply under the spell of these tales. It was not enough for him to *read* them, the word is too tame: he *devoured* them, just as Wordsworth was later to *devour* the *Thousand and One Nights*. 'My father', Crabbe's son later wrote,

> devoured without restraint whatever came into his hands, but especially works of fiction – those little stories and ballads about ghosts, witches, and fairies, which were then almost exclusively the literature of youth, and which, whatever else might be thought about them, served, no doubt, to strike out the first sparks of imagination in the mind of many a youthful poet. Mr Crabbe retained, to the close of life, a strong partiality for marvellous tales of even this humble class.[46]

George Crabbe not only retained a strong and unapologetic partiality for such tales throughout his adult years, when, many people would have said, he should have known better, but he also celebrated their powerful charm in his own writing. Here is a specific and vivid record from *The Parish Register*:

> Unbound and heap'd these valued works beside,
> Laid humbler works, the pedler's pack supplied;
> Yet these, long since, have all acquir'd a name;
> The *Wandering Jew*, has found his way to fame:
> And fame, denied to many a labour'd song,
> Crowns *Thumb* the great and *Hickerthrift* the strong.
> There too is he, by wizard-power upheld,
> *Jack*, by whose arm the giant-brood were quell'd . . .
> No English blood, their pagan sense could smell,
> But heads dropt headlong, wondering why they fell.

These hear the parent Swain, reclin'd
With half his listening offspring on his knees.[47]

Crabbe recognized the essential *frisson* – the pleasurable terror – of such moments, and on occasions he slily introduced resonant little echoes of this protean world into his own verse;

Yet sometimes comes a ruffling cloud to make
The quiet surface of the Ocean shake;
As an awakened Giant with a frown,
Might shew his wrath, and then to sleep sink down.[48]

In such ways, Crabbe, partly out of a deep and unquestioned commitment to story-telling, maintained his contact with the rude tales of the chap-books: it seems that their primal energies served to re-invigorate him. And certainly there is no evidence whatever that they in any way unsettled his mind. It was, in fact, of Samuel Johnson that Bishop Percy remarked that as a boy 'he was immoderately fond of reading romances of chivalry, and he retained his fondness for them through life', even though Johnson himself attributed to those 'extravagant fictions that unsettled turn of mind which prevented his ever fixing in any profession'.[49]

4

Boswell, more typically, lost touch with the tales of his early years, and then by chance at the age of twenty-three came upon them again. It was an unexpected meeting with old friends:

. . . some days ago I went to the old printing office in Bow Church-yard kept by Dicey, whose family have kept it fourscore years. There are ushered into the world of literature *Jack and the Giants, The Seven Wise Men of Gotham*, and other story-books which in my dawning years amused me as much as *Rasselas* does now. I saw the whole scheme with a kind of pleasing romantic feeling to find myself really where all my old darlings were printed. I bought two dozen of the story-books and had them bound up with this title, *Curious Productions*.[50]

Boswell's inscription on this collection reads thus:

Having, when a boy, been much entertained with *Jack the Giant-Killer* and such little story-books, I have always retained a kind of affection for them, as they recall my early days. . . . I shall certainly some time or other write a little story-book in the style of these. It will not be a very easy task for me; it will require much nature and simplicity and a great acquaintance with the humours and traditions of the English common people. I shall be happy to succeed, for he who pleases children will be remembered with pleasure by men.[51]

As far as we know, Boswell never realized this intention, but what is remarkable about this note is the evidence it offers of Boswell's immediate sensitivity to the intrinsic linguistic difficulty of the enterprise, a linguistic challenge that is part of a larger cultural question. He is clearly aware, not merely of his own distance from childhood, but also of a cultural divide, as Addison had been when encountering 'The Two Children in the Wood'. An extreme case of this divide was offered by Dr Harwood's efforts in 1768 to 'clothe the vulgar version [of the Bible] in the vest of modern elegance': Corinthians 1, 13 – 'Charity suffereth long, and is kind . . .' – became: 'Benevolence is unruffled, is benign. . . . It preserves a consistent decorum. . . It throws a vail of candour over all things. . . . In fine, the virtues of superior eminence are these three, but the most illustrious of these is benevolence.' Boswell, unlike Harwood, recognized and respected 'nature', but unlike Addison, he did not find there a '*despicable* simplicity', or a '*poorness* of expression'. On the contrary, he breathed not a word of condescension, but hinted, rather, at the possibility of some kind of retrieval, the retrieval of 'nature', of 'simplicity'. Like Steele, Boswell seems to have found it easy to like children and to respect their likes. As for the question of linguistic idiom, of the primal idiolect of the tales, one is reminded of Hazlitt's observation, that

> Johnson's colloquial style was as blunt, direct, and downright, as his style of studied composition was involved and circuitous. As when friends knocked him up at his chambers, at three in the morning, and he came to the door with the poker in his hand, but seeing them, exclaimed, 'What, is it you, my lads? Then I'll have a frisk with you!' What words to come from the mouth of the great moralist and lexicographer!

Johnson could not of course have *written* so colloquial an expression: as Goldsmith remarked, 'If he were to write a fable of little fishes, he would make them speak like great whales.'

Boswell's retroactive, salvaging operation would then have been to set out to reclaim the 'frisk' of the 'vulgar' tongue, the expressive, even poetic, tribal language of little fishes, and to discard the rotund, periphrastic, latinized declamations of whales on their best public behaviour. It is to his credit that he was sensitive to the issue, even though nothing seems to have come of his scheme. But there was, in fact, an exemplary precedent for such an attempt at de-sophistication, such a return to the 'natural'. It was offered by Perrault's *Histoires ou Contes du temps passé* of 1697. Like Galland's French version of the *Thousand and One Nights*, these tales of Perrault soon passed into England, and in Robert Samber's translation were frequently reprinted throughout the eighteenth century.

Marc Soriano has given us what must be, for some time, the last word on Perrault, and his findings are very much to the point.[52] Charles Perrault was a distinguished member of the French Academy when he published the *Histoires*, and the question that intrigued Soriano was this: how could a sophisticated, lettered and urbane elderly man, living in a society characterized by emphatic cultural divides, produce a text that was so idiomatic, simple, vigorous, even ostensibly naive? For Soriano, part of the answer had turned up in 1953, when a manuscript of the *Histoires*, dated 1695, came to light; Jacques Barchilon, who edited this manuscript for publication, noted that, where in the 1697 text mention was made of *reading* the tales, in the manuscript of 1695 the term used was *listening*; the earlier version also contained notes on the story-teller's gestures and tones of voice. (Authentic support for Walter Benjamin's insistence that 'storytelling, in its sensory aspect, is by no means a job for the voice alone. Rather, in genuine storytelling, the hand plays a part which supports what is expressed in a hundred ways with its gestures trained by work.'[53]) Perrault's manuscript was, then, at least in part, a notation, a transcript, of stories that were being *heard*, not *read*. In addition, some of the tales could be seen to derive from early chap-book versions, dating back at least to the sixteenth century. It was in response to such 'models' that Perrault set himself the Boswellian task, to 'rediscover his "naivety"',[54] and the language that he shaped for his narratives was tacitly and tactfully an artful, finely gauged 'reconstruction of common language rather than that language itself'.[55] It appears that Darmancour, Perrault's son, collected the tales, both from story-tellers and from chap-books, and that Perrault then 'tuned' the language to a finely judged pitch – never over-elegant, over-refined, never grossly coarse or crude, or locked away inside the opacity of an extremely non-standard dialect, but achieving an extraordinary illusion of directness, idiomatic liveliness, and 'nature', the most elusive quality of all. So, Perrault effected a discreet marriage of 'la littérature savante' and 'la littérature orale'.[56]

Robert Samber's 1729 translation of Perrault managed to translate and preserve this liveliness of language:

> The poor girl bore all patiently, and dared not tell her father, who would have rattled her off; for his wife governed him entirely. . . . Now it happened that the King's son gave a ball, and invited all persons of quality to it: our young ladies were also invited; for they made a very great figure.

So much the worse, one might add, for 1977 which produced this from Angela Carter:

> The poor girl bore everything patiently and dared not complain to her father because he would have lost his temper with her. His new wife ruled with a rod of iron. . . . The King's son decided to hold a ball to which he invited all the aristocracy. Our two young ladies received their invitations, for they were well connected.[57]

Thomas Percy, Bishop of Dromore, recognized the existence of a deep cultural divide between educated, cultivated, genteel readers, on the one hand, and folk, 'primitive' or 'gothic' literature, on the other: a division which was in certain respects co-extensive with the division between adults and chidren.[58] Hence his frequent references, in his *Reliques of Ancient English Poetry* (1765), to the fact that many of the metrical romances that he was thereby reclaiming from dusty vellum for the benefit of an adult readership were still currently popular with children, to whom they had in effect been relegated. Of *Sir Guy of Warwick*, for example, he remarked: 'though now very properly resigned to children, it was once admired by all readers of wit and taste: for taste and wit had once their childhood.'[59] Similarly, of the story of St George:

> chiefly taken from the old story-book of the Seven Champions of Christendome; which, though now the play-thing of children, was once in high repute. . . . The Seven Champions, though written in a wild inflated style, contains some strong Gothic painting; which seems, for the most part, copied from the metrical romances of former ages.[60]

As Walter Scott was to remark, a little later, 'Mr [William] Godwin may have himself read Valentine and Orson, while at school; but during the eighteenth century, romances were the amusement of grown gentlemen.'[61] It was Scott, too, who expressed the view that Joseph Ritson's charge against Percy, of 'adulterating' the texts he had collected 'by modern improvements', was 'urged with far too much grossness': but Scott was careful to add: 'We do not, indeed, approve of this species of sophistication, by which the man of taste is sometimes a gainer at the expense of the antiquary.'[62] But Percy himself had entertained some scruples about publishing the romantic and gothic ballads at all, however smartened up to make them presentable. 'As most of them are of great simplicity, and seem to have been merely written for the people, he was long in doubt, whether, in the present state of improved literature, they could be deemed worthy the attention of the public.'[63] Rather as if the yokels had been pushed awkwardly into the best sitting-room of gentlefolk and told to entertain them. Fortunately, Johnson and William Shenstone were importunate in their encouragement of Percy's enterprise.[64]

When Percy gave his attention to the 'Ancient Ballad of Chevy-Chase', he recognized 'nature' as Addison had in 'The Two Children in the Wood':

> The fine heroic song of Chevy-Chase has ever been admired by competent judges. Those genuine strokes of nature and artless passion, which have endeared it to the most simple readers, have recommended it to the most refined; and it has equally been the amusement of our childhood, and the favourite of our riper years.[65]

It is interesting and instructive to compare Percy with that much more commonplace, vulgar and representative mind, that seems to encapsulate, albeit in a distinctively boring way, the conventional wisdom of an unquestioning acceptance of cultural subordination – Lord Chesterfield, who sustained the role of Mr Worldly Wiseman at inordinate length:

> There is, likewise, an awkwardness of expression and words, most carefully to be avoided; such as false

47

English, bad pronunciation, old sayings, and common proverbs; which are so many proofs of having kept bad and low company. If . . . you should let off a proverb . . . everybody would be persuaded that you had never kept company with anybody above footmen and house-maids.[66]

Again: 'Proverbial expressions and trite sayings are the flowers of the rhetoric of a vulgar man . . . a man of fashion never has recourse to proverbs. . . .'[67] Odd to see an aristocrat expressing the cultural anxiety and insecurity of a petty bourgeois!

In his 'Essay on the ancient Metrical Romances', Percy remarks of the romance *Libius Disconius* that if an epic poem may be defined as 'a fable related . . . to excite admiration, and inspire virtue, by representing the action of some one hero, favoured by heaven, who executes a great design, in spite of all the obstacles that oppose him' – if that is a proper definition of an epic poem, then it follows that the title, the status, of epic poem *must* be accorded to this romance despite its 'barbarous unpolished language'. Thus a 'vulgar' romance, hitherto consigned by the polite to outer darkness, enters the same ranks as *Paradise Lost*.

It is an ingenious trap, cunningly prepared, and perfectly convincing: and it serves to bridge the gap between the high and the ostensibly low: in a similar spirit Richard Graves, in his novel *The Spiritual Quixote* (1772), remarked on the similarity between adventures of Bunyan's Christian and those of Jack the Giant-Killer and Tom Hickathrift: and one is immediately reminded of the obvious fact that may be too easily overlooked – that *Pilgrim's Progress* was a popular masterpiece partly because its picaresque narrative was close indeed to that of the romances, just as many of its events were as dramatic and glamorous as the wonders of the old tales. Bunyan, moreover, had achieved precisely what Wrangham hoped for in the writer of tracts: 'narrative and precept' were indeed intimately blended, inextricably so; and the whole was 'rendered interesting by incident, or dialogue, or general vivacity of composition'. But writers like Bunyan didn't exactly grow on trees, for he had enjoyed the benefit of drawing preconsciously on the prose of the King James Bible and on the colloquial language to be found on the more vigorous, ruder side of the cultural divide: his prose has the sinews and idioms of someone who grew up among 'vulgar' story-tellers.

5

In 1797, Coleridge offered his friend, Thomas Poole, some remarkable autobiographical notes, offering an account of his formative years in the late 1770s and early 1780s:

> . . . the School-boys drove me from play, & were always tormenting me – & hence I took no pleasure in boyish sports – but read incessantly. . . . I read thro' all the gilt-cover little books that could be had at that time, & likewise all the uncovered [i.e. chap-book] tales of Tom Hickathrift, Jack the Giant-killer, &c & &c &c &c –/– and I used to lie by the wall, and *mope* – and my spirits used to come upon me suddenly, & in a flood – & then I was accustomed to run up and down the church-yard, and act over all I had been reading on the docks, the nettles, and the rank-grass.[68]

Just as the young Thomas Bewick and his friends 'became' the 'savages' in *Robinson Crusoe*, so Coleridge became Hickathrift and Jack.[69]

But his early reading did not always give rise to such pleasurable fantasy-play:

> At six years old I remember to have read Belisarius, Robinson Crusoe, & Philip Quarle [Quarll] – and then I found the Arabian Nights' entertainments – one tale of which (the tale of a man who was compelled to seek for a

pure virgin) made so deep an impression on me (I had read it in the evening while my mother was mending stockings) that I was haunted by spectres, whenever I was in the dark – and I distinctly remember the anxious & fearful eagerness, with which I used to watch the window, in which the books lay. . . .[70]

Norman Fruman has cast severe doubt on the reliability of this account:[71] Coleridge, he argues, could not have found the tale of a man in search of a virgin in the *Thousand and One Nights*, for such a tale is not to be found there. As with his famous reference to Goody Two-Shoes, Coleridge's memory is at fault, or he is inventing a plausible fiction. But Fruman goes further and hints at the basic undependability of Coleridge's claim that he could have been reading such books at the age of six. The improbability disappears if we recall that Coleridge was the youngest of ten children and that the texts he mentions were all available in compressed form as chapbooks. What less improbable than a shared-reading experience in such circumstances? Even today, in large families, it is not uncommon for three- or four-year-olds to enjoy the illusion of actually reading in this way. As for the night-fears, Coleridge seems to have derived some kind of satisfaction from describing them: 'Frequently have I, half-awake & half-asleep, my body diseased and fevered by my imagination, seen armies of ugly Things bursting in upon me, & these four angels keeping them off'[72] – the four angels being, of course, those from the traditional rhyme:

> Matthew, Mark, Luke, & John,
> Guard the bed that I sleep on,
> Four angels round my bed,
> Two at the foot and two at the head.

The image of the child's body 'diseased & fevered by [his] imagination' is of course conventional eighteenth-century psychology, such as one finds in Maria Edgeworth's tales.

When he was eight years old, young Coleridge took the

wonders of the heavens in his stride: in the company of his father:

> I remember, that at eight years old I walked with him one winter evening from a farmer's house, a mile from Ottery – & he told me the names of the stars – and how Jupiter was a thousand times larger than our world – and that the other twinkling stars were Suns that had worlds rolling round them – & when I came home, he shewed me how they rolled round –/. I heard him with a profound delight & admiration; but without the least mixture of wonder or incredulity. For from my early reading of Faery Tales, & Genii &c &c – my mind had been habituated *to the Vast* – & I never regarded *my senses* in any way as the criteria of my belief. I regulated all my creeds by my conceptions not by my *sight* – even at that age.[73]

To a modern reader that last phrase, 'even at that age', may seem odd, or even misguided. We might well expect, 'especially at that age'. But the degree to which the child's perceptions are formed by inner necessity, fantasy and preconception was not something that eighteenth-century empiricism was altogether ready to accept.

But what of the larger effects on children of reading fantastic, gothic tales? What of the moral, intellectual, emotional, epistemological effects? On the whole, Coleridge was in no doubt that they were essentially beneficial:

> Should children be permitted to read Romances, & Relations of Giants & Magicians, & Genii? – I know all that has been said against it; but I have formed my faith in the affirmative. – I know no other way of giving the mind a love of 'the Great', & 'the Whole'. – Those who have been led to the same truths step by step thro' the constant testimony of their senses, seem to me to want a sense which I possess – They contemplate nothing but *parts* – and all *parts* are necessarily little – and the Universe to them is but a mass of *little things*. It is true, that the mind

may become credulous & prone to superstition by the former method – but are not the Experimentalists credulous even to madness in believing any absurdity, rather than believe the grandest truths, if they have not the testimony of their own senses in their favor? – I have known some who have been *rationally* educated, as it is styled. They were marked by a microscopic acuteness; but when they looked at great things, all became a blank & they saw nothing – and denied (very illogically) that any thing could be seen; and uniformly put the negation of a power for the possession of a power – & called the want of imagination Judgment, & the never being moved to Rapture Philosophy![74]

Are there, then, sharp contradictions between that effectively concessive 'even at that age' and the rhapsodic anti-materialism of the subsequent paragraph? Is Coleridge over a philosophical barrel? It seems more than likely. For in the same week as he offered those autobiographical reflections to Tom Poole, he wrote to another friend, John Thelwall, about the very same matter, but in a spirit of painful confession and a sense of very present crisis of mind and spirit:

I can *at times* feel strongly the beauties you describe – in themselves, & for themselves – but more frequently *all things* appear little – all the knowledge that can be acquired, child's play – the universe itself, what but an immense heap of *little* things? – I can contemplate nothing but parts, & parts are all *little* –! My mind feels as if it ached to behold & know something *great* – something *one & indivisible* – and it is only in the faith of this that rocks or waterfalls, mountains or caverns give me the sense of sublimity or majesty! – But in this faith *all things* counterfeit infinity![75]

His 1797 memory of his childhood idealism, its sense of wholeness, of a universe that was all of a piece, coherent and charged with benign meaning – that memory is clearly affirmative. But when, to a different friend, he turned his mind to his present condition, the same questions clearly provoked pain, a deep or at least intense sense of fragmentation and of pettiness – a kind of epistemological malignity giving rise to a sense of deprivation and depravation of meaning.[76]

The discrepancy between past and present seems to offer an instance of the familiar distinction between the seamlessness of the child's unquestioning, pre-critical, pre-conceptual ways of knowing – the epistemology of Innocence, so to speak – and the distancing, the alienation, that come with the development of adult, critical thought, and seem so often to be the inevitable by-product of an education in which we are 'compelled to number footsteps upon the sand'.[77] Certainly Coleridge was only too familar with such a dialectic. But a more immediate, more specific, even banal, explanation is available to us in Coleridge's letter to John Prior Estlin, of 30 December 1797, in which he gave Estlin an account of his recent vocational uncertainties: Tom Wedgwood had invited him and Wordsworth to participate in a bizarre educational experiment – the controlled, experimental supervision of a solitary child's development in what were to be virtually laboratory conditions. (See Chapter Nine, pp. 278–80, for a fuller account of this.) In order effectively to participate in such an experiment, Coleridge was characteristically convinced that he would need to know far more than he already did; and there is evidence to suggest that he actually set about the task of amassing the requisite knowledge – 'the Mathematical Branches, chemistry, Anatomy, the laws of Life, the laws of Intellect, & lastly, thro' universal History, arranging separately all the facts that elucidate the separate states of Society, savage, civilized & luxurious. . . .' Eighteen months later, he was still in pursuit of his omniscient will-o'-the-wisp. He wrote to Josiah Wedgwood, Jr: 'I have attended the lectures on Physiology, Anatomy, and Natural History, with regularity. . . .'[78]

So Coleridge crammed himself, desperately, with useful knowledge, sitting astride a deep contradiction between two ways of knowing. And it was only when he became a privileged reader of the manuscript of *The Prelude* that his tensions, at least on this score, began to abate under the calming influence of Wordsworth's confident and steady character, and of the coherence and authority of Wordworth's philosophical meditations on childhood and learning.

So, in May 1808, under the influence of the less clever and more intelligent poet, Coleridge offered the following thoughts to the audience at his lecture on education:

> In speaking of Education as a means of strengthening the character, he opposed our system of 'cramming' children. . . . He censured the practice of carrying the notion of making learning easy much too far, and especially satirised the good books in Miss Edgeworth's style. 'I infinitely prefer the little books of "The Seven Champions of Christendom", "Jack the Giant-Killer", etc., etc., – for at least they make the child forget himself – to your moral tales where a good little boy comes in and says, "Mama, I met a poor beggar man and gave him the sixpence you gave me yesterday. Did I do right?" – "O, yes, my dear, to be sure you did." This is not virtue, but vanity; such books and such lessons do not teach goodness, but – if I might venture such a word – goodyness. . . . Instructors should be careful not to let the intellect die of plethora.'[79]

A year later, in *The Friend*, he poked fun at both Robert Hooke's 'multifarious recipe for the growth of science',[80] and his 'appalling catalogue of preliminary knowledges' which had to be mastered before one could presume to construct any theories at all (echoes here of Coleridge's schemes in the 1790s!), and at Isaac Watts's essay, 'The Improvement of the Mind', where Watts's advice was:

> Furnish yourself with *a rich variety of Ideas*. Acquaint yourselves with *things* ancient and modern; *things* natural, civil, and religious; *things* of your native land, and of

foreign countries; *things* domestic and national; *things* present, past, and future,; and above all, be well acquainted with God and yourselves; with animal nature, and the workings of your own spirit. *Such a general acquaintance with things will be of a very great advantage.*[81]

It is indeed difficult to extract anything of value from such tushery, as Samuel Johnson claimed to have done, but the manic touch of omniscience is again not unlike the plans that Coleridge had in the 1790s.

In 1811 he returned once more, and more than a little divergently, to the question of literature in childhood. He deplored the growth of a didacticism that involved 'so many miserable little beings taught to think before they had the means of thinking'. And he leapt to defend 'natural infantile prattle'. As for the best books, he exclaimed,

> Give me the works which delighted my youth. Give me the History of St George and the Seven Champions of Christendom, which at every leisure moment I used to hide myself in a corner to read. Give me the Arabian Nights' Entertainments, which I used to watch till the sun shining on the bookcase approached it, and glowing full upon it gave me courage to take it from the shelf. I heard of no little Billies, and sought no praise for giving to beggars, and I trust that my heart is not the worse, or the less inclined to feel sympathy for all men, because I first learnt the powers of my nature, and to reverence that nature – for who can feel and reverence the nature of man and not feel deeply for the afflictions of others possessing like powers and like nature.[82]

One may feel tempted to ask, 'Why "Give *me*"?' One may feel provoked to wince at the way in which Coleridge offers a garbling of *The Prelude*. And one may marvel at Coleridge's sheer capacity for repeating himself, or, rather, his capacity for repeating Wordsworth: here is part of his lecture on 'Dr Bell's New System of Education' – a system with which Coleridge was for a time intensely infatuated:

Nothing should be more impressed on parents and tutors than to make children forget themselves; and books which only told how Master Billy and Miss Ann spoke and acted, were not only ridiculous but extremely hurtful; much better give them Jack the Giant-Killer, or the Seven Champions, or anything which, being beyond their own sphere of action, should not feed their self-pride.[83]

The numerous debts to Wordsworth's *Prelude*, book V, in Coleridge's lectures, between 1808 and 1813, are not merely peripheral; they are often a matter of a lecture's central argument. But Wordsworth's poem was still safely tucked away in manuscript, so the debts could pass off completely unacknowledged. The pity is that it was a matter, not only of extensive plagiarism, but of garbling: of translating a complex and subtle 'Argument', such as one finds in book V of *The Prelude*, into a lecture-room rhetoric characterized by an egregious capacity for wandering from the point – which is not always easy to identify – and by a persistent inclination to self-reference, almost verging on solipsism. Coleridge's main themes in the lectures that concern us appear to be these: the forcing of children into a premature display of quasi-adult rationality; the cult of self-conscious virtue, which drew the attention of the child to its own virtue; and the relative neglect or contempt shown toward the repertoire of traditional tales: all three figure large in book V of *The Prelude*. So also does a fourth issue to which Coleridge turned his mind in the *Biographia Literaria* of 1817: why, or how, did such flimsy little stories come to acquire such a remarkable capacity for survival? Characteristically, Coleridge overlooked the obvious explanation – that children, grandparents and peasants are in their several ways extremely conservative. Coleridge posed the more specifically literary question of whether this survival was related to the fact that for many centuries many of the tales had been cast in metrical form – the form, in fact, in which Walter Scott preferred to read and hear them.[84]

Certainly, the supporting frames of rhythm and of rhyme
would do a great deal to sustain oral/aural transmission and
retention; but Coleridge was not entirely convinced of this,
and in the event he simply abandoned the question and broke
off, to celebrate the spectacle of a giant's great beard:

> I am not convinced by the collation of facts, that the
> 'Children in the Wood' owes either its preservation, or its
> popularity, to its metrical form. Mr Marshal's repository
> affords a number of tales in prose inferior in pathos and
> general merit, some of as old a date, and many as widely
> popular. 'Tom Hickathrift', 'Jack the Giant-Killer',
> 'Goody Two-Shoes', and 'Little Red Riding-Hood' are
> formidable rivals. And that they have continued in prose,
> cannot be fairly explained by the assumption, that the
> comparative meanness of their thoughts and images
> precluded even the humblest forms of metre. The scene
> of Goody Two-Shoes in the church is perfectly sus-
> ceptible of metrical narration; and, among the most
> extraordinarily miraculous miracles or wonders even of
> the present age, I do not recollect a more astonishing
> image than that of the 'whole rookery, that flew out of the
> giant's beard', scared by the tremendous voice, with
> which this monster answered the challenge of the heroic
> Tom Hickathrift![85]

For over a century, such tales had survived in a state almost
of outlawry: they were contrary to reason, they were vulgar,
and they were of very dubious morality. Yet, even as
Coleridge celebrated Hickathrift, the tales were threatened as
never before by the cult of useful knowledge. One could argue
till the cows came home about when and how this cult started.
Certainly it was a movement to reckon with by the 1770s, but
it assumed formidable proportions in the early nineteenth
century, acquiring power, prestige, proof and legitimacy from
the indisputable fact that industrialization, the application of
useful knowledge, could create wealth. And it did not escape
Coleridge's pansophistical attention:

Whatever scruples may arise to its being an enlightened age, there can be no doubt that it is an enlightening one – an era of *enlighteners*, from the Gas Light Company to the dazzling Illuminati in the Temple of Reason – not forgetting the diffusers of light from the Penny-Tract-pedlary, nor the numberless writers of the small, but luminous works on arts, trades, and sciences, natural history, and astronomy, all for the use of children from three years old to seven, interwoven with their own little biographies and nursery journals, to the exclusion of Goody Two Shoes, as favouring superstition, by one party; and of Jack the Giant Killer, as a suspicious parody of David and Goliath, by the other.[86]

There is no virtue like that of the converted sinner; once more one thinks ironically of Coleridge's earlier pursuit of the many keys to all the mythologies, and one notes, too, his carelessness in thinking that *Goody Two-Shoes* could ever be exposed to suspicion on the grounds of superstition, when that is precisely and explicitly what it speaks out against. Coleridge's weakness for the showy and dismissive rhetorical effect, his carelessness, and his frequent ignorance – all make it all the more regrettable that publication of *The Prelude* was so long deferred.

6

There could be no greater contrast than that between Coleridge and Clare. One, egomaniacal, the star performer at dinner-parties, his head lumbered with a crazy heterogeneous olla podrida of 'knowledge', and sophisticated enough to put on an impressive public face; the other, awkward, diffident, deeply learned in matters of local nature, a green provincial. But one thing they had in common: a love of Hickathrift! The peculiar value of Clare's report on folk-culture is that it was given from inside; its intimacy is that of one who writes from within the community of those who could barely read, rather than of a *spectator ab extra*. He recorded the culture of the provincial rural poor, as a member of the tribe, albeit one with an often painful sense of being set apart by the itch to rhyme. In his *Village Minstrel*, for all the poem's debts to Beattie's gothic farrago, he wrote truly of the day-long, back-breaking work in the fields, and of how the women, with small children clustered at their feet and ankles, would snatch a rest:

> When old women, overpowered by heat,
> Tucked up their clothes and sickened at the toil,
> Seeking beneath the thorn the mole-hill seat,
> To tell their tales and catch their breath awhile,
> Their gabbling talk did Lubin's cares beguile;
> And some would tell their tales, and some would sing,
> And many a dame, to make the children smile,
> Would tell of many a funny laughing thing,
> While merrily the snuff went pinching round the ring.

> Here Lubin listened with awe-struck surprise,
> When Hickathrift's great strength has met his ear,
> How he killed giants as they were but flies,
> And lifted trees as one would lift a spear,
> Though not much bigger than his fellows were;
> He knew no troubles waggoners have known,
> Of getting stalled, and such disasters drear;
> Up he'd chuck sacks as one would hurl a stone,
> And draw whole loads of grain unaided and alone.[87]

It is worth noting that Hickathrift, the miraculously power-ful peasant-boy, the scourge of giants and the saviour of his community, belonged to the same world as the audience, precisely. So the fantasies of his prodigious strength must have been specially appealing to them. And Clare perceived that such tales were as naturally indigenous, and consistently so, from year to year, generation to generation, as the very weeds themselves:

> robin hood
> And giant blue heard and such tales
> That live like flowers in rural vales

Natural as last years faded blooms
Anew with the fresh season comes
So these old tales from old to young
Take root and blossom where they sprung
Till age and winter bids them wane
Then fond youth takes them up again . . .[88]

For Clare, such tales were not only as natural, native, and permanent as wild flowers, but they were also 'poetry': in Edwin Morgan's phrase, they were 'a poetry before poetry'.[89] Clare wrote:

> I was fond of books before I began to write poetry. These were such that chance came at – 6py Pamphlets that are in the possession of every door-calling hawker, and found on every bookstall at fairs and markets, whose titles are as familiar with every one as his own name. Shall I repeat some of them – 'Little Red Riding Hood', 'Valentine and Orson', 'Jack and the Jiant' . . . 'The Seven Sleepers', 'Tom Hickathrift', 'Johnny Armstrong' . . . and many others. Shall I go on? No, these have memorys as common as Prayer Books and Psalters with the peasantry. Such were the books that delighted me and I saved all the pence I got to buy them for they were the whole world of literature to me and I knew of no other. I carried them in my pocket and read them at my leisure and they was the never weary food of winter evenings, ere Milton Shakespeare and Thomson had ever existed in my memory, and I feel a love for them still. Nay, I cannot help fancying now that Cock Robin, Babes in the Wood, Mother Hubbard and her Cat, etc., etc., are real poetry in all its native simplicity and as it should be. I know I am foolish enough to have fancys different from others and childhood is a strong spell over my feelings but I think so on and cannot help it.[90]

That strikes me, despite its concluding diffidence, as a testimony of great natural authority, the authority of personal knowledge and of a clear uninsistent honesty. It also offers the peculiar virtue of coming from below the cultural divide. As such, it is the first voice of its kind that we have so far heard.

Like flowers and games, the tales had their seasons, and, as one might expect, Clare had an intimate appreciation of the way in which the tales helped the villagers to get through their long winter evenings, by the flickering light of the fire and perhaps a rush-light. He often recalled the deeply ambivalent frisson of delight and terror that he had known as a child. After the telling of such tales, children retired unwillingly to the darkness of the bedroom: they

> hide their heads beneath the cloaths
> And try in vain to seek repose
> While yet to fancys sleepless eye
> Witches on sheep trays gallop bye
> And faireys like to rising sparks
> Swarm twittering round them in the dark. . . .[91]

He recalled many such occasions with a vivid sense of the way in which they had been charged with a potent mixture of wonder, delight and apprehension – a tingling of nerves, an almost unbearable intensity of feeling. What, then, had supervened, to petrify, to deaden, to dull, such charged moments?

> O spirit of the days gone bye
> Sweet childhoods fearful extacy
> The witching spells of winter nights
> Where are they fled wi their delights . . .
> Breathless suspense and all their crew
> To what wild dwelling have they flew
> I read in books but find them not
> For poesy hath its youth forgot. . . .[92]

Was there any cause in nature for such a falling-off? Why had nature, once so rich, apparently inexhaustible, become so flat and stale? What was the root cause of such disenchantment, such painful disinheritance? Was it a radical neurotic failure to 'grow up', a failure to carry over into maturity the energy of earlier years? Was it a retreat into a regressive need to cling to pre-conscious ways of being? Was it a failure to incorporate new ways of knowing, more 'critical', more detached, more thoughtful, less passional? Was it inevitable that, for Clare, learning the Linnean system of botanical classification should have the effect of reducing nature to 'collections of dried specimens like carcasses in glass cases'? Could his incorrigibly green mind not cope with the abstracting, cool clear understanding offered by Reason's 'sterner lore'?

> Where are they gone the joys and fears
> The links the life of other years
> I thought they bound around my heart
> So close that we could never part
> Till reason like a winters day
> Nipt childhood visions all way . . .
> Memory may yet the themes repeat
> But childhoods heart doth cease to beat
> At stories [that] reasons sterner lore
> Turneth like gossips from her door. . . .[93]

In the event, he was left with a demythologized, vacant world, drained of spirit, of felt life, of meaning –

> Those truths are fled and left behind
> A real world and doubting mind[.][94]

It is tempting to see Clare's predicament as merely personal, as belonging only to a green man – green in many senses – who failed lamentably to come to terms with an unaccommodating world, and who therefore lapsed into various futile attempts to escape, backwards and inwards, into his own infantile self. But we must acknowledge that his crisis occurred at a particular moment in history, a moment when other equally tender, but better supported or more resourceful, minds were oppressed, confused, or disturbed by the way the world was beginning to wag. The status accorded to various forms of knowledge was undeniably changing: 'poetry', construed both literally and metaphorically, was undergoing devaluation, and the epoch was characterized variously by those discomfited by the change, as an 'iron time', and a 'mathematical age'. Scott, Wordsworth, Hazlitt, and with hindsight, Ruskin, Carlyle and Dickens, all concurred in registering such a shift; and, like Coleridge before him, and John Stuart Mill a generation later, Clare went through a peculiarly painful crisis of knowledge, which involved necessarily a crisis of faith. It was nothing more nor less than a matter of feeling at home in the world, that is, of not any longer feeling at home. Coleridge and Mill had much to sustain them. Clare, unsupported, retreated into a kind of private reality that was identified as insanity.

In 1860, at the age of sixty-seven, institutionalized for over twenty years, he had only himself and his memories to talk to; and it was Jack the Giant-Killer that he recalled – the myth of the green lad pitting his wits against overbearing, blundering and stupid powers: it is difficult to believe that he could any longer find any truth in such a fantasy:

To John Clare

Well honest John how fare you now at home
The Spring is come and birds are building nests
The old cock robin to the stye is come
With olive feathers and its ruddy breast
And the old cock with wattles and red comb
Struts with the hens and seems to like some best
Then crows and looks about for little crumbs
Swept out by little folks an hour ago
The pigs sleep in the sty the bookmen comes
The little boys lets home close nesting go
And pockets tops and tawes where daiseys bloom
To look at the new number just laid down
With lots of pictures and good stories too
And Jack the jiant killers high renown[.][95]

NOTES AND REFERENCES

1 On Tom Wedgwood, see R.B. Litchfield, *Tom Wedgwood, the First Photographer* (London: Duckworth, 1903).

2 Wrangham had been a contemporary of Wordsworth at Cambridge, and at the time of this correspondence was an important member of the Anglican establishment in York and the East Riding. In 1816 he published *Sermons Practical and Occasional*, 3 vols (London: Baldwin, Cradock & Joy). His advocacy of education for the poor began when the Blagdon controversy over Hannah More's village school was raging. He established a village library at Hunmanby and claimed that of its hundred or so volumes there were rarely more than half a dozen on the shelves.

3 *Westminster Review*, vol. LXVI (July 1856), p. 51; reprinted in *Essays*, ed. T. Pinney (London: Routledge & Kegan Paul, 1963), p. 266.

4 Litchfield, op.cit., p. 44.

5 Wrangham's attitude to the people is unapologetically paternalistic. On pseudo-egalitarianism at this time, see E.P. Thompson, *Education and Experience* (Leeds: Leeds University Press, 1968).

6 *A Defence of Poetry*, ed. J. van Dorsten (London: Oxford University Press, 1975), p. 39.

7 Cf. Bishop Percy's observations, in *Reliques of Ancient English Poetry*, ed. H.B. Wheatley, 3 vols (London: Swan Sonnenschein, 1876–7), vol. I, p. lviii.

8 Wordsworth's awareness of the *oral* dimension of cultural transmission marks him off from most of his contemporaries. See *The Excursion*, bk 1, ll. 162 ff.

9 Cf. the French 'livrets de colportage': '"canards" annonçant toujours d'étonnantes et horrifiques nouvelles, almanachs pleins de reçettes fantaisistes, de remèdes de bonne femme, de formules frôlant la magie, livrets de colportage contenant d'extraordinaires histoires, adaptations trés simplifiées d'oeuvres plus élaborées souvent passées de mode' (Marc Soriano, *Les Contes de Perrault; culture savante et traditions populaires*, Paris: Gallimard, 1968, p. 94). Cf. Philippe Ariès, *Centuries of Childhood* (Harmondsworth: Penguin Books, 1973), pp. 93–6; and John Ashton:

> Whether men and women are better now than they used to be, is a moot point, but things used to be spoken of openly, which are now whispered, and no harm was done, nor offence taken, so the broad humour of the jest-books was,

after all, only exuberant fun, and many of the *bonnes histoires* are extremely laughable, though to our own thinking equally indelicate. (*Chap-books of the Eighteenth Century*, London: Chatto & Windus, 1882, p. xi).

10 James Kendrew of Colliergate, York, started his business in 1801, specializing in chap-books for children.

11 *Spüren*, quoted by F. Jameson in *Marxism and Form* (Princeton, NJ: Princeton University Press, 1974) p. 124.

12 The best account of the early diffusion of chap-book tales is given by Margaret Spufford in *Small Books and Pleasant Histories* (London: Methuen, 1981).

13 In a draft of some lines for *The Prelude*, subsequently abandoned, Wordsworth recalled the power and glamour of the *Thousand and One Nights*:

When summer comes, no more within himself
Marvels what summer is; and when in fine
That great Magician, the unresting year,
Hath play'd changes off, till less and less
They excite in us a passionate regard;
Then attestations new of growing life,
Distinct impressions and unbounded thought,
To appease the absolute necessities
That struggle in us, opportunely come
From the universe of fable and (romance?) –
Trees that bear gems for fruit, rocks spouting milk,
And diamond palaces, and birds that sing
With human voices, formidable hills,
Or magnets which, leagues off, can witch away
Iron, disjointing in a moment's space
The unhappy ship that comes within their reach,
Enchanted armour, talismanic rings,
Dwarfs, Giants, Genii, creatures that can shape
Themselves and be or not be at their will;
Others, the slaves and instruments of these,
That neither are beast, bird, insect or worm,
But shapes of all, and powers intemperately
Upon each other heap'd, or parcell'd out
In boundless interchange.

(Wordsworth, *Poetic Works*, ed. E. de Selincourt, Oxford: Clarendon Press, 1940–9, vol. v, p. 573).

14 Florence V. Barry, *A Century of Childen's Books* (London: Methuen, 1922), p. 18, and Soriano, op. cit., pp. 137 and 163.

15 Cf. Vladimir Propp, *Morphology of the Folk-Tale* (Austin, Tex.: University of Texas Press, 1969).

16 Or, as Walter Scott put it: 'the heroes are no doubt sufficiently savage, they shed much blood in battle, and are determined enemies to giants and wizards' ('Essay on Metrical Romances'). Cf. Percy, op.cit., vol. 1, pp. xxxii–iii.

17 *The Prelude*, bk v. See below, p. 287.

18 This was by no means universal. Sabine's edition of *Guy of Warwick*, c.1780, ran to 144 pages.

19 *The Excursion*, bk 1, ll. 181–4.

20 *Edinburgh Review* (1806), p. 16.

21 Reprinted in R.M. Dorson, *Peasant Customs and Savage Myths* (London: Routledge & Kegan Paul, 1968).

22 As in the syntax of stories told or written by young children: a and b and c and d and e and f and g. . . .; in most European languages the words for 'tale' and for 'count' come from the same root.

23 Cf. *Rambler*, no. 177 (November 1751): *The Works of Samuel Johnson*, vol. 5 (New Haven, Conn., and London: Yale University Press, 1969), p. 168.

24 George Orwell, quoted in Victor E. Neuburg, *The Penny Histories* (London: Oxford University Press, 1968), p. 17.

25 *The Speaker* (12 October 1901). Chesterton asserted: 'Fairy tales are the only true accounts that man has ever given of his destiny' (*The World*, 27 September 1904).

26 Cf. Seamus Heaney, 'Rhymes', in *Worlds: Seven Contemporary Poets*, ed. G. Summerfield (Harmondsworth: Penguin Books, 1974).

27 Cf. Hugh Rhodes: 'reading of fayned fables, vayne fantasyes, and wanton stories, and songs of love . . . bring much mischiefe to youth' (*The Boke of Nurture, or Schoole of Good Manners*, 1577).

28 Cf. Ted Hughes: 'all imaginative writing has to do with the neglected and the forbidden' (*Poetry in the Making*, London: Faber & Faber, 1967, p. 51).

29 *Tatler*, no. 95 (17 November 1709).

30 The humour of Steele's narrative depends on a simple ironic reversal of roles: it is not the adults who frighten the children, but vice versa.

31 Cf. Sidney, above, p. 25.

32 *Spectator*, no. 85 (7 June 1711).

33 Cf. *Rambler*, no. 177 (26 November 1751): *The Works of Samuel Johnson*, vol. 5, p. 171. *Guy of Warwick* was one of the most popular tales issued in both metrical and prose versions. Scott preferred the metrical versions.

34 Walpole to Miss M. Berry (4 December 1793).

35 One young reader who bent his mind to this matter was George
    Canning; at the age of sixteen, while at Eton, he wrote a rather
    witty, slightly showy, essay for the *Microcosm*, a periodical
    which he and four friends had started in 1786. In no. 30 (14 June
    1787), he produced a neat parody of Addison's Essay on 'The
    Children in the Wood'. Just as Addison had invoked a compari-
    son with Horace, so Canning produced some preposterous
    comparisons between Tom Thumb's sleeplessness and Homer's
    decription of Agamemnon in the *Iliad*, bk 10; and between the
    ogre's seven-league-booted journey in *Thumb*, and Neptune's
    passage from Samothrace to Troy, in Homer. What, or who, one
    wonders, was the butt of this mock-heroic joke? Could it have
    been Addison's essay of 1711, or some unfortunate classics
    teacher?

36 Hester Lynch Piozzi (Mrs Thrale), *Anecdotes of the Late Samuel
    Johnson* (London: T. Cadell, 1786), p. 13.

37 ibid., p. 14.

38 Cf. Edgeworth, below, p. 129.

39 Cf. Lawrence Stone, *The Family, Sex and Marriage in England,
    1500–1800* (Harmondsworth: Penguin Books, 1979).

40 The Story of St George appeared not only in chap-books but
    also on horn-books. See William Shenstone, 'The School-
    Mistress'.

41 Laurence Sterne, *The Life and Opinions of Tristram Shandy*, 9
    vols (York, later London, 1760–7), vol. 1, ch. XIV.

42 Scott, op.cit., p. 19.

43 *The Pleasures of Imagination*, bk 1, ll. 255 ff.: *The Poetical Works
    of Mark Akenside*, ed. A. Dyce (London, 1845, repr. AMS Press,
    New York, n.d.), p. 93.

44 *Dichtung und Warheit*, bk 1.

45 Op.cit, bk 2, ch. 3. Carlyle's views on this matter may well have
    influenced Dickens.

46 *Poetical Works*, ed. George Crabbe, Jr, 8 vols (London: John
    Murray, 1834) vol. 1. Crabbe again offered chap-book tales as an
    important element in a child's imaginative life, in *Silford Hall*,
    one of his posthumous tales (ibid., vol. 8, p. 8):

    > He sought his Mother's hoard, and there he found
    > Romance in sheets, and poetry unbound;
    > Soft Tales of Love, which never damsel read,
    > But tears of pity stain'd her virgin bed.
    > There were Jane Shore and Rosamond the Fair,
    > And humbler heroines frail as these were there;
    > There was a tale of one forsaken Maid,
    > Who till her death the work of vengeance stay'd;

Her Lover, then at sea, while round him stood
A dauntless crew, the angry ghost pursued;
In a small boat, without an oar or sail,
She came to call him, nor would force avail,
Nor prayer; but, conscience-stricken, down he leapt,
And o'er his corse the closing billows slept;
All vanish'd then! but of the crew were some,
Wondering whose ghost would on the morrow come.
  A learned Book was there, and in it schemes
How to cast Fortunes and interpret Dreams;
Ballads were there of Lover's bliss or bale,
The Kitchen Story, and the Nursery Tale.
His hungry mind disdain'd not humble food,
And read with relish keen of Robin Hood;
Of him, all-powerful made by magic gift,
And Giants slain – of mighty Hickerthrift;
Through Crusoe's Isle delighted had he stray'd
Nocturnal visits had to witches paid,
Gliding through haunted scenes, enraptured and afraid.

47 *Poems* (London: J. Hatchard, 1807), pp. 38–9.
48 *The Borough*, general decription, letter 1.
49 'Extravagant': wandering outside, beyond.
50 *Boswell's London Journal, 1762–1763*, ed. F.A. Pottle (London: Heinemann, 1950), p. 299; the entry for Sunday 10 July 1763.
51 ibid., p. 299, n. 6.
52 Soriano, op.cit.
53 See Walter Benjamin, 'The Storyteller', in *Illuminations*, trans. Harry Zohn (London: Fontana, 1973), p. 108.
54 Soriano, op.cit., p. 123.
55 ibid., p. 111.
56 ibid., p. 53.
57 *Histories, or Tales of Past Times*, a revision of the trans. of Guy Miège, dedication signed by Robert Samber (London: J. Pote & R. Montagu, 1729); *The Fairy Tales of Charles Perrault*, trans. Angela Carter (London: Gollancz, 1977).
58 Cf. Lord Chesterfield's letter of February 1750 to his son, then seventeen:

> Many people lose a great deal of time by reading; for they read frivolous and idle books; such as the absurd romances of the last two centuries, where characters that never existed are insipidly displayed, and sentiments that were never felt, pompously described; the oriental ravings and extravagances of the Arabian Nights ... or the new flimsy *brochures* that now swarm in France, of Fairy Tales. ...

He goes on to contrast these with books of 'rational amusement' (*Letters*, London: Dent, 1929, p. 155).

On Chesterfield, Carlyle wrote well: 'the flattery, the dissimulation, and paltry cunning that he is perpetually recommending. . . .'; 'I must mention my having read Cicero de Officiis . . . if we compare the steady, affectionate, unbending precepts of the venerable Roman with Chesterfield's Advice, we shall blush for the eighteenth century' (letters to R. Mitchell, 25 March 1815 and 15 July 1816).

59 Percy, op.cit., vol. 1, p. 101.

60 ibid., p. 216.

61 Op.cit., p. 59.

62 ibid., p. 25.

63 Percy, op.cit., vol. 1, p. 1. Percy was acutely aware of widely held prejudices against folk-proverbs.

64 See A.R. Humphreys, *William Shenstone* (Cambridge: Cambridge University Press, 1937), p. 114.

65 Percy, loc.cit.

66 Chesterfield, op.cit., letter of July 1741.

67 ibid., letter of September 1749.

68 *Letters*, vol. 1, p. 347.

69 The peculiar appeal of Hickathrift for children must lie partly in the fact that even as a 'small' child he was exceptionally strong (in a purely physical sense) and therefore wielded power. Cf. Eric Rabkin, *Fantastic Worlds* (New York: Oxford University Press, 1979), pp. 29–30, on the 'illusion of central position'.

70 *Letters*, vol. 1, p. 347.

71 See *Coleridge, The Damaged Archangel* (London: Allen & Unwin, 1972), p. 550.

72 *Letters*, vol. 1, p. 348.

73 ibid., vol. 1, p. 354: letter endorsed 16 October 1797, covering the period October 1779 to October 1781.

74 ibid., vol. 1, pp. 354–5.

75 ibid., vol. 1, p. 349: letter dated 14 October 1797.

76 Cf. M. Moorman, *Wordsworth, The Early Years* (Oxford: Clarendon Press, 1957), p. 438.

77 Blake, *Tiriel*, sect. 8.

78 Ed.cit., vol. 1, pp. 215 and 283: letters of 30 December 1797 and 21 May 1799.

Another plan presented itself; that of joining . . . in a project of tuition. Our scheme was singular & extensive, for we proposed in three years to go systematically, yet with constant reference to the nature of man, thro' the mathematical Branches, chemistry, Anatomy, the laws of Life, the laws of Intellect, & lastly, thro' universal History, arranging separately all the facts that elucidate the separate states of Society, savage, civilized & luxurious: singular, for we proposed ourselves, not as Teachers, but only as Managing Students. If by this plan I could at once subsist my family for three years, and enable myself to acquire such a mass of knowledge, it would doubtless be preferable to all other modes of action for me, who have just knowledge enough of most things to feel my ignorance of all things. (30 December 1797)

79 *Coleridge's Shakespearean Criticism*, ed. T.M. Raysor, 2 vols (London: Constable, 1930), vol. 2, p. 13: 'Lecture on Education' (3 May 1808), as reported by H.C. Robinson in a letter to Mrs Clarkson (7 May 1808).

80 We refer the reader to the Posthumous Works of Robert Hooke, M.D. F.R.C. &c. FOLIO, published under the auspices of the Royal Society, by their Secretary, Richard Waller: and especially to the pages from p. 22 to 42 inclusive, as containing the preliminary knowledges requisite or desirable for the naturalist, before he can form 'even a foundation upon which anything like a sound and stable *Theory* can be constituted'. As a small specimen of this appalling catalogue of preliminaries with which he is to make himself conversant, take the following:– 'The history of potters, tobacco-pipe-makers, glaziers, glass-grinders, looking-glass-makers or foilers, spectacle-makers and optic-glass-makers, makers of counterfeit pearl and precious stones, bugle-makers, lamp-blowers, colour-makers, colour-grinders, glass-painters, enamellers, varnishers, colour-sellers, *painters, limners, picture-drawers, makers of baby-heads, of little bowling-stones or marbles*, fustian-makers (query whether *poets* are included in this trade?), music-masters, tinsey-makers, and taggers. – The history of schoolmasters, writing-masters, printers, book-binders, stage-players, dancing-masters, and vaulters, *apothecaries, chirurgeons, seamsters, butchers, barbers, laundresses*, and *cosmetics*! &c. &c. &c. &c. (the true nature of which being actually determined) WILL HUGELY FACILI-TATE OUR INQUIRIES IN PHILOSOPHY!!!'

81 *The Friend*, 2 vols, ed. B.E. Rooke (London: Routledge & Kegan Paul, 1969), vol. 1, p. 484.

82 *Coleridge's Shakespearean Criticism*, vol. 2, p. 110: 'Lectures on Shakespeare and Milton' (Crane Court, Fleet Street, beginning 18 November 1811), fifth lecture, as reported by J. Tomalin.

83 ibid., vol. 2, p. 293: 'Lecture on "New System of Education"' (18 November 1813).

84 *Edinburgh Review* (1806).
85 *Biographia Literaria* (1817), ch. 18.
86 'The historie and gests of Maxilian', *Blackwood's Magazine* (January 1822). Cf. Carlyle:

> not only the Torch of Science still burns, and perhaps more fiercely than ever, but innumerable Rush-lights and Sulphur-matches, kindled thereat, are also glancing in every direction, so that not the smallest cranny or doghole in Nature or Art can remain unilluminated. (*Sartor Resartus*)

87 John Clare, *The Village Minstrel.*
88 'A Sunday with Shepherds and Herdboys', *Selected Poems and Prose of John Clare*, ed. E. Robinson and G. Summerfield (London: Oxford University Press, 1978), p. 96.
89 In *Worlds: Seven Contemporary Poets*, p. 228.
90 *Selected Poems and Prose*, p. 100.
91 'January: A Cottage Evening', *The Shepherd's Calendar*, ed. E. Robinson and G. Summerfield (Oxford: Oxford University Press, 1973), pp. 17–18.
92 ibid., p. 18.
93 ibid., p. 19.
94 ibid., p. 21.
95 Clare MSS., Peterborough Museum.

CHAPTER THREE

TEACHING THE YOUNG IDEA HOW TO SHOOT

But you always did provoke people into doing
the dirty human thing to you by insisting that
they should do the Goody Two-Shoes bit.
(Saul Bellow, *Humboldt's Gift*, 1975)

Goody, goody-goody: mawkishly good;
weakly benevolent or pious.
(*Chambers's Twentieth Century Dictionary*)

1

An ethos of finer sensitivity, amenity, refinement and lenity –
that is what Locke and Addison in their various ways helped
to create, at the beginning of the eighteenth century. Locke
offered a coherent blueprint for the task of forming a child's
mind, appealing to reason in fostering the growth of reason,
and delicately attentive to the childlikeness, the distinctive
sensibility, of the child as child, and not as plaything or dwarf
adult. Addison marked out a place in civilized life for the
imponderable claims of the life of the imagination, and
proposed such claims in so urbane a way as to reassure his
readers. As Johnson later testified, he 'purified intellectual
pleasure, separated mirth from indecency, and wit from
licentiousness', and 'taught a succession of writers to bring
elegance and gaiety to the aid of goodness'.[1]

Isaac Watts likewise applied his talents to the 'aid of
goodness', civilizing the Dissenters, helping them to succeed
in the world by amending, not their morals, but their
manners. He started, as was the wont of many eighteenth-
century reformers, with the still malleable soft wax of the

child. Johnson squeezed Watts into his *Lives of the Poets*, but had to admit that 'his devotional poetry is, like that of others, unsatisfactory. . . . It is sufficient for Watts to have done better than others what no man has done well.'[2] Of Watts's *Improvement of the Mind* (essays on education, in Locke's sense of the word) Johnson had a higher opinion, and indeed wrote of it 'Few books have been perused by me with greater pleasure'[3] – which is difficult to believe – but also remarked that the book owed all its 'radical principles' to Locke's *Conduct of the Understanding* – which is easy to believe, for Watts was an incorrigible plagiarist.

Just as Watts's prosings owed most of their sense to Locke, so his poetry for children was heavily indebted to Bunyan's *Book for Boys and Girls*. The *Divine Songs, Attempted in Easy Language for the Use of Children*, were published in 1715, and reprinted over two hundred times in the next hundred years. In the same league of popularity, *Pilgrim's Progress* owed its popular success to Bunyan's genius as a story-teller, and its intimate connections with the chap-book tradition. How, then, to account for the success of Watts's *Divine Songs*? If poets were made, not born, we could claim that Watts was well prepared for his task. His father was a deacon of the Independent Meeting House in Southampton, i.e. a Congregationalist. As a committed dissenter, he was prepared to pay a price for his conscience, and may well have been in prison when his son, Isaac, was born in 1674.

The boy started to learn Latin at the age of four, Greek at nine, and Hebrew at thirteen. He became convinced of his sinfulness at fourteen, and began to trust in Christ's redeeming power at fifteen. He was educated at grammar school, and at Newington Green (Dissenting) Academy. In 1696, at twenty-two, he became tutor to the son of a wealthy dissenter – the Independents were at the prosperous and respectable end of the spectrum of dissent – and in 1712 he went to stay for a week with Sir Thomas and Lady Abney, also rich dissenters; he remained for thirty-six years. Lady Abney took good care of him until his death in 1748, and she followed him in 1750.

Dr. WATTS'S
Divine Songs,
FOR
CHILDREN.

A flow'r when offer'd in the bud,
Is no vain sacrifice. See Page 10.

BANBURY:

Printed and Sold by J. G. Rusher,

BRIDGE-STREET.

Price One Penny.

Why should I love my sport so well, so constant at my play?—

He was a prolific author, most of his writings being devoted to how to get to heaven and how to get on in the world – theology, devotional prayers, sermons, hymns, handbooks on reading and writing, and on moral and social education; he is remembered today for some of his hymns, especially 'Our God our help in ages past' (modified in a moment of rhetorical insight by John Wesley to 'O God . . .'), 'When I survey the wondrous cross' and 'Jesus shall reign where'er the sun'.

In his *Discourse on the Education of Children and Youth*, he warned his readers: 'LET not any Persons that are near them [i.e. children] terrify their tender Minds with dismal *Stories of Witches and Ghosts, of Devils and evil Spirits, of Fairies and Bugbears in the Dark*',[4] and we know immediately that we are spiritual and emotional light-years away from the kind of benign ethos described by Richard Steele, in which such questions are ventilated by a delicate and generous humour. Watts, in the event, was not at all averse to subjecting children to a grisly display of dire terrors, and the clue to the apparent contradiction may be found in the Preface to his *Horae Lyricae* of 1706.[5] His argument here is that poetry's origins were divine:

> *Pierian Muses, fam'd for Heavenly Lays,* .
> *Descend, and sing the God your Father's Praise –*

but, alas, poetry had since become 'enslav'd to Vice and Profaneness . . . ingaged in the Interests of Hell'. As a result of this degradation, this profanation, 'many of the Writers of first Rank in this our Age of National Christians have to their Eternal Shame surpassed the vilest of the Gentiles'. Watts's moral stance was not conspicuous for its moderation, and his vision of the damage caused by such poetic depravity is almost apocalyptic in its stress: 'Unthinking Youth have been allured to Sin beyond the Vicious Propensities of Nature, plung'd early into Diseases and Death, and sunk down to Damnation in Multitudes.' Why, he asks, have such writers as Dryden, Otway, Congreve and Dennis expended their talents on pagan subjects? If they genuinely desired a really sublime and

extensive subject for their verse, a theme much richer than
'Ancient Fables or Later Romances',[6] it was waiting for them
in the Bible. 'The Heaven and the Hell in our Divinity are
infinitely more delightful and dreadful than the Childish
Figments of a Dog with three Heads . . . the Furies with
Snaky Hairs, or all the Flowr'y Stories of *Elysium*.' The Bible
story was 'Divinely True', whereas the neo-classical and
romance repertoire was a 'Medly of Fooleries which we can
never believe'. Above all, the Bible's story lay under the
'Command of an Harmonious Pen, whose every line . . . is the
very Life or Death of his [the reader's] Soul.'

If willing were inspiration, then such theocentric aspirations should have generated great verse, but here, as proof of
the pudding, is Watts's account, divinely sanctioned no doubt,
of a disobedient child:

> What heavy Guilt upon him lies!
> How cursed is his Name!
> The Ravens shall pick out his Eyes,
> And Eagles eat the same.

So much for punishment in this life; but the next world offers
much more ingeniously contrived terrors:

> There is a dreadful Hell,
> And everlasting Pains,
> There Sinners must with Devils dwell
> In Darkness, Fire, and Chains.

Punishment for telling lies is characteristically disproportion-
ate to the offence:

> The Lord delights in them that speak
> The Words of Truth; but every Lyar
> Must have his Portion in the Lake
> That burns with Brimstone and with Fire.

And Watts's God is like a strict, petty-minded schoolmaster,
counting up each pupil's offences:

Then let me always watch my Lips,
Lest I be struck to Death and Hell,
Since God a Book of Reckoning keeps
For every Lye that Children tell.

Even the relatively trivial misdemeanours of childhood
receive the most severe retribution:

Cross Words and angry Names require
To be chastiz'd at School;
And he's in danger of Hell-fire,
That calls his Brother, Fool.

But Lips that dare be so prophane
To mock and jeer and scoff
At Holy Things or Holy Men,
The Lord shall cut them off.

Watts balances his po-faced humourlessness and his retribu-
tive sadism pretty evenly:

When Children in their wanton Play
Serv'd old *Elisha* so,
And bid the Prophet go his way,
"*Go up, thou Bald-head, go*
God quickly stopt their wicked Breath,
And sent two raging Bears,
That tore them Limb from Limb to Death,
With Blood and Groans and Tears.[7]

Watts's preoccupation with punishment and pain carries an
unmistakable whiff of sadistic gratification; however elevated
his moral intentions, there is persistent unpleasantness in the
man, a relishing of power and authority, used to mainly
punitive ends. His visions of terror, for all their artistic
gaucheries, must have disturbed the slumbers of many a child.
Addison, in his ninth essay on the pleasures of the imagination, looked back through history from the vantage point of a
time 'enlightened by learning and philosophy' to those dark

ages when 'pious frauds were made use of to amuse mankind, and frighten them into a sense of their duty.'[8] Watts, of course, never set out to amuse anyone, though his sycophantic addresses to his patrons doubtless gratified them, but *Divine Songs* offers an exemplary case of a pious divine setting out 'to frighten [children] into a sense of their duty' and represents that emotional perversion and philistinism that Sydney Smith was to castigate a century later in the Methodists.

In Watts's *Discourse on the Education of Children and Youth*, published posthumously,[9] there is an ambivalent amalgam of Locke, of 'utility', and of religious enthusiasm. His advice offers a comprehensive policy to ensure that those who adopt it will prosper both in this world and in the next. Watts's aspiration were both worldly and other-worldly, but the two elements are rarely integrated in a convincing way: he is simultaneously a joiner, a social conformist, and a Separatist. Although of an austere and ascetic temper, he lived comfortably with people who were, in worldly terms, extremely successful. When, therefore, he offers his prescriptions for child-rearing, he walks a tightrope, between God and Caesar. The term 'Puritan', he insisted, 'is to this day a name of lasting glory.' Therefore, 'it is better to look like a Puritan, and stand almost alone' than to 'follow the multitude in the road that leads to iniquity and mischief.' For 'there are some things in which you must dare to be singular, if you would be Christians, and especially in a corrupt and degenerate age.' On the other hand, one must recognize that

> there is a certain fashion and appearance of things that belongs to every age: modes of conversation and forms of behaviour, are ever changing in this life; and it is no improper thing for persons, according to their rank and figure in life, to conform themselves to the present customs.

That seems to have been written with a sidelong glance at the people to whom he was beholden: it is measured, judicious and hedging. But when he turns to, or perhaps one should say 'on', children, his tone is very different. Their very limbs are potentially 'wild Instruments of Madness and Mischief', so their *Thoughts and Fancies should be brought under early Government.*' They must 'call in their wandering Thoughts, and bind them to the Work in Hand.' Where Locke had construed the tasks of learning so that they should draw on the mental animation and physical energies of 'play', Watts – with a much cruder, even Manichaean, psychology – transformed play into a form of severe instruction, a kind of perpetual and unrelieved standing to attention. But he had taken from Locke the notion that children should be given 'clear ideas of things' and so he insisted that they must quickly learn to distinguish between 'Truth and Falsehood, between Good and Evil, between Trifles and Things of Importance'. Thus, unlike Locke, he fell into the inevitable trap of imposing on the child the adult view of what constitutes a 'trifle' and of what is 'important'. These discriminations, he argued, 'are the most valuable Pieces of Knowledge and Distinction which can be lodged in the young Understandings of Children.' Thus it was imperative that the lineaments of the Devil should not be confused with bugbears and other heathenish spirits.[10] Servants, therefore, had to be watched very carefully, for their idle chatter was likely to sow the seeds of dire metaphysical confusion:

> Let not Nurses or Servants be suffered to fill their Minds with *silly Tales and with senseless Rhimes,* many of which are so absurd and ridiculous that they will not bear to be represented in a grave Discourse. The Imagination of young Creatures is hereby flattered and deceived: Their Reason is grossly abused and imposed upon: And by this Means they are trained up to be amused with Follies and Nonsense, rather than to exercise their Understanding, which is the Glory of human Nature.
>
> LET not any Persons that are near them terrify their tender Minds with dismal *Stories of Witches and Ghosts, of Devils and evil Spirits, of Fairies and Bugbears in the Dark.* [An echo here of Bunyan's hymn, 'To be a

pilgrim'?] This hath had a most mischievous Effect on some Children, and hath fixed in their Constitutions such a rooted Slavery and Fear, that they have scarce dared to be left alone all their Lives, especially in the Night.

It is to be expected that someone of so humourless a temper as Watts should object to senseless rhymes, but what of his objections to ghost stories and fairy-tales? Is he moved here by a benign compassion, by humanity? Perhaps so; but what he is at pains to prevent is an embarrassing confusion of pagan devils and the Christian's demonology:

> These Stories have made such a deep and frightful Impression on their tender Fancies, that it hath ener- vated their Souls, it hath broken their Spirits early, it hath grown up with them, and mingled with their Religion, it hath laid a wretched Foundation for Melan- choly and distracting Sorrows.

Watts, then, wants to have it both ways; to expel the pagan bugbears, but to keep the Christian bugbear of the Devil. To borrow a phrase from Pope, he proves himself to be 'himself one vile antithesis'. And he draws heavily on Locke, to resolve the matter by deferring it: 'Let these Sort of Informations be reserved for their firmer Years, and let them not be told in their Hearing, till they can better judge what Truth or Reality there is in them, and be made sensible how much is owing to Romance and Fiction.' Again, to prove once more that his right hand did not know what his left hand was doing, the man who introduced lurid images of terror and pain into his *Divine Songs* enters this appeal:

> NOR let their little Hearts be frighted at three or four Years old with *shocking and bloody Histories, with Massa- cres and Martyrdoms, with Cuttings and Burnings, with the Images of horrible and barbarous Murders, with Racks and redhot Pincers, with Engines, of Torment and Cruelty, with mangled Limbs, and Carcases drenched in Gore.*

But Watts does rather dwell on them, does he not? And, of course, they must come to them later: 'It is Time enough, when their Spirits are grown a little firmer, to acquaint them with these Madnesses and Miseries of Human Nature.' And, one might add, judging by the revealing tone of such passages, Watts will be more than ready and willing to so acquaint them.

Posterity has not been just to Watts. It has been absurdly indulgent. To read many of the histories of children's literature, one would conclude that the images of pain and violence in the *Divine Songs* were eccentric little lapses, and that he had made a fine contribution to the repertoire of poetry for children. At this late hour, there is nothing to be gained from beating about the bush: his writings for children are essentially pernicious.

2

In November 1748, Lord Chesterfield wrote to his son:

> To show you that a very wise, philosophical, and retired man thinks upon that subject [social graces] as I do, who have always lived in the world, I send you the famous Mr Locke's book upon education, in which you will find the stress that he lays upon the Graces, which he calls (and very truly) good-breeding.

Three years later, in 1751, Jennings and Doddridge published posthumously the second part of Watts's *Improvement of the Mind* and his *Discourse on the Education of Children and Youth*. They observed in their Preface that several 'eminent persons and learned societies' had been pressing for their publication. The guidance offered by Watts's vulgarization of Locke was clearly still meeting a felt need and thus proliferating in mid-century.

Seven years earlier, in 1744, one of the most preposterous efforts at such popularization had appeared in the unlikely shape of a book for children, *A Little Pretty Pocket-Book*,[11] published by John Newbery. The Preface, addressed to parents, offered a series of moral and educational commonplaces, a selection of Locke's thoughts, reduced to a level of irreducible banality. Where Locke was scrupulously attentive to the gradients, gradations and graduations of a child's evolving mind, Newbery – or the hack that need for money had pressed into his service – generalized in a remarkably bland, not to say fatuous, manner. 'Would you have a *Virtuous* Son, instil into him the Principles of Morality early, and encourage him in the Practice of those excellent Rules, by which whole Societies, States, Kingdoms, and Empires are knit together': an appeal for submission to patriarchal principles. Again: 'Would you have a *Wise* Son, teach him to reason early' – a kind of Old Moore's parody and garbling of Locke. As for the child's reading, 'make him understand what he reads [*sic*]. No sentence should be passed over without a strict Examination of the Truth of it' – nothing more than a fatuous cliché, a threadbare scrap of the conventional wisdom. And the *Pocket-Book* itself conspired to defeat any such intention, as we shall see, for much of it is no more than abject rubbish.

Its ostensible aim was to promote socially advantageous virtues, beginning with the root of the matter: submission to the rule of reason and the subjugation of the 'Passions'. When Newbery addresses his young readers directly, he praises them for their obedience, kindness and complaisance; for their refusal to swear, lie and use obscenities; and for their pious and sycophantic acceptance of adult advice. The arch and insinuating tone he uses is itself enough to give virtue a bad name, but worst of all is his insistence that the child's virtue will gain the love of others: to be good is thereby to be loved; virtue is *not* its own reward; we can expect payment in the form of affection, or at least a display of affection, and material rewards also. Again and again he insists that people will love you, and that you will prosper, if you are good. His tone is ingratiating, coy, disingenuous, and subtly threatening – he comes across as repulsively anxious to succeed, and as worldly wise. There is a persistent whiff of calculation in all his prosy moralizings, and a clear note of mercantilism. At his worst, he is downright silly, and unpleasantly so; as when he advises parents to have their son study mankind – 'study Mankind; shew him the Springs and Hinges on which they move.' Like Chesterfield, Newbery speaks in the accents of Mr Worldly Wiseman, his eye on the main chance, preparing to do business in the city of Carnal Policy, and served by Mr Legality, 'a very judicious man', and his ingratiating son, 'a very pretty young man, whose name is Civility'. Not that Newbery's manners always served him as well as his business acumen; when he and his wife visited their son at Oxford, Newbery insisted on parading his son's compendious useful knowledge to the embarrassment of nearly everyone present.

His letters to his child-readers, one for girls and one for boys, signed fraudulently, as Dickens would have re-marked,[12] with the misappropriated name of Jack the Giant-Killer, are patronizing and mock naïve. The postscript reads:

> When you are tired with playing, I have added, for your further Amusement, a Collection of pretty Songs, which your Nurse will take Care to teach you; and I must insist on your getting them perfectly, because the Knowledge of these Songs will recommend you to the Favour of all the Gentlemen and Ladies of England who sing in that Manner.

This ingratiating cant invites the child to offer a precocious attention to the dubious matter of 'How to Win Friends and Influence People'; in its fake-Lilliputian tones, it speaks for a mercantile knowingness, keen to initiate children into acceptabe social conformity, calculated patterns of conduct, designed to yield a due return of social and business success.

The centre of the *Pocket-Book* is a series of woodcuts depicting various games, almost exclusively boys'; underneath each picture is a feeble quatrain, describing the game, and then another quatrain, or a couplet, offering a gloss, a moral, or a 'Rule of Life'. The game of chuck-farthing, for example:

As you value your Pence,
At the Hole take your Aim;
Chuck all safely in,
And you'll win the Game.

Which is moralized thus:

Chuck-Farthing, like Trade,
Requires great Care;
The more you observe,
The better you'll fare.

And this is doubtless an entirely appropriate moral for a man who made a fortune out of a rather dubious patent medicine.

Four rather indifferently rhymed fables follow, for each of which a moral is provided, again ostensibly by the spuriously misappropriated Jack the Giant-Killer: the stress is again on how to gain 'the love and esteem of the whole world' – is this, one begins to ask, Newbery's own neurotic obsession? – on 'the folly and wickedness of telling lies', and similar questions. But the moral core of the book is still to come, in the form of letters to the author: they appeal quite nakedly to a desire for wealth and worldly success. Here is the one for the attention of ambitious little boys:

Sir, There was in my Country a little Boy, who learned his Book to that surprising Degree, that his Master could scarce teach him fast enough, for he had his Lesson almost as soon as it was pointed out to him; which raised the Attention of every Body; and as he was also very dutiful to his Parents and obliging to his Playmates, every Body loved him. His Learning and Behaviour purchased him the Esteem of the greatest People, and raised him from a mean State of Life to a Coach and Six, in which he rides to this Day. Learning is a most excellent Thing, and is easily acquired too, when little Boys set themselves earnestly about it. I know several Masters at this Time, who all bid fair for the same Honour the above Gentleman enjoys.

The great G *Play.*

Hop, Step, *and* Jump.

Hop fhort, and *Step* fafe,
    To make your *Jump* long;
This Art oft has beat
Th' Efforts of the Strong.

Moral.

This old Maxim take,
    T' embellifh your Book;
Think well are you talk,
    And, ere you leap, look.
                    C   Boys

The ideal girl is equally successful, and gains the approval
of Lady Meanwell, who gives her a gold watch, and declares
that she shall ride in her own coach; there is a slight ambiguity
here, since it is not clear whether the deserving girl is to ride in
her own coach or in that of Lady Meanwell, but presumably
either mode of conveyance represents a consummation de-
voutly to be wished!

A section on piety – prayers and benevolence – follows, then
four fustian pieces of verse on the seasons; a moralized
emblem, 'Time's Address to Plutus and Cupid'; and finally
four pages of proverbs, many of them prudential, and some of
them both inappropriate and incomprehensible to children.

Whatever the archaeological interests of this and other Newbery volumes – and they are clearly considerable for some bibliographers – the philistinism of the *Pocket-Book*, the smell of the shopkeeper that pervades the volume, has received remarkably little attention. Wittingly or unwittingly, it is a sneaky piece of work, and serves only to show how calamitous the didactic book for children could be, even when free of the gloomy puritanism of such as Watts. Whoever wrote the *Pocket-Book*, it is the work of a thoroughly trivial, commercial, and disinherited mind, and its continuing *succès d'estime* is something of a mystery.

3

Could a woman perhaps do better? Assuredly, she could not do worse.

Because of their unsettled family circumstances, Henry Fielding, born in 1707, and his sister, Sarah, born in 1710, seem to have enjoyed an unusually unconstrained childhood, a kind of benign or insouciant neglect. They were able to browse freely, not in Aesop or Watts, but in the great chapbook tales – *Tom Hickathrift*, *The Seven Champions*, *Guy of Warwick* and *Jack the Giant-Killer*. Like George Canning, two generations later, Henry probably discovered them during his early years at Eton, providing an oasis in a desert of Greek hexameters.

In 1706, Isaac Watts had argued that writers should turn from the 'Medley of Fooleries' of neo-classical paganism, to the great dramas of the *Bible*, 'the Heaven and Hell of our Divinity'. In an ironic and provocative spirit, Fielding, in his early career as a writer, issued a similar rebuke:

> It is with great Concern, that I have observed several of our Tragical Writers, to Celebrate in their Immortal Lines the Actions of Heroes recorded in Historians and Poets, such as Homer or Virgil, Livy or Plutarch, the

Propagation of whose Works is so apparently against the Interests of our Society; when the Romances, Novels, and Histories, *vulgo* called Story-Books, of our own People, furnish such abundant and proper themes for their Pens; such are Tom Tram, Hickathrift, &c.[13]

Fielding returned to this mock-heroic theme again, in *The Jacobite's Journal*, when he directed his irony at Thomas Carte, a hack-writer who was churning out a periodical history of England, subsidized by the coffers of the City of London. The whole enterprise would fare much better, Fielding argued, if Carte would 'deal forth his excellent work' in penny-numbers,

> in the same manner with those true and delectable Histories of Argalus and Parthenia, Guy Earl of War-wick, The Seven Champions, etc., in which form, at the price of 1d each, when embellished by our Frontispiece, I make no doubt of assuring him as universal a Sale, as the inimitable *Adventures of Robinson Crusoe* formerly had throughout this Kingdom.[14]

Defoe's book had appeared in 1719, at a time when the trade in chap-books was booming, and their publishers were disposed to cannibalize any good story. The fundamental type of the chap-book romance was that of the adventurous journey: only by leaving home and setting off into the unknown could one encounter danger, marvels, monsters and giants; and, at a deeper level, explore the sub-text of the picaresque mode, to answer the call to the quest, to face tests, endure, and gain autonomy. Just as the stories of the *Thousand and One Nights* had made their appearance in chap-books by 1708, and the French fairy-tales of Madame D'Aulnoy been 'done into English' by 1700, so the appropriation of *Robinson Crusoe* by the penny histories was inevitable, rapid and infallible. It was entirely characteristic of Fielding's spirit, that he should seize on this case of extreme popularity, to make fun of what was a rather pretentious enterprise.

It was again in a spirit of teasing mockery that Fielding began to write his parody of Richardson's pruriently moral *Pamela*, and ended by producing *Joseph Andrews*. A man of Fielding's irreverent temper must have groaned and hooted simultaneously when struggling through the heavily sententious moralizings that Richardson paraded to justify his lubricious sexual fantasies in terms of moral instruction and the reformation of manners. The lively, nimble and genial *sprezzatura* of Philip Sidney's *Defence* had yielded place to a pious and often hypocritical canting, as in Richardson. So it was with an ironic fake-deference that Fielding began his first novel, and slotted it into a native tradition, characterized by unimpeachable moral example:

> our own language affords many [biographies] of excellent use and instruction, finely calculated to sow the seeds of virtue in youth, and very easy to be comprehended by persons of moderate capacity. Such as the history of John The Great, who, by his brave and heroic actions against men of large and athletic bodies, obtained the glorious appellation of the Giant-killer; that of an Earl of Warwick, whose Christian name was Guy; the lives of Argalus and Parthenia; and above all, the history of those seven worthy personages, the Champions of Christendom. In all these, delight is mixed with instruction, and the reader is almost as much improved as entertained.[15]

It is a deft and unsettling argument; the wild reckless tales, totally innocent of any didactic aim, are thus endorsed as impeccably moral, and effectually so: 'calculated to sow the seeds of virtue in youth'. Addison had persuasively legitimized the pleasures we derive from the vast, the strange, and the beautiful – an unwitting typology of the chap-book romance; Steele had shown how, through such tales, a child 'had his thoughts insensibly moulded into the notions of discretion, virtue and honour'; and Fielding, with ambiguous humour, joins their company, beating the moralists at their own game.

In the light of Fielding's recurrent, almost obsessive, espousals of the chap-book tales, it is hardly surprising that, in the *Grub Street Journal* of 18 November 1731, he was credited with responsibility for 'the fame of Hickathrift and brave Tom Thumb'; or that Thackeray, reviewing W.J. Thoms's reprint of *Hickathrift* in 1846,[16] should have confidently fathered the tale on Fielding. But if it is undeniable that the energy, vivacity and picaresque extravagating of such prototypes left their mark on Fielding's novels, what then of his sister's work?

As Jill Grey has observed,[17] Sarah Fielding's *The Governess* was the first English novel written expressly for young readers; but what kind of animal is this pioneering work? Certainly, it derived from a world very different from that of the chap-book tales, and that essential fact is made abundantly clear in both the novel's Dedication and the Preface. Its avowed intention was 'to cultivate an early Inclination to Benevolence, and a Love of Virtue, in the Minds of young Women' whose best interests lay in 'cherishing and improving those amiable Dispositions into Habits; and in keeping down all rough and boistrous Passions'. Sarah Fielding wished for the 'strictest observance' of those social duties appropriate to 'the Female Character', and aimed to purge all tender minds of 'all those Desires and Passions which Vanity or Ambition might inspire'. The true use of books, she averred, was to make their readers, especially young readers, 'wiser and better'. And she proposed to do this by offering them 'Fable and Moral'.

Jill Grey has suggested that, in her design for *The Governess*, Sarah Fielding was strongly influenced by Fénelon's *Instructions for the Education of a Daughter*, translated into English in 1707, but for the morality one need look no further than Watts's *Discourse*, published in the early 1750s. On the face of it, this may seem ridiculous, for *The Governess* appeared in 1749, but my point is that both Fénelon and Watts were dealing in the social and moral commonplaces of the early eighteenth century's mercantile classes, and ringing rather predictable changes on the ideals of self-control, duty, truth-telling, modesty, good manners and usefulness. Filtered through the provocatively ironic tempers of such men as Sterne or Fielding, even this could be made to yield a lively and unpredictable fiction, but Sarah, under the unfortunate influence of Richardson, had by this time become rather well-meaning.

In order to get a woman – rather than a man – into the centre of her action, she realized that it would be appropriate and useful, not least to her moral scheme, to give her heroine plenty of years of discretion and the opportunity for relatively independent action; in other words, a widow would be most appropriate. The Rev. Mr Teachum had died after nine years of married life, but during those years he had taken 'great Delight in improving his wife'. Her 'chief pleasure' had of course come from receiving his Instructions. Widowed, with two daughters, she 'called forth all her Resolution to conquer her Grief,' but then – it never rains but it pours – her two daughters died, and her banker, who held her life-savings, went broke. Thus ruined, she then applied her powers of fortitude and judgement to the task of opening a small school for nine female pupils.

The story – if that is not too strong a word – opens with Mrs Teachum's turning her back in order to allow some action to take place. The girls quarrel over some apples, in a display of regressive passion, and 'they fell to pulling of Caps, tearing of Hair, and dragging the Cloaths off one another's Backs. Tho' they did not so much strike, as endeavour to scratch and pinch their Enemies.' They then 'fought, scratched, and tore, like so many Cats, when they extend their Claws to fix them in their Rival's Heart.' When Mrs Teachum returns, they have almost torn the clothes off each other's backs. Compared with Newbery's sneakiness, this is at least an honest way of ensuring that you get your apple, and there is an undeniable sense of exhilaration in the fight; one recalls Keats's observation: 'though a quarrel in the streets is a thing to be hated, the energies displayed in it are fine.'[18] Such an affirmation of delight in the experience of arousal is one that Henry Fielding would have endorsed, and Sarah is clearly of the same party, allowing her pleasure in sheer energy to have its head. But the 'better' part of her knew only too well that such a quarrel was also a 'thing to be hated', and it is Mrs Teachum's judgement on it that provides the springboard for Sarah's prudent didacticism.

Jenny Peace, the head-girl, who did not join in the fray – hence her name, or *vice versa* – takes the girls to the arbour in the garden, and tells them the story of 'the cruel Giant Barbarico, the good Giant Benefico, and the pretty little Dwarf Mignon', a Frenchified and factitious fairy-tale with an extremely feeble story-line. Mrs Teachum casts her eye over it – it is written down, which further underlines its remoteness from the oral tradition – and delivers a judgement on its acceptability:

> I have no Objection, Miss Jenny, to your reading any Stories to amuse you, provided you read them with the proper Disposition of Mind not to be hurt by them. A very good Moral may indeed be drawn from the Whole, and likewise from almost every Part of it; and as you had this Story from your Mamma, I doubt not but you are very well qualified to make the proper Remarks yourself upon the Moral of it to your Companions. But here let me observe to you (which I would have you communicate to your little Friends) that Giants, Magic, Fairies, and all Sorts of supernatural Assistances in a Story, are only introduced to amuse and divert: For a Giant is called so only to express a Man of Great Power. . . .

Jenny duly communicates Mrs Teachum's warning to the other girls:

> Our good Governess last night not only instructed me in this Moral I am now communicating to you, but likewise bid me warn you by no means to let the Notion of Giants or Magic to dwell upon your Minds; for by a Giant. . . .

Not only does Jenny dutifully repeat Mrs Teachum's words *verbatim*, but she also follows her in carefully de-mythologizing the story, in much the same way as Charles Lamb was to do, fifty years later.[19]

The other eight girls then tell their stories. Sukey Jennett, who had been left as a child 'to the Care of an old Servant', has an appropriately judicious story of conceit to tell; by this time it was well-known that servants had an invariably depraving effect on children. The girls then go for a walk, and discover a poor woman thrashing a child for telling lies – 'For tho' I am but poor, yet I will breed up my Child to be honest, both in Word and Deed', and, needless to add, 'Miss Jenny could not but approve of what the poor Woman said'. The girls' stories are confessions of falsehood, deceit, lying, envy, jealousy, false pride, affectation, greed, vanity and malice: Mrs Teachum is pleased with them all, for they prove to her 'how much they were in Earnest in their Design of Amendment'. Jenny Peace tells a very complicated, seemingly interminable, and quite unmagical fairy-tale, which Mrs Teachum anato-mizes, step by step, for three pages, in order to reveal each of the morals it offers. Again, she is at pains to remind them that 'the Fairies are only introduced by the writers of these Tales, by way of Amusement to the Reader'. Miss Jenny, paragon of virtue, thanks Mrs Teachum on behalf of everyone, 'for her kind Instructions, and promised that they would endeavour, to the utmost of their Power, to imprint them on their Memory for the rest of their Lives'. It is oddly revealing that, in order to remember such things, they had to make an effort to remember them. It is the same phenomenon, of overt consciousness and effort of the will, that characterizes their notion of influence: unless the 'good' influence can be explicitly charted, and discretely accounted for, it is not recognized or seen to exist at all. The dominant characteristic of Sarah Fielding's sober pioneering fiction, apart from the severe limits within which appropriate experience is seen to be found, is an unrelieved self-consciousness. The girls have always to *know* that they are becoming improved, more controlled, more rational. And affection is meted out only to those who are clearly seen to deserve it, because they are virtuous.

4

The *reductio ad absurdum* of this kind of didacticism came with the book that gave our language a continuingly useful piece of shorthand:[20] *The History of Little Goody Two-Shoes*, published by Newbery in 1765. The extent of Oliver Goldsmith's involvement in Newbery's numerous publishing ventures has given rise to a great deal of speculation, especially about the authorship of *Goody Two-Shoes*. Darton characterized the book as the work of a 'sentimental democratic conservative'[21] – some of the salient characteristics of Goldsmith – and Welsh observed that the world of Goody's father bore a striking resemblance to that of Goldsmith's *Deserted Village*. John Ginger has recently argued that 'the case for Newbery himself as author is stronger as the story contains a real-life incident which had been used as the starting point for an article in [Newbery's] *The Midwife*'.[22] But if negative evidence is of any use, one may note that *Goody Two-Shoes* has many of the same egregious faults as Goldsmith's novel, *The Vicar of Wakefield*. The novel is a weirdly confused concoction – a serio-comic pastiche of the Book of Job, with elements of chap-book romance thrown into the melting-pot to provide a miraculous and benevolent *deus ex machina*, to reward virtue, and to tie up the numerous loose ends of Goldsmith's feeble plotting. Indeed, the novel is so confused that from page to page, almost from paragraph to paragraph, the tone is so inconsistent and uncertain that it is continuously difficult to know whether or not to take it seriously as a formed work of art, and if so, how. When one does succumb to its sentimental strain, and is led to be moved, as by the 'death' of the vicar's daughter, it is only to discover that one has been the victim of a contrived and tasteless ruse.

Goldsmith's authorial relationship with his fiction is at best uncertain and at worst disastrous; it was Boswell – not the severest of judges – who remarked of Goldsmith, that he 'had no settled system of any sort'; and to read through Goldsmith's complete works is to encounter a lively, sometimes trivial, often conventional, and chronically unsettled and undisciplined mind. Many of his essays read like indifferent hack-work, offering the contemporary reader what Goldsmith presumably thought he wanted to see – a mirror-image of his own conventional wisdom. And this is often a worldly commercial canniness, as in his essay, 'On Education', of 1759:

> Instead of romances, which praise young men of spirit, who go through a variety of adventures . . . there should be some men of wit employed to compose books that might equally interest the passions of our youth, where such an one might be praised for having resisted allurements when young, and how he at last became lord mayor; how he was married to a lady of great sense, fortune, and beauty: to be as explicit as possible, the old story of Whittington, were his cat left out, might be more serviceable to the tender mind, than either Tom Jones, Joseph Andrews, or an hundred others, where frugality is the only good quality the hero is not possessed of.[23]

In accordance with orthodox notions of cultural subordination, he insists that 'nurses, footmen and such, should be driven away [from the presence of children] as much as possible', and yet at other times he displays symptoms of a nostalgia for that other culture that lay beyond the pale of polite society: in 'The Traveller' (1765), for example, he offers a touching cameo:

> Blest that abode, where want and pain repair,
> And every stranger finds a ready chair;
> Blest be those feasts with simple plenty crown'd,
> Where all the ruddy family around

> Laugh at the jests or pranks that never fail,
> Or sigh with pity at some mournful tale . . .[24]

and earlier, in a letter of 1757 to a friend in Ireland, he confesses that when he goes to the opera in London, 'I sit and sigh for Lishoy fireside, and Johnny Armstrong's Last Good Night.'[25] In 1765, he criticizes Shakespeare for having Hamlet say 'Ay, there's the rub', which he condemns as a 'vulgarism beneath the dignity of Hamlet's character',[26] but praises him for Macduff's 'He has no children', for this he perceives as 'the energetic language of simple Nature, which is now grown into disrepute'. Why? How so? Because 'by the present mode of education we are forcibly warped from the bias of nature, and all simplicity in manners is rejected.' As a result, he argues, 'we are totally changed into creatures of art and affection . . . our minds lose their native force and flavour. The imagination, sweated by artificial fire, produces nought but vapid bloom.'[27]

The nostalgia for a simpler, less complicated beauty, for what, borrowing from the French, he calls *naïveté*, is then transformed into a social and cultural critique, an examination of the hypertrophy of polite culture: 'A clear blue sky, spangled with stars, will prove an insipid object to eyes accustomed to the glare of torches and tapers, gilding and glitter.'[28] He sees, therefore, a state of 'depravity' in which 'a gaudy silken robe, striped and intersected with unfriendly tints, that fritter the masses of light and distract the vision, pinked into the most fantastic forms, flounced, and fur-belowed, and fringed with all the littleness of art' is preferred to 'the ingenuous blush of native innocence, the plain language of antient faith and sincerity'[29] – a view that will later be pushed to extremes by Thomas Day.

It is such a blush, such a language, that we find in the story of Little Margery (Goody) Meanwell, published in the same year as Goldsmith's lament for lost simplicity. Margery's parents die as a result of the distress forced on them by the squire, Sir Timothy Gripe, and the covetous Farmer

Graspall. Margery and her brother, Tommy, are cared for by
Mr Smith, a convenient benefactor, analogous to Sir William
Thornhill in *The Vicar*. But the villains lean on her again, and
she is turned loose in the world. No such adventures ensue as
in the old tales: frequenting the hedgerows, she somehow –
the story is recklessly vague on this score – learns to read and
write, and becomes convinced that 'the Tales of *Ghosts*,
Witches and *Fairies* are the Frolicks of a distempered Brain',[30]
rather than a form of 'antient faith'; eventually she does Gripe
a favour, and her shining virtues are duly rewarded when she
becomes headmistress of a little school. Ironically, it is now,
when she has turned her back firmly on the 'Gothick
Mythology of Elves and Fairies', and Fortunatus and his
magical wishing-cap have been consigned to outer darkness,
that Goody, enlightenedly invoking science and technology to
help her neighbours cope with the vagaries of the weather at
harvest-time, devises a 'weather-glass' – a barometer – and is
accused of witchcraft. Needless to say, she survives, Reason
and Benevolence triumph, and she marries a rich husband, a
reward for her virtue. He obligingly dies, she inherits his
wealth, and her apotheosis is a life of genteel affluence and
social acceptance in the City of London, as Lady Jones; and
not a cat in sight!

In his essay, 'On Deceit and Falsehood',[31] of 1759,
Goldsmith deals explicitly with the vexed question of witchcraft, and he is happy to point out that the ironic, bantering
and 'ludicrous' tone of his essay is a modern privilege; for it
'used to be managed with all possible gravity, and even terror'.
He tackles the question psychologically, and argues that
'deceit and falshood' are only possible because we are
irrational: our imaginations are 'amused and entertained' by
fictions, and take no delight in 'homely truth'. Our passions
are let loose and inflamed by our fancy, 'credulity is a much
greater error than infidelity, and it is safer to believe nothing
than too much'.[32] And he points to the paradox that – as in
Goody Two-Shoes – 'many have been condemned as witches
. . . for no other reason but their knowing more than those

who accused them'. It is imperative, he argues, that we exercise our reason and understanding in order to gain control over our '*wondering quality*' – Goldsmith's italics – for it is this part of us that enjoys 'huge gratification when we see strange feats done', especially when we cannot understand how the trick is performed.

If, in the event, we do find out what the 'natural causes' are, then, alas, 'our delight dies with our amazement'. But it is children who are especially inclined to indulge in 'wonder': an old woman's 'rueful figure' frightens a child into 'the palpitation of the heart; home he runs, and tell his mamma, that goody such a one looked at him, and he is very ill. The good woman cries out, her dear baby is bewitched, and sends for the parson and the constable.' The victims of such misjudgement are often women 'of strong imaginations and little understandings', who are therefore predisposed to accept the views of their accusers, but fortunately for everyone, the spread of education and enlightenment is improving matters: 'An old woman may be *miserable now*, and not be *hanged* for it.'[33]

Tabart's 1804 edition of *Goody Two-Shoes* is at pains to reassure its young readers that 'in this happy country, the poor are to the full as much protected by our excellent laws, as are the highest and the richest nobles in the land; and the humblest cottager enjoys an equal share of the blessings of English liberty with the sons of the King themselves.' This kind of cant seems to have had two purposes: one would be to assure the reader that the injustices of 1765, that drove Margery into her peculiar resourcefulness, could no longer occur; the second would be rather more sinister, a slick attempt to obliterate or deny the fact that the previous decade had witnessed savage repression, the suspension of habeas corpus, paranoid treason-trials, the imprisonment of the publisher Joseph Johnson and others, and the Combination Acts of 1799! Tabart's edition also attempts to catch up with other changes that had taken place since 1765: the spread of Sunday schools, for example; as the story notes, 'the poor are indebted to Mrs Hannah More and Mrs Trimmer, who have written many pretty books for these useful institutions'. But such changes are all seen as relatively superficial. At a deeper level, the divine plan goes on as ever; Providence is always there:

> God Almighty heaps up blessings for all those who love him; and though for a time he may suffer them to be poor and distressed, and hide his good purposes from human sight, yet in the end they are generally crowned with happiness here, and no one can doubt that they are so hereafter.[34]

Mrs Trimmer, recognizing cannily enough that books for children could contain social and political messages, insisted that the text of *Goody Two-Shoes* must be modified, for the most urgent social reasons: there was far more political unrest and turmoil at the turn of the century than there had been in the 1760s:

> This book is a great favourite with us on account of the simplicity of style in which it is written, yet we could wish some parts to be altered, or omitted. It was the practice of Mr Newbery's writers to convey lessons to those whom they facetiously called Children of six feet high, through the medium of children's books; and this has been done in the little volume we are examining. But in these times, when such pains are taken to prejudice the poor against the higher orders, and to set them against parish officers, we could wish to have a veil thrown over the faults of oppressive squires and hard-hearted overseers. Margery and her brother might have been represented as helpless orphans, without imputing their distress to crimes of which young readers can form no accurate judgment; and should these readers be of the lowest class, such a narration as this might tend to prejudice their minds against those whose favour it may be their future interest to conciliate, and who may be provoked by their

insolence (the fruits of prejudice) to treat them with harshness instead of kindness.[35]

And so, implicitly, don't say you weren't warned!

One such reader of the 'lowest class' was Robert Bloomfield, born in 1766, a year after Goody Two-Shoes. Like Sarah Fielding's Mrs Teachum, his mother was early widowed and subsequently ran a dame's school in Suffolk. Young Robert learned his letters there, and then went to ply his trade of shoemaker in London, where he began to write verse. He later acquired an uncertain veneer of polite learning and was for a time a successful writer, having gained the patronage of Capel Lofft, a literary member of the Suffolk squirearchy. Darton notes that Bloomfield learned to disown his earlier attachment to *Jack the Giant-Killer*, and all its 'abominable absurdities',[36] thus offering an instructive contrast to John Clare. Similarly, in his 'Anecdotes and Observations', published posthumously in 1824, Bloomfield recalls having had his fancy 'set to work' by what later struck him as a 'strange and ridiculous song' which as a child he had heard 'sung to the thrum of the spinning-wheel' – a Suffolk version of the great ballad, 'The False Knight on the Road'.[37] But, if he is to be believed, his enlightenment, or disenchantment, must have set in quite early; for, in his critical note, 'Children's Books', apart from praising virtuous tushery such as *Jemima Placid* and *Virtue in a Cottage*, he recalls:

> My mother read *Goody Two-Shoes* to me and my sister, when very young, and enforced its precepts, and its excellent hits at superstition, in a manner which I shall ever esteem the greatest of her favours, and the most unquestionable proof of her love and her understanding.[38]

To appreciate Bloomfield's gratitude for such an early liberation from dark superstition, it helps to bear in mind that the effusiveness of tone – something that he came to identify as a token of gentility – does not rule out the presence of real feeling: only fifteen years before his birth, the people of Tring had 'seized on two superannuated wretches, crazed with age, and overwhelmed with infirmities, on a suspicion of witchcraft; and, by trying experiments, drowned them in a horsepond.'[39] Less extreme superstitions, but equally affecting, stuck in Bloomfield's memory: his

> good old aunt Austin had many sickly children; burying nine under three years old. With one of them . . . a superstitious cure was attempted. I remember an old woman being employed to 'cut the child from the spleen.' The child's ear was cut so as to bleed, and the blood was applied to the temples *in the form of a cross*, and, as I believe, with something repeated by way of *charm*. . . . The child died.[40]

For Bloomfield it is clear that the desperate climb from the cobbler's bench to the writing-desk, the escape from near penury and squalor to the benign and genteel drawing-rooms of his patrons, involved him in a radical shift from a world of proverbs, 'ridiculous' ballads, charms and old wives' tales to the clear light of reason and enlightenment. And his reading of *Goody Two-Shoes*, together with his mother's prudent reinforcements, was an important step on that difficult journey. His tragedy was that he ended up in a social and cultural no-man's-land: he seems to have been only too happy to abandon, slough off, his own peasant culture, but he never became a truly naturalized citizen of the polite world. He died in poverty, in debt, and in a state of deep mental confusion.

5

Bloomfield's life and work offer a conspicuously futile and painful case of cultural and social disruption – of profound dislocations ending in failure. Conversely, for a confident, even magisterial, expression of the late eighteenth-century mind in a state of transition, we can perhaps turn to no better examples than those of John Aikin (1747–1822), and of his sister, Anna, Mrs Barbauld (1743–1825). They both enjoyed long and eminently useful lives: he was a doctor of medicine, and for a time a colleague of Joseph Priestley at Warrington (Dissenting) Academy; she ran a school for dissenters with her husband in Suffolk. Her *Lessons for Children from Two to Three Years Old* (1780) was a remarkable pioneering work, and very well regarded by the Edgeworths,[41] but her most considerable didactic work for children was one in which she collaborated with her brother – *Evenings at Home* (1792–6).[42] Its six volumes ran to over 900 pages, and, as Cecil Hartley claimed in his 1866 edition, it 'contained an almost exhaustless store of interesting material for the unfatiguing exercise of mind, from the state of infancy to that of adolescence.' The contents comprised 40 instructive dialogues, 30 stories, 10 fables, 9 plays and 8 poems. The fact that the book continued to be reprinted frequently throughout the nineteenth century, with few emendations, testifies to its extraordinary popularity and timeliness: it perfectly caught and encapsulated certain interests, values and beliefs that continued to appeal to a sizeable public for three-quarters of a century.

The pretext for *Evenings* is set out in the Introduction, where we are given an account of a genial mercantile home and family, rather in the same spirit as the one Steele offered to our inspection in 1709; but where Steele's ideal parents left their children to read tales of unimpeachable insouciance, stories for stories' sakes, the essentially earnest Fairbornes – how auspicious a name! – are committed to evenings of sober and sensible, indeed useful, instruction:

> The mansion-house of the pleasant village of Beechgrove was inhabited by the family of Fairborne, consisting of the master and mistress, and a numerous progeny of children of both sexes. Of these, part were educated at home under their parents' care, and part were sent out to school. The house was seldom unprovided with visitors, the intimate friends or relations of the owners, who were

entertained with cheerfulness and hospitality, free from ceremony and parade. They formed, during their stay, part of the family; and were ready to concur with Mr and Mrs Fairborne in any little domestic plan for varying their amusements, and particularly for promoting the instruction and entertainment of the younger part of the household. As some of them were accustomed to writing, they would frequently produce a fable, a story, or dialogue, adapted to the age and understanding of the young people. It was always considered as a high favour when they would so employ themselves; and when the pieces were once read over, they were carefully deposited by Mrs Fairborne in a box, of which she kept the key. None of these were allowed to be taken out again till all the children were assembled in the holidays. It was then made one of the evening amusements of the family to rummage the budget, as their phrase was. One of the least children was sent to the box, who putting in its little hand, drew out the paper that came next, and brought it into the parlour. This was then read distinctly by one of the older ones; and after it had undergone sufficient consideration another little messenger was dispatched for a fresh supply; and so on, till as much time had been spent in this manner as the parents thought proper. Other children were admitted to these readings; and as the Budget of Beechgrove Hall became somewhat celebrated in the neighbourhood, its proprietors were at length urged to lay it open to the public. They were induced to comply.

In such a situation, said Maria Edgeworth, 'the mind is opened to extensive views', but what did the views contain? What was there to catch and hold the attention? Were they 'vast, strange, and beautiful'?

As with most of the stories emanating from dissenting and enlightened circles at this time, the little fictions are moralized tales, after the fashion popularized by Berquin and Madame de Genlis.[43] Arnaud Berquin, who died in 1791, had been awarded a 'prize for usefulness' by the French Academy; his *Ami des Enfants* – a typically ingratiating title – first appeared in monthly parts, in 1782–3, and spread like a plague in the nurseries and apartments of Europe. An English version, *The Looking Glass for the Mind*, had sold over 20,000 copies by 1800. Like those of Madame de Genlis, his worthy and tediously prosing books were compounded of a predictable prudential moralizing and large servings of useful knowledge. As Jane Austen drily remarked to her sister Cassandra, 'Having just finished [Mme de Genlis'] *Les Veillées du Château*, I think it a good opportunity for beginning a letter to you, while my mind is stored with ideas worth transmitting.'[44] Perfectly characteristic of her generation – almost exactly contemporary with Aiken and Barbauld – Madame de Genlis was possessed by what Sainte-Beuve called 'verve de pedagogie poussée jusqu'á la manie', and had never deviated from the path of didactic duty that she had first trodden at the age of seven when she gathered the local peasant children together and rammed instruction down their throats. A Goody Two-Shoes with a vengeance!

Apart from the moralized tales, *Evenings* gives much space to instruction in science, technology and manufactures. In a tone of low-keyed reasonableness and almost indefatigable material curiosity, it lays open the order of the created world. The terms of its explanations, definitions and classifications are those of the empirical sciences. Aikin offers cool reason rather than rapture, natural curiosity tinged with respect for a sensible and efficient deity: the voice of Linnaeus rather than that of Traherne: the creator's works are regarded with a rational admiration rather than with any sense of noumenous wonder. Indeed, one of the most notable features of the book is its consistent tendency to promote the language of science as more precise, more appropriate to a sensible account of the physical world, than the *lingua franca* of layman's talk. So 'Philosophy' in *Evenings* is not so much the love or pursuit of wisdom as 'the knowledge of Things Natural, grounded upon

Reason and Experience':[45] and the uses of philosophy that we encounter here are tending not only towards a 'system upon which natural effects are explained', but also in the direction of 'the course of sciences now read in the schools'.[46]

Child's play is turned by the omniscient tutor into an occasion for explanation:

> *George:* Harry, can you blow off all these dandelion feathers at a blast?
> *Harry:* I will try.
> *George:* See, you have left almost half of them. . . .
> *Tutor:* A pretty child's play you have got there. Bring me one of the dandelion's heads, and let us see if we can make no other use of it.

But, of course, he does not mean 'no other use'. On the contrary, he proceeds to give a scrupulous and enlightening botanical demonstration of 'the compound-flowered plants', and concludes: 'They are a difficult class to make out botanically . . . you must get acquainted with them.' Similarly, tea-time is transformed into a chemistry lesson:

> *Tutor:* You have assisted in tea-making a great many times, and yet I dare say you never considered what sort of operation it was.

He explains that it is a chemical process: 'O – there are many things in common life that belong to the deepest of sciences. Making tea is the chemical operation called *infusion*. . . .' He follows this up with decoction, maceration, diffusion, solution, evaporation, exhalation, saturation and distillation. It is a lucid and comprehensive lecture, proving that science lies about us, even in our infancy, and that it is not only possible but also desirable for young persons to 'speak philosophically'. In a similar spirit, when they shelter from the rain in a blacksmith's shed, the tutor seizes the occasion for an excellent lecture on mineralogy and metallurgy, in the course of which George naïvely remarks: 'I have read of rivers rolling sands of gold. Is there any truth in that?' Predictably, the tutor replies: 'The poets, as usual, have greatly exaggerated the matter.'

Not that there is any serious conflict between the arts and the sciences; as Harry's father, a sensible Whig, points out in a lecture on the manufacture of paper: 'The invention of paper has been of almost equal consequence to literature, with that of printing itself; and shows how the arts and sciences, like children of the same family, mutually assist and bring forward each other.' The exemplar of such a happy union that *Evenings* holds up for our respect, is Josiah Wedgwood, 'an excellent chemist, and a man of great taste', who has moulded more clay 'into all the forms of grace and beauty that are to be met with in the precious remains of the Greek and Etruscan artists'. As a result of his marriage of art and science, 'he has given to our houses a classic air, and has made every saloon and every dining-room schools of taste.' So Wedgwood is offered as a hero of a melioristic England's glory, creating wealth and prosperity, founded surely on his mastery of mechanics and chemistry. In the same league is Sir Richard Arkwright, inventor of the spinning-frame: 'as in this country every one is free to rise by merit,' the barber who shaved people for a penny apiece eventually 'acquired the largest fortune in the country . . . and had leave given him by the king to put *Sir* before his name.' The father reports Arkwright as saying that, 'if he had time to perfect his inventions, he would put a fleece of wool into a box, and it should come out broad-cloth.' Since this is a dialogue in which the child-auditor is allowed to interpose useful questions, Henry asks, 'What did he mean by that? Was there any fairy in the box to turn it into broad-cloth with her wand?' This of course is the perfect opportunity for the father to reply firmly: 'He was assisted by the only fairies that ever had the power of transformation – Art, and Industry.'

In the same spirit, Mr C. takes his son, Arthur, to a 'place where a number of workmen were employed in raising a prodigious mound' – they are canal-navvies, and in the midst of them is 'a very plain-dressed man, awkward in his gestures,

uncouth in his appearance, and rather heavy in his countenance – in short, a mere countryman like the rest'. As David
Piper has observed of the portraits painted at this time, 'There
are no industrial faces, as such, but occasionally one does get a
glimpse of a face that is bluntly tough, with an atmosphere
that has not been caught before',[47] such as those of John
Wilkinson, the iron-master, and Arkwright. Mr C. tells
Arthur that this is 'a great man. . . . Yes, a very great man.' It
is none other than the canal-builder James Brindley, in the
process of achieving a totally unmagical and very useful
realization of the Biblical prophecy, 'Every valley shall be
exalted. . . .' In the rapturous words of Mr C., 'He is doing
things that were never done or even thought of in this country
before. He pierces hills . . . and is likely to change the whole
face of the country, and to introduce improvements the value
of which cannot be calculated.' Arthur must, then, not be
misled by appearances: Brindley 'looks like a rustic, it is true,
but he has a soul [*sic*] of the first order, such as is not granted to
one out of millions of the human race.'

Such recognition is characteristic of the politics of
Evenings: democratical, demystifying, utilitarian, even Ben-
thamite, and excited by the whiff of bank-notes. If young
Arthur is to determine whether or not a 'great' man is truly
great, he must 'strip him, in . . . imagination, of all the
external advantages of rank and power, and see what a figure
he would have made without them.' And imperial glory and
territorial aggrandizement are similarly stripped of their
deceptive trappings.

> *Edward:* I have read of taking possession of a newly
> discovered country by setting up the king's standard,
> or some such ceremony, though it was full of in-
> habitants.

His father replies: 'Such was the custom; and a more
impudent mockery of all right and justice cannot be conceived. Yet this, I am sorry to say, is the title by which
European nations claim the greatest part of their foreign

settlements.' Colonization comes in for especially severe criticism: 'the natives were deprived, on various pretexts, of their most fertile grounds . . . the whites spread death and desolation throughout the country.' In one typical case, the white invaders lure the natives to a meeting for making a treaty of co-existence, then shoot them down in cold blood. 'Of the hundreds who had there assembled, only one escaped to tell the children how their fathers fell by the treachery of the whites.' As for domestic politics, the primary criterion is economic growth!

At home, 'order, peace, and union' constitute the ideal, for without these, manufactures cannot prosper. Where you see prosperous manufactories, you can assume that 'property is accurately ascertained and protected'. The drift of the book is consistently in the direction of peaceableness, and the settlement of differences by the use of patience and reason: the use of force is seen as entirely abhorrent. In this respect, one of the most attractive, effective – and Swiftian – features of the book is its trick of presenting familiar phenomena under the guise of the unfamiliar, so that the reader's eyes are scrubbed clean of habitual ways of seeing, the mind deprived of unexamined assumptions, and the unquestioned is seen critically. There is no better example of this than 'Things by their Right Names':[48] the opening lines of this also exemplify two other virtues of *Evenings*, namely that children are occasionally allowed to speak naturally, even cheekily, and to reveal their real enthusiasms:

> *Charles:* Papa, you grow very lazy. Last winter you used
>   to tell us stories, and now you never tell us any; and we
>   are all got round the fire, quite ready to hear you. Pray,
>   dear Papa, let us have a very pretty one.
> *Father:* With all my heart – What shall it be?
> *C.:* A bloody murder, papa!
> *F.:* A bloody murder! Well, then – Once upon a time,
>   some men, dressed all alike –
> *C.:* With black crapes over their faces.

F.: No; they had steel caps on: – having crossed a dark heath, wound cautiously along the skirts of a deep forest –

C.: They were ill-looking fellows, I dare say.

F.: I cannot say so; on the contrary, they were as tall, personable men as most one shall see; – leaving on their right hand an old ruined tower on the hill –

C.: At midnight, just as the clock struck twelve; was it not, papa?

F.: No, really; it was on a fine balmy summer's morning; – they moved forward, one behind another –

C.: As still as death, creeping along under the hedges.

F.: On the contrary . . . they gloried in what they were about. – They moved forward, I say, to a large plain, where stood a near pretty village, which they set on fire –

C.: Set a village on fire, wicked wretches!

F.: And while it was burning, they murdered – twenty thousand men! . . .

C.: How should these men kill twenty thousand people, pray?

F.: Why not? the *murderers* were thirty thousand.

C.: O, now I have found you out! you mean a battle.

F.: Indeed, I do. I do not know any murders half so bloody.

It is a deft performance, and relates to another key issue in the book, which rests on the knowledge that naming is crucial not only in matters of moral judgement, but also in the act of knowing anything. The epistemology of *Evenings* is clearly derived, as one might expect, from Locke: 'A great deal of the delicacy of language depends upon an accurate knowledge of the specific meaning of single terms, and a nice attention to their relative propriety'; and 'nothing is more useful, than to learn to form ideas with precision, and to express them with accuracy'. It is the dialogue that ends with that last proposition that epitomizes the effective drift or tendency of

Evenings: a dialogue entitled, 'A lesson in the Art of Distinguishing'. Here is a representative extract:

> *F.:* Come hither, Charles; what is that you see grazing in the meadow before you?
> *C.:* It is a horse.
> *F.:* Whose horse is it?
> *C.:* I do not know; I never saw it before.
> *F.:* How do you know it is a horse, if you never saw it before? . . .
> [One of the pleasures of being an adult is that one can tell people who ask questions like that where to go; but C., poor boy, is trapped.]
> Later, much later:
> *F.:* You see, therefore, that large and small are relative terms.
> *C.:* I do not well understand that phrase.
> *F.:* It means that they have no precise and determinate signification in themselves, but are applied differently according to the other ideas which you join with them, and the different positions in which you view them.

What all this constitutes is a kind of hypertrophy of explanation, which was to characterize instructional books for children even to the present day. The father's moment of pedagogical consummation, in this instance, comes with his climactic definition of a definition! But to be fair to Aikin, always on the alert for a void to fill, this dialogue on definitions *is* the most relentless thing in the whole work, and Maria Edgeworth was no more than just when she commended the 'agreeable manner' in which *Evenings* communicated its useful knowledge. The pity is that it spawned many imitators, and those had few of the virtues of *Evenings*, but all of its vices, and more besides. Within a few years the children of England were reeling under a maniacal deluge of useless 'useful' knowledge; as Jane Austen observed with characteristic good sense:

Fanny could read, work, and write, but she had been taught nothing more; and as her cousins found her ignorant of many things with which they had been long familiar, they thought her prodigiously stupid, and for the first two or three weeks were continually bringing some fresh report of it into the drawing-room. . . .' I cannot [said one] remember the time when I did not know a great deal that she has not the least notion of yet. How long ago it is, aunt, since we used to repeat the chronological order of the kings of England, with the dates of their accession, and most of the principal events of their reigns!'

'Yes,' added the other; 'and of the Roman emperors as low as Severus; besides a great deal of the Heathen Mythology, and all the Metals, Semi-metals, Planets, and distinguished philosophers.'

'Very true, indeed, my dears, but you are blessed with wonderful memories, and your poor cousin has probably none at all.'[49]

A generation later, Dickens was to take such satire much further, and with more cause for feeling provoked into ridicule. Meanwhile, *Evenings at Home* forms an appropriate conclusion to the century that began with Locke: it is lucid, reasonable, sensible most of the time, empirical, useful, and short on imagination and poetry. Samuel Johnson's judgement of Locke may also be passed on John Aikin and Anna Barbauld: 'Locke's plan gives too much to one side and too little to the other; it gives too little to literature.'

NOTES AND REFERENCES

1 Samuel Johnson, 'Joseph Addison', in *Lives of the Poets* 2 vols (London: Oxford University Press, 1961), vol. 1.
2 'Isaac Watts', ibid., vol. 2.
3 ibid.
4 Isaac Watts, *The Improvement of the Mind*, 2 pts (London: J. Buckland & T. Longman; T. Field; C. Dilly; 1782).

5 *Horae Lyricae* (London: John Lawrence, 1706). The Preface is reprinted in the facsimile edition of *Divine Songs*, intr. by J.H.P. Pafford (London: Oxford University Press, 1971), pp. 97–107. A more persuasive form of Watts's argument was offered by John Dennis:

> One of the principal Reasons that has made the modern Poetry so contemptible is that, by divesting itself of Religion, it is fallen from its Dignity . . . from the greatest Production of the Mind of Man, it is dwindled to an extravagant and vain Amusement. (*The Grounds of Criticism in Poetry*, 1704)

6 Dryden's *Fables Ancient and Modern* (from Ovid, Boccaccio, Homer and Chaucer) appeared in 1700.

7 *Divine Songs* (London: M. Lawrence, 1715), Song XXIII, st. iii, p. 33; Song XI, st. ii, p. 16; Song XV, sts v and vi, p. 23; Song XVIII, sts ii-v, pp. 26–7. For details of a facsimile reproduction of this first edition, see n. 5 above.

8 *Spectator* (1 July 1712).

9 In *The Improvement of the Mind*, pt 2, pp. 100–236; ibid., pt 2, pp. 104, 124–5, 111–12, 166–7.

10 Cf. Vicesimus Knox, in *Winter Evenings: or, Lubrications on Life and Letters*, 3 vols (London, Charles Dilly, 1788), vol. LXII; reprinted in *The British Essayists*, 45 vols (London: T. & J. Allman, 1823), vol. 43, p. 116.

11 *A Little Pretty Pocket-Book, Intended for the Instruction and Amusement of Little Master Tommy, and Pretty Miss Polly . . .* (London: J. Newbery, 1744). The 10th edition appeared in 1760. For full bibliographical details see M.F. Thwaite's edition, with her introductory essay and bibliography (London: Oxford University Press, 1966).

12 See Dickens's essay, 'Frauds on the Fairies', *Household Words*, no. 184 (1 October 1853).

13 Preface to *Tom Thumb*, in *The Criticism of Henry Fielding*, ed. Ioan Williams (London: Routledge & Kegan Paul, 1970), p. 4.

14 *The Jacobite's Journal and Related Writings*, ed. W.B. Coley (Oxford: Clarendon Press, 1974), p. 177.

15 *Pamela*, ch. 1.

16 *Fraser's Magazine* (April 1846), pp. 495–502. F. Homes Dudden notes that Fielding was indeed acquainted with the adventures of the 'young English Hercules', and that *The Grub-Street Journal* of 18 November 1731 contains a poem, 'The Modern Poets', which attributes to Fielding 'The fame of Hickathrift, and brave Tom Thumb', but, Dudden argues, 'that he ever wrote them up, or turned them into a farce, is both unproved and extremely

improbable' (*Henry Fielding, His Life, Works, and Times*, Oxford: Clarendon Press, 1952).

17 See her edition of *The Governess* (London: Oxford University Press, 1968) and *Fénelon on Education*, ed. H.C. Barnard (Cambridge: Cambridge University Press, 1966).
18 Keats, *Letters*, ed. Robert Gittings (London: Oxford University Press, 1970), p.230.
19 See below, Chapter Eight, p.255.
20 See, for example *Radio Times* (24 January 1981), p.18.
21 F.J. Harvey Darton, *Children's Books in England*, 2nd edn (Cambridge: Cambridge University Press, 1958), p.130.
22 John Ginger, *The Notable Man: The Life and Times of Oliver Goldsmith* (London: Hamish Hamilton, 1977), p.385.
23 *The Bee*, no. VI (10 November 1759). Reprinted in *Works*, ed. A. Friedman (Oxford: Clarendon Press, 1966), vol.1, p.461.
24 *Works*, ed. Friedman, vol.4, p.249.
25 *Works* (London, 1801), vol.1, p.43. Reprinted in *Collected Letters*, ed. K.C. Balderston (Cambridge: Cambridge University Press, 1928), pp.29–30. And cf 'Happiness', *Works*, ed. Friedman, vol.1, p.385.
26 *Works* (1801), vol.IV, p.423, essay XVI.
27 ibid., p.377, essay XII.
28 ibid., p.378.
29 ibid., p.380.
30 *The History of Little Goody Two-Shoes* (London: J. Newbery, 1765), p.56.
31 *The Bee*, no. VIII (November 1759). Reprinted in *Works* (1801), vol.IV, p.277.
32 *Works* (1801), vol.IV, p.283.
33 For an ironic essay on witchcraft, see *The Lounger*, no. 41 (November 1785).
34 *Popular Stories for the Nursery*, vol. III (1809). The illustrations are dated September 1804.
35 *The Guardian of Education: containing Memoirs of Modern Philosophers, both Christian and Infidel ... also Abstracts of Sermons on some of the Most Important Points of Christian Doctrine; together with Extracts from other Works of Established Reputation, Religious and Moral, and A Copious Review of Modern Books for Children and Young Persons*, 5 vols (London: J. Hatchard, June 1802–September 1806 – monthly 1802–3 except September–December 1803; quarterly 1804–6).
36 Darton, op.cit., p.97.
37 Bloomfield, *Remains*, ed. J. Weston (London: Baldwin, Cradock

& Joy, 1824), vol. II, p. 87. Cf. the 'Child Ballads', no. 3.

38 ibid., p. 120.

39 Gilbert White commented on this in his *Natural History of Selborne*; and cf. *The Midwife*, ed. Christopher Smart (London: J. Newbery, 1750).

40 Op. cit., vol. II, p. 87.

41 See below, p. 122.

42 On her hymns for children, see Chapter Seven.

43 On Berquin and Mme de Genlis, see Marc Soriano, *Guide de Littérature pour la Jeunesse* (Paris: Flammarion, 1975). On Mme de Genlis see also Mary Wollstonecraft, *The Rights of Women*, ch. V, sect. iv.

44 Letter of 8 November 1800.

45 *Bailey's English Dictionary*, 17th edn (London, 1757).

46 Walker's *Dictionary*, 14th edn (London, 1814).

47 David Piper, *The English Face* (London: National Portrait Gallery, 1980), p. 224.

48 Cf. Ruskin:

> But the Johnsonian vanity of wishes is triumphantly and with bray of penny trumpets and blowing of steam-whistles, proclaimed for the glorious discovery of the civilized ages, by Mrs Barbauld, Miss Edgeworth, Adam Smith, and Co. There is no God, but have we not invented gunpowder? – who wants a God, with that in his pocket? . . . No man can owe more than I to both Mrs Barbauld and Miss Edgeworth. . . . Nevertheless, the germs of all modern conceit and error respecting manufacture and industry, as rivals to Art and to Genius, are concentrated in *Evenings at Home* and *Harry and Lucy* – being all the while themselves works of real genius, and prophetic of things that have yet to be learned and fulfilled. See for instance the paper, 'Things by their Right Names'. ('Fiction Fair and Foul', in *Works*, ed. E.T. Cooke and A. Wedderburn, London, George Allen, 1908, vol. XXXIV, pp. 303 and 314)

49 *Mansfield Park*, ch. 2.

CHAPTER FOUR

FATHER, DAUGHTER, AND LEARNED LUNATIONS

What we needed was a new radiance altogether.
(Saul Bellow, *Humboldt's Gift*, 1975)
How many souls hoped for the strength and
sweetness of visionary words to purge
consciousness of its stale dirt.
(ibid.)

1

'Prudence' and 'Reason' – two of Newbery's most conspicuous values, and recurrent elements of eighteenth-century mercantile morality, at least in theory – figure early and prominently in Rousseau's Émile, translated into English as *Emilius and Sophia*.[1] And here they are stood on their heads. He addresses his gospel of nature to the 'tender and provident mother . . . who is prudent enough. . . .' In terms of the conventional wisdom of the 1750s, we can predict how that sentence will end; but Rousseau concludes: 'prudent enough to leave the beaten road'.[2] It is the first of his barrage of provocative paradoxes. As for reason, many of our most respectable conventions, founded ostensibly on an appeal to reason or judgement, are 'idle and ridiculous',[3] and even 'the most sagacious instructors' make the fundamental mistake of 'always expecting the *man* in the *child*'.[4]

As a polemical writer, Rousseau was blessed with some attractive, and – for many readers – disarming, even irresistible, gifts. In this first English translation, by William Kenrick, a sympathetic admirer, the argument is nervously alive, lightly and deftly agile; his stance *vis à vis* the reader is provoking, unsettling, and insouciant – rather like Sterne, without the wilder nonsense. His essential premise is maddeningly, or intoxicatingly, simple: everyone before him had totally misunderstood the nature of the task of rearing children. The essential wisdom was only to be found in an uncompromising, unapologetic, fearless, radical appeal to nature.

His appeal was partly existential: prudential forethought – concern for the security of our future – has conspired to rob us of our lives. If we live at all, it must be in the present moment; but where are we, most of the time, inside our careful heads? We are anxiously staking out the future, so that we shall be prepared to meet whatever may happen the day after tomorrow! At the age of sixty, we 'wake up' and realize that we have lived, not in our lives, but in some illusory envisioned future, which fails to arrive in the way our prudential schemes presumed. Such policy has particularly damaging effects on children, for childhood is *par excellence* a time for being and for growing. So Rousseau took the age of reason's conventions of child-rearing, and with an often exhilarating iconoclastic enthusiasm he showed them to be committed to factitious appearances rather than to inner realities. They were devoted to producing pseudo-adults, and in the process they failed to allow for a natural maturation, and so failed to help children grow into a full adulthood, with all gifts and talents come to rich fruition: 'Forward, prating children usually make but ordinary men.'[5] Examine your precious prodigy, he insisted, and

> you will sometimes conceive him possessed of an amazing genius, an active and penetrating spirit, capable of soaring to the clouds; and yet you will more often find this very genius inactive, indolent, insipid, dull, and, as it were, wrapt in a thick fog. Sometimes he will fly before you, and at others, remain motionless and immoveable. At one instant, you will admire him as a prodigy of wit

and ingenuity, and the next, despise him for a fool; you
will in both, however, be equally mistaken: he is neither a
genius nor a blockhead, but a child. . . . Treat him,
therefore, agreeable to his age, notwithstanding appearances. . . .[6]

With canny aptness, he took the simplest of La Fontaine's
Fables, 'The Fox and the Crow' – staple fare for infantine
reasoners, and representative of what enlightened French and
English parents approved as polite nursery literature[7] – and
proceeded to expose it as incomprehensible, ridiculous, false,
soaked in the irrational fictions of old mythologies, over-
sophisticated, over-subtle, and riddled with all manner of
covert complex ideas, each of which would have to be
explained before the child could in any way be said to
understand it!

It is a virtuoso performance on Rousseau's part, and a
pioneering example of close analysis of the encounter of small
child and print. If one takes him seriously – and his analysis *is*
persuasive – then the consequences are indeed far-reaching,
for what must follow is a totally fresh start from first
principles. His central charge was that 'whatever pains we
take to render them [the implicit ideas] simple, the instruction
we would deduce from them is attended with other ideas
above his [the child's] capacity.'[8] *Impasse!* And as for the
'morals' of the fable, the morals which serve to legitimize it,
morals such as Newbery and his like were dispensing in vast
quantities, even in this matter, where the explicit seemed so
clear and unambiguous, children had an incorrigible and
natural habit of turning them upside down, inside out, back to
front! When it was blandly assumed that they were learning
from La Fontaine's fable of 'The Raven and the Fox' to be on
their guard against the cunning flattery of the fox, motivated
by self-interest, they were actually falling in love with the
wicked animal. 'In reading the fable above-cited . . . children
laugh at and despise the silly raven; but they are fond of the
fox.'[9]

As for all the strategies that pedagogues and tutors had devised for teaching children to read, Rousseau gave them short shrift: in a seeming parody of 'Habe caritatem et fac quidquid vis', he insisted that the only 'certain method' was to excite in children a desire to learn. Give a child this desire, and do as you will with your cards and dice [i.e. visual aids]; any method will then be sufficient. The grand motive, indeed the only one that is certain and effectual, is present interest.'[10] As for the serious task of teaching a child to write, 'I am ashamed of descending to such trifling objects in a treatise on education.'[11] Where the judicious, moderate Locke had placed this very low on his list of priorities, Rousseau simply refused to give it any attention.

Uncosseted, unpampered, hardened by exposure to the elements, actively impelled by a natural curiosity and genuine need, the Rousseauesque child was nevertheless to be given a literary education: just one solitary book, the remarkable eighteenth-century record of a man living by his wits, his resourcefulness, his natural talents, in a state of nature, reclaiming his right to the title of 'noble savage'. Who else but Robinson Crusoe? If Crusoe had not already been invented, it would have been apropos for Rousseau to invent him.

> I would have him [Emilius] indeed personate the hero of the tale, and be entirely taken up with his castle, his goats and his plantations; he should make himself minutely acquainted, not from books but circumstances, with every thing requisite for a man in such a situation. He should affect even his dress, wear a coat of skins, a great hat . . . in short, he should be entirely equipt in his grotesque manner, even with his umbrello. . . . I would have him when at a loss about the meaures necessary to be taken for his provision or security . . . examine the conduct of his hero . . .: for I doubt not but he will form a project of going to make a like settlement. . . . What opportunities of instruction would such an amusement afford an able preceptor, who should project it only with

a view to that end! The pupil, eager to furnish a magazine for his island, would be more ready to learn than his tutor to teach him. He would be solicitous to know every thing that is useful, and nothing else: You would in such a case have no more occasion to direct; but only to restrain him.[12]

On principles derived from Locke – the recognition of effective learning in forms of play – but irradiated here by Rousseau's distinctive enthusiasm, Defoe's fiction was thus transformed into a handbook for survival, a guide to self-sufficiency: not merely economic, but also of the spirit. The pupil would thus be prepared, at the age of twelve or thirteen, to enter society, having known only the company of his tutor, reinforced by the exemplary role-playing of Crusoe: ready to enter the world of men, armed with an independent spirit, a rich personal resourcefulness, and a healthy mind in a healthy body.

Such a paragon would not be deceived by words, by appearances, by fine rhetoric, but would be quick to appeal directly to actuality, to the substantial realities that he himself knew through direct unmediated contact. On all fronts, the artifice of civilization would yield to the irresistible power, vividness, and integrity of uncorrupted nature. We now know all the objections, moral, philosophical and practical, to this oddly theoretical vision; especially do we know that for human beings 'nature' is essentially social, that without all the buzz of social interactions our language and mind would fare poorly. But it is clear that a 'new radiance altogether' was what Rousseau seemed to many to offer a society suffering from a hypertrophy of 'civilization', of refinement, of artifice. His vision, proffered so feelingly, without hedging, without carefully contrived rationale, seemed to 'purge consciousness' of stale custom, of grey judgement, of over-prudential reason. Its appeal transcended the cooler levels of understanding and went straight to the heart, to the sensibility. Little wonder that the readers of the 1760s responded in extreme ways – some with a snarl of revulsion or a groan of disgust, others with a rhapsodic embrace.[14]

2

The deepest revulsion came from those who for fundamental sectarian reasons found essential heresy in his basic assumption of original innocence in unsocialized, unformed human nature: those who sustained, throughout the eighteenth century, the severity of conscience that linked late seventeenth-century puritanism and late eighteenth-century evangelicalism: in Wesleyan circles, for example, Rousseau was regarded with abhorrence. Conversely, those who rushed into uncritical discipleship, keen to swallow hook, line and sinker, were mostly young, injudicious, hungering for emotional intensities, and idealistic enough to entertain the possibility of a radically new beginning. Such indeed were Richard Lovell Edgeworth and Thomas Day.

In 1762, Sterne's Walter Shandy spoke out extravagantly for the generation of Edgeworth and Day when he enthused about his vision of a 'North-west passage to the intellectual world', his belief that 'the soul of man has shorter ways of going to work, in furnishing itself with knowledge and instruction, than we generally take with it.'[15] Walter, naïve and eccentric, unwittingly prophetic of Bentham and James Stuart Mill, envisaged a clear explicit path through the tangle of the mind and its hitherto haphazard and ineffectual nurture. A year later, Rousseau's trail-blazing to a state of natural fullness and fulfilment appeared in England; and in 1765, the pragmatic Lunar Society was founded. It was a heady time to be young, and Richard Edgeworth was headier than most.[16] It was Rousseau that he discovered and espoused first.

Born in 1744, Edgeworth eloped with Anna Maria Elers, and their first child, Richard, was born in 1764. Two years later, Edgeworth met Day, and in 1767 Edgeworth began to apply Emilian principles to the task of rearing young Richard. In this risky business, he clearly received far more encouragement from Day than from Anna Maria. The boy grew up to be virtually uncontrollable, and would listen to no one but his father. With a nice sense of irony, when Edgeworth took the boy to see the great Rousseau himself, young Richard was extremely rude to the sage, and laid on a rather ugly display of gross chauvinism. But it was in 1766 that Edgeworth also came into contact with the major formative influence of his adult life: through Erasmus Darwin, with whom he had corresponded about the improved design of carriages, he was introduced to the Lunar Society. The Society, a year old, was to flourish in Birmingham, the centre of scientific and technological innovation, for about forty years. It met on the Monday nearest to the full moon – hence its name – so that its members could travel to, or rather, from meetings, with the benefit of its light to illuminate their way; and its members formed the most powerful gathering of intellectual, scientific and technological talent, genius indeed, in the world.[17] It was their various and indefatigable enquiries that formed the basis, the theoretical and scientific basis, for the industrial revolution. Matthew Boulton, James Watt, Erasmus Darwin, Samuel Galton, James Keir, Josiah Wedgwood, William Withering and Joseph Priestley were among its most celebrated members; and, together with Darwin, Edgeworth and Day were its most literary members.

The Lunatics met to conduct experiments, to exchange ideas, to solve problems and to discuss innovations; they corresponded with other such societies in various parts of the world, and enjoyed visits from distinguished foreigners: F.R. Raspe, subsequently famous as the author of *Baron Münchausen*, was one such visitor.

Under the influence of the Lunatics, and of their motto – *Observare* – Edgeworth sloughed off most of his Rousseauism, and evolved a pragmatic, empirical approach to questions that, in Rousseau, generated rather more warmth than light. Of Rousseau's principles he retained three: the importance, in learning, of interest; the importance of close and disinterested scrutiny of conventional 'wisdom', especially in relation to children and learning; and the view that, in certain situations, the child could be said to know best.

Maria, Edgeworth's eldest daughter, was born in 1768, and in 1773 his first wife, for whom he had felt little genuine affection or respect, died. He subsequently married Honora Sneyd, of Lichfield, and she died of tuberculosis in 1780; then her sister, Elizabeth, who died in 1797; and finally Frances Beaufort. In all, there were twenty-two children. He inherited the family house and estate, Edgeworthstown, in Ireland, in 1770; and his days came to be increasingly devoted to the management and improvement of the estate, the invention of various machines, relatively unsuccessful excursions into politics, and – above all – an indefatigable involvement in the education of his family.

Honora, his second wife, was a severe and intensely moral woman, and it was with her that Edgeworth began to give close attention to the children's education. In 1796, he observed that for a long time education had been 'classed amongst the subjects of vague and metaphysical speculation; but of late, it has attained its proper station in experimental philosophy',[18] and again, in 1798, he affirmed: 'To make any progress in the art of education, it must be patiently reduced to an experimental science.'[19] He realized that in order to do this, his first task was to define and isolate the distinctive elements of the skills and competences that children were to acquire, and to observe and record their performances very carefully, in a spirit of cool detachment and with a pragmatic acceptance of the various ups and downs of trial and error. Like his contemporaries, Thomas Reid, Jeremy Bentham and Tom Wedgwood, he coveted a complete inner and outer record of a child's development:

> If we could obtain a distinct and full history of all that
> hath passed in the mind of a child, from the beginning of
> life and sensation, till it grows up to the use of reason . . .

this would be a treasure of natural history, which would probably give more light into the human faculties, than all the systems of philosophers about them, since the beginning of the world.[20]

Edgeworth was not slow to recognize the difficulties of such an enterprise, though it was typical of the man's grand ambitions that he should think it feasible, and a sign of his hubristic cleverness that he should think it desirable; he saw the possible snags not so much in the inherent difficulty of accurate measurement as in the partiality, affections and vanity of the child's parents. If they were to conduct the experiment, would they not be tempted to arrange their findings so as to prove that they had produced exemplary offspring? In the event, he devoted a great deal of his time, during his early thirties, to just such a task. Honora, in fact, did most of the work – Edgeworth was a great delegator – and she also preserved a measure of scientific detachment and cool aloofness that struck some of the children as cold severity. Just as Rousseau had misconstrued the *social* roots of learning, so Richard failed to see that the demands of parent and of empiricist were in truth irreconcilable, or at least that their merging would set up problematic confusions in the minds of the subjects! Edgeworth proceeded to scrutinize about forty books for children, in his search for suitable reading-matter, and was forced to conclude:

> I could not select three pages that were suited to their capacities; and there is scarcely any folly or any vice, of which they might not learn the Rudiments, in this collection, if it were written in language which they could comprehend.[21]

But then he lit on Mrs Barbauld's *Lessons for Children from Two to Three Years Old*, which not only earned his approval for its effectiveness as a first reader, but also served as a useful model for the first essays that he and Honora made in producing a text for young readers. Psychologically reinforced by the teachings of Locke and of Hartley, as mediated by Joseph Priestley of the Lunar Society, they wrote their first children's book in 1779: it set out to exemplify, as simply as possible, 'ideas of analogy, causation, and utility',[22] and was the first stage of a larger, more ambitious plan to 'introduce . . . the first principles of many sciences or rather the facts upon which those principles are founded', and to 'inculcate the plain precepts of morality, not by eloquent harangues' but by offering pictures of real life so as to arouse the spirit of emulation in the child's mind. Every word of the text would be clearly and explicitly attached, by the aid of a glossary, to 'a clear and accurate idea'. The whole enterprise was to be founded on the secure empirical basis of close objective observations; thus, the effects of different forms of instruction could be compared and evaluated, and 'real proficiency' clearly distinguished from the merely apparent show of the same.[23] The essential instrument, the tool of 'experimental science', was to be a detailed register of each child's progress.[24] So, the world of infantine learning was to be reformed, root and branch.

In 1782, two years after Honora's death and Edgeworth's precipitate remarriage, Maria returned to Edgeworthstown from school in London. She was fourteen, and already an accomplished story-teller.

> Maria was remembered by her companions at school for her entertaining stories, and she learned with all the tact of an improvatrice to know which tale was most success-ful by the unmistakable evidence of her auditors' wake-fulness . . . she recollected only one which was specially applauded: of an adventurer who had a mask made of the dried skin taken from a dead man's face, which he put on when he wished to be disguised, and kept buried at the foot of a tree.[25]

She returned to a household firmly committed to a schematic and systematically didactic view of the learning of reading, in part a kind of posthumous tribute to the memory of Honora, and to a pioneering curriculum of science for juveniles. But her own unredeemed head was full of exciting, romantic, even gothic stories. How, then, did she take her place in her father's educational enterprise? She had come through a very difficult childhood. When she was four she was placed with her mother's aunts in London, while her mother went off to join Edgeworth who was engaged in a civil engineering scheme in France. In 1773, her mother died, and four months later her father had a new and severe wife. Maria was unhappy, disturbed and difficult for months, possibly years. Edgeworth was obsessed with Honora, and Honora with Edgeworth. Moreover, she was an exacting and awesome stepmother, who meted out due portions of 'affection' in a rather calculating way, in proportion to a child's deserts, or apparent deserts. In 1775, Maria was packed off to school, first in Derby, then in London; and for the rest of her long life she was intensely, almost obsessively, committed to domestic happiness, and disposed to the overt display of affection: she needed very badly to know that she was loved, and loved especially by her father.

How better to win his affection than by pleasing him? How better to please him than to become more like him by imitation? She learned this lesson well, too well, and committed herself to didacticism so decisively that in her mature years it was her father who had to warn her against overplaying her moralizing hand in her fiction. In effect, she made too good a job of internalizing the demands of his demanding ego. Within weeks of her return to Edgeworthstown, she had serious work to do: her father set her the task of translating Madame de Genlis' *Adèle et Théodore: ou Lettres sur l'Éducation*, and she also became involved in the instruction of the younger children. Gradually she began to write stories and plays for the family's use, and this apprenticeship bore fruit, in the 1790s, in a variety of ways, in *The Parent's Assistant, or stories for children* (1796); in *Practical Education* (1798); and in scientific 'stories', published in 1801, as *Harry and Lucy* (*Early Lessons*).

On and off, for about thirty years, she and her father were
involved in a peculiarly close collaboration, which continued
right up to 1817, the year of his death. We can judge
Edgeworth's views on literature for children by the preface
that he wrote for the *Continuation of Early Lessons* (1814): it
takes the form of an 'Address to Mothers', for he had learned
from Rousseau to address himself to women. It is a remarkable performance for a man of almost seventy, who could have
been resting on his laurels. But he was indeed indefatigable.
His preface is judicious, candid, disinterested and lucid. And
it is Rousseauesque in conceding a remarkable degree of
discretion and judgement to children: 'We defer implicitly to
their opinion; well educated children are, in fact, best judges
of what is fit for children.'[26] He allows himself to reminisce:
'When I was a child, I had no resource but Newberry's [*sic*]
little books and Mrs Teachum [i.e. *The Governess*]', and he
notes the remarkable proliferation of books for children that
was such a feature of late eighteenth-century publishing; but
he finds them a mixed blessing, for too many of them are very
confused. Learning and reading, he insists, have to be made
agreeable to the child: the 'universal and rational incentive to
application' – success – has to be 'perceived by the learner'.
His golden rule is radical and simple: 'Whenever a child, who
has in general a disposition for instruction, shows a dislike for
a book, lay it aside at once.'[27] Ignorance is to be preferred to
'confused and obscure instruction', and a little knowledge is
'far preferable to a string of ready-made answers to specific
questions, which have been merely committed to memory'.

Neither he nor Maria, who had imbibed many of his views,
had any time for mere rote-learning, accompanied by an
incapacity for combining or in any way internalizing knowledge so acquired. Once children could read fluently, the first
priority was not so much to find entertaining and instructive
books for them to read, as to prevent them from 'reading too
much, and indiscriminately'. They were to be allowed access
only to such books as 'cultivate the moral feelings, and create a
taste for knowledge, while they, at the same time, amuse and

interest'.[28] A sufficient library, in Edgeworth's view, would comprise: *Fabulous Histories, Evenings at Home,* Berquin's *Children's Friend, Sandford and Merton, Little Jack, The Children's Miscellany, Bob the Terrier, Dick the Poney* [*sic*], *The Book of Trades, The Looking-Glass, or History of a young Artist, Robinson Crusoe, The Travels of Rolando* and *Mrs Wakefield on Instinct. Rolando* he mentioned with some hesitation because 'though it contains much knowledge . . . yet it is too much mixed with fiction', whereas he recommended *Instinct* 'with more confidence', on the grounds that 'the facts and the fiction are judiciously separated; so that the reader is in no danger of mistaking truth for falsehood'. Truth and Falsehood: as Samuel Johnson remarked,

> Truth is, indeed, not often welcome for its own sake. . . . For this reason many arts of instruction have been invented, by which the reluctance against truth may be overcome, and as physic is given to children in confections, precepts have been hidden under a thousand appearances, that mankind may be bribed by pleasure. . . .

But in Johnson's allegory on the subject,[29] it was not only Falsehood that wore a robe to captivate her admirers: Truth also wore one, woven by the Muses on the loom of Pallas, and whenever she put it on, she was recognized under the name of Fiction.

Johnson's reconciliation of reason and fiction was not, however, Edgeworth's, whose bias was consistently scientific and empirical: he himself seems to have felt virtually no need for those things for which we turn to fiction. A clear demonstration of his temper is to be found in his discussion of elementary science: the Lunar Society, like other of the Literary and Philosophical Societies that were such a marked feature of later eighteenth-century society, had domesticated scientific experiment, as one can see in some of the remarkable paintings of Joseph Wright of Derby, such as 'An Experiment on a Bird in the Air Pump' and 'A Philosopher giving a

Lecture on the Orrery'. Children could be initiated into the disciplines of scientific method, and actually conduct experiments at quite an early age, given appropriate guidance: the effect of such an experience could prove immeasurable, as George Eliot later remarked:

> To see a chemical experiment gives an attractiveness to a definition of chemistry, and fills it with a significance which it would never have had without the pleasant shock of an unusual sequence such as the transformation of a solid into gas, and *vice versa*.[30]

Unfortunately, the supply of scientific tutors and itinerant lecturers was very limited in Edgeworth's time, so books had to serve as surrogates. Hence the appearance of Mrs Marcet's *Chemical Dialogues* (1806), and Jeremiah Joyce's *Scientific Dialogues* (1807), not to mention *Harry and Lucy*. Such books could at least help to establish correct 'habits of thinking', Edgeworth thought, and he instanced the case of one of his daughters who, at the age of ten, was in a state of serious confusion:

> One of my children had early acquired such an eager taste for reading, as had filled her mind with a multitude of facts, and images, and words, which prevented her from patient investigation, and from those habits of thinking, and that logical induction, without which no science, nor any series of truths, can be taught.[31]

(It is amusing, for us, to note how his remarks about his children have the tone of a headmaster's end-of-term report.) The poor girl was put on a regular diet of *Chemical Dialogues*, which 'produced the most salutary effects in her education. Romantic ideas, poetic images, and some disdain of common occupations, seemed to clear away from her young mind; and the chaos of her thoughts formed a new and rational arrangement.' There speaks the Edgeworth of the Lunar Society; 'romantic' and 'poetic' are terms to be used pejoratively, not merely in this context on the grounds of inappropriateness, but generally as inferior, irrational, or sub-rational, even regressive, ways of knowing, or of even declining to know, as when compared to the empirical, the measurable, the objective. And it may not be entirely fortuitous that the culprit in this instance is a girl, one of the 'weaker' sex.

As for Edgeworth's other voice – the vestigial echo of his erstwhile infatuation with Rousseau – it can be heard in his condemnation of those who 'load the memories of children with answers to every possible question in geography and history, and with all such learning as is to be found in *task books*', i.e. text-books, or work-books. In elementary books for children, he argued,

> what is purely didactic, and all general reflections, ought, as much as possible, to be avoided. Action should be introduced – Action! – Action! Whether in morals or science, the thing to be taught should seem to arise from the circumstances in which the little persons of the drama are placed.[32]

The bait for the child must be 'entertaining story, or natural dialogue': what the instructing adult had to fold or tuck away inside this, was 'useful instruction'. And again we find a trace of the persisting influence of Locke and Rousseau in his insistence that children would learn most effectively through contact with immediate experience, through direct observation and through talk: 'by the senses', and by 'oral communication'.[33] Books, as supplementary resources, should then be used 'to recall, arrange and imprint what is learnt by the senses'.

Both Locke and Rousseau had recommended that circumstances be devised, wherein the child could not help but be provoked into observing, enquiring and reflecting. Something of this sort clearly occurred at Edgeworthstown. But the juvenile science-books were written in order to provide rather a pale simulacrum of such situations – an illusion, even a fiction, of such experience, accompanied or followed by instructive dialogue which, at least theoretically, 'seemed to arise' from the experimental observations.

Edgeworth and Maria, therefore, like Joyce and Mrs Marcet, slipped into a contradiction: however empirical or sense-derived their recommended procedures, however firmly they deplored rote-learning, the long-term effect of their juvenile science-books was to contribute to a tradition of science task-books which would serve in part to counteract or severely dilute many of their decent original intentions. As for the other, complementary, life of the mind, variously known as 'imagination' and 'fancy', Edgeworth himself had no difficulties in cleaning out the stable. In the Preface to *The Parent's Assistant*, he asked: 'Why should the mind be filled with fantastic visions, instead of useful knowledge? Why should so much valuable time be lost? Why should we vitiate their taste and spoil their appetite by suffering them to feed upon sweetmeats?' As for the unfortunate influence of the sagacious Samuel Johnson, and his notorious affection for fairy-tales, 'It is hoped that the magic of [his] name will not have power to restore the reign of fairies.'[34]

Could Maria share this dismissive view of fantasy? Her own attitude was most clearly laid out in her contributions to *Practical Education*, the theoretical rationale composed to accompany and fortify the stories for children which Edgeworth and Honora had initiated in the 1770s. Edgeworth himself wrote the chapters on Tasks, Grammar, Classical Literature, Geography, History, Arithmetic, Geometry and Mechanics. Dr Thomas Beddoes, of the Pneumatic Institution, Bristol, contributed most of the chapter on Toys, and one of the Edgeworth sons, Lovell, the chapter on Chemistry. Maria wrote more than half, including the chapter on books for children.

3

The keynote of Maria's views on literature for children was prudence. Although she herself had certainly had a taste for the sublime, the fantastic, and even for the gothic – as witness her schoolgirl story of the mask of dead-man's flesh – she had clearly acquired a more rational attachment to restraint and circumspection. Children, therefore, should not be exposed to extreme states of awe, excitement or amazement, such as the one found displayed in Akenside's poem (see above, p. 39). In this 'poetic description of the beldame telling dreadful stories to her infant audience,' Maria complained, 'we hear only of the pleasures of the imagination. We do not recollect how dearly these pleasures must be purchased by their votaries.' It may well look exciting, such a scene of open-mouthed awe and possession, but 'no prudent mother' would allow either the old woman or her stories anywhere near a well-conducted nurery.[35]

She returned to this theme in her novel, *Harrington*, published in 1817, nearly twenty years later. Henry, her step-brother and 'special protégé',[36] born in 1782, had suffered 'childhood terrors',[37] and died in 1813, insane, in Clifton Asylum. Marilyn Butler, Maria's best biographer, offers us no further information on this sad affair: we do not know what was thought to have given rise to those childhood terrors or how they were dealt with, though Mrs Butler does observe that Maria wrote to Charlotte Sneyd in 1787, expressing concern lest she should have communicated her own 'coward-ice' to the boy: Maria was indeed notoriously diffident and tongue-tied in company, for many years, but there is surely a wide gulf between extreme childhood terrors and the social gaucheness of an adolescent girl, overawed by a severe step-mother and a powerful and egotistical father.

In *Harrington*, the eponymous hero is left to the insensitive 'mercies' of his mother's maid, while the mother goes out in search of amusement. At the age of six, the boy is aroused, mystified and haunted by the street-cries of an old Jewish rag-and-bone man: the old man calls out, 'Old clothes, old clothes!' but the child cannot make out the words. Fowler, the maid, discovers this, and uses the child's fear as a way of controlling him through threat, after the fashion of those in

Locke who cried 'Raw-Head and Bloody-Bones'; 'If you don't come quietly this minute, master Harrington, I'll call to Simon the Jew there, and he shall come up and carry you away in his great bag.' Subsequently, she tells the child blood-curdling stories of 'Jews who had been known to steal poor children for the purpose of killing, crucifying, and sacrificing them at their secret feasts and midnight abominations.' The worst such story is of a Jewish couple in Paris who tempt children into their cellar, kill them, and use them in pork-pies. As a result of being subjected to such macabre nonsense, the child, as he lies in bed, suffers an 'indescribable agony of terror'; he sees faces around him, 'grinning, glaring, receding, advancing', and invariably ends with a 'roar and scream' until his mother tells Fowler to stay with him until he is fast asleep. In the novel Maria used this episode explicitly and rather tendentiously to underline the power of the 'association of ideas' and also, unwittingly, to reinforce one's sense that when the imagination looms large in her writing, it is invariably as a symptom or a vehicle of error, aberration, distress, mental disorder or illness.

The plot subsequently twists and turns, more or less implausibly, to exemplify her 'moral', which is that Jews are just as human as Christians – for *Harrington* is a *roman-à-thèse* – and Harrington finally exorcises his terrors, which do, however, persist well into his adult life, but become, in the process, less and less convincing: the adult Harrington 'shudders with horror', 'starts back . . . with vehement gestures', is prey to 'nervous tremors' – all in broad daylight, and in the company of friends. The effect is, alas, all too gothic. And the psychological explanations – 'restless imagin-ation . . . this superfluous activity of imagination' – are both intrusive and reductive, just as a lengthy quotation from Akenside, in the course of a conversation, seems rather forced, and has the feeling of a hobby-horse being ridden too hard.

Fowler is finally brought to book, and is shipped off to America – due punishment for miscreant servants. And in the cooler air of *Practical Education*, too, servants were dealt with very severely. Maria repeated, with a distinctive intensity of seriousness, the advice of Locke, Watts, Helvetius, Mrs Bonhote[38] and many another, by now the orthodox wisdom: the less children had to do with servants, the better. It was from the servants that they learned 'awkward and vulgar tricks', so all opportunity of intercourse should be cut off, so that the servants would come to consider 'the children as beings moving in another sphere'. If the servants, as a result, found the childen to be cold, stand-offish, and reserved, so much the better, for not only were most servants foolish and vulgar, but they possessed a vast store of vulgar stories with which to pollute the children's minds. As Gilbert White wrote in 1776:

> It is the hardest thing in the world to shake off superstitious prejudices; they are sucked in, as it were, with our mother's milk; and, growing up with us at a time when they take the fastest hold and make the most lasting impressions, become so interwoven into our very constitutions, that the strongest good sense is required to disengage ourselves from them. No wonder, therefore, that the lower people retain them their whole lives through, since their minds are not invigorated by a liberal education, and therefore not enabled to make any efforts adequate to the occasion.[39]

For reasons such as this, the prudential *cordon sanitaire* was carefully erected, but sometimes a remnant of the older magic slipped through, and had to be rendered harmless, defused by enlightened intervention:

> We were once present when a group of speechless children sat listening to the story of Blue-beard, 'breathing astonishment'. A gentleman [Edgeworth himself?] who saw the charm beginning to operate, resolved to counteract its dangerous influence. Just at the critical moment, when the fatal key drops from the trembling hands of the imprudent wife, the gentleman interrupted

the awful pause of silence that ensued, and requested permission to relate the remainder of the story. Tragi-comedy does not offend the taste of the young, so much as of old critics; the transition from grave to gay was happily managed. Blue-beard's wife afforded much diversion, and lost all sympathy the moment she was represented as a curious, tattling, timid, ridiculous woman. The terrors of Bluebeard himself subsided when he was properly introduced to the company; and the denouement of the piece was managed much to the entertainment of the audience; the catastrophe, instead of freezing their young blood, produced general laughter. Ludicrous images, thus presented to the mind of the audience which has been prepared for horror, have an instantaneous effect upon the risible muscles: it seems better to use these means of counteracting the terrors of the imagination, than to reason upon the subject whilst the fit is on; reason should be used between the fits. Those who study the minds of children know the nice touches which affect their imagination, and they can by a few words change their feelings by the power of association.[40]

What chance would Macbeth's witches have in such disen-chanting company?

Maria, like her step-mothers, was always on the watch for error, nonsense or irrationality. Honora had never hesitated to use the scissors when some passage in an otherwise inoffen-sive book struck her as less than sensible or logical. And when Maria found Mrs Barbauld writing, in her *Lessons for Children*, 'Charles shall have a pretty new lesson', she tapped the author smartly on the knuckles and, once again invoking the laws of association, remarked firmly: 'In this sentence, the words *pretty* and *new* are associated; but they represent ideas which ought to be kept separate in the mind of the child.'[41] She disapproved, too, of Mrs Barbauld's lapses into poetical language: 'The moon shines at night, when the sun is gone to bed' provoked this comment:

'When the sun is out of sight' would be more correct, though not so pleasing, perhaps to the young reader . . . we should not give so false an idea as that the sun is gone to bed. Every thing relative to the system of the universe is above the comprehension of a child.[42]

One wonders what the eight-year-old Coleridge's father would have had to say to that!

Consistently, Maria's criteria in judging books for children were reason, morality and utility. Useful knowledge, she claimed, 'enlarges the view of human life, and of human nature, and teaches by the experience of the past, what we may expect in the future.' As for reason, 'Without the habit of reasoning, the best dispositions can give us no solid security for happiness; therefore we should early cultivate the reasoning faculty, instead of always appealing to the imagination.' When, years later, Mrs S.C. Hall recalled her meetings with Maria, she noted that 'She did not see, so clearly as I saw, the value of the imaginative in Literature for the young . . . and argued strongly for truth in fiction.' Or, as Maria herself wrote to her Utilitarian friend Étienne Dumont, in 1813: 'There is a *security* and sense of reality in studying from life, which the most inventive imagination can never attain.'[43] (My italics; but note the stress again on security.) In the same year, she was sympathetically impressed by William Roscoe's philistine assertion that 'Writers of secondary powers, when they are to describe or represent either objects of nature or feelings of the human mind, always begin by simile: they tell you not what the thing *is*, but what it is *like*.'

Late in her career, in 1830, Maria wrote to her good friend Walter Scott, asking for his advice about the inclusion of a silly affected Scots chieftain in *Helen*, the novel she was then working on; would it, she asked, be 'useful and moral' to include such a figure?[44] It was a perfectly characteristic question; and four years later, Matthew Stewart, son of the philosopher Dugald Stewart, wrote a very carefully considered letter about *Helen* to her friend Mrs Stark. In the same spirit as the response of Constable to Daguerre's Diorama, and of Rodin to instantaneous photographs of people walking, Stewart argued that a careful rendering of actuality, a feat of verisimilitude, did not necessarily ensure an effect of truth: 'Le vrai peut quelquefois n'être pas vraisemblable.' He praised Maria's 'power of observation' – a Lunar virtue – but argued that 'it is not the way in which a power can be acquired of giving a sustained and decided impression of unity to fictitious characters.'[45] Mrs Stark then sent Stewart's letter to Maria, who admitted: 'I *know* I feel how much *more is to be done, ought to be done* by suggestion than by delineation, by creative fancy than by facsimile copying',[46] but she went on to justify her own methods as being best suited to her talents and predispositions.

On one occasion, she 'broke off on the side of a letter to her stepmother to exclaim in mock alarm: "I have not yet done talking of *persons* – what will my father say to me?"' Was this a wry admission of some supposed feminine weakness? Or is it rather that the persons who figure in our letters have a life of their own, which we can appreciate only by exercising our sympathetic imaginations, and at the deepest level of intensity, by being possessed by them, as Morgann insisted in his 'Essay on Falstaff'?[47] Maria's uncertainty in her relationship with 'creative fancy' was such that she 'collected' facts – idiolects, mannerisms, idiosyncrasies, appearances and so on – and 'used' them to 'moral and useful' ends, as her plan demanded. She remained mostly external to her characters, just as the domesticated scientist remained external to her apparatus: and both were severally in pursuit of the same useful ends.

Nowhere are the prudential constraints on imagination more evident than in her remarks on the fantasy of travel and adventure, the stock-in-trade of the chap-book tales, and the root of much of the greatest fiction of the eighteenth century:

> There is a class of books which amuses the imagination of children without acting upon their feelings. We do not

allude to fairy-tales, for we apprehend that these are not now much read, but we mean voyages and travels; these interest young people universally. Robinson Crusoe, Gulliver, and the Three Russian Sailors, who were cast away upon the coast of Norway, are general favourites. No child can ever read an account of a shipwreck, or even a storm, without pleasure. A desert island is a delightful place. . . . Savages, especially if they happen to be cannibals, are sure to be admired, and the more hair-breadth escapes the hero of the tale has survived, and the more marvellous his adventures, the more sympathy he excites.[48]

It is impossible to grasp exactly what she intended by that phrase 'without acting upon their feelings'. On the face of it, it is tempting to dismiss her remark as nonsense, for anyone who has read *Crusoe* in childhood is not likely to forget the urgency of involvement that it aroused, not to mention the irresistible fantasy-play that it could inspire: Thomas Bewick, for instance, as a boy, ran with friends stark-naked across the fells, in imitation of 'the savages' in *Crusoe*, 'like mad things, or like Bedlamites who had escaped'.[49] The most plausible explanation is perhaps that Maria was referring to *moral* feelings – the feelings that inform our actual social ife, and constitute the elements of our moral development as social animals – selfishness, generosity, patience, tolerance and so on. But her recognition of the delight that young readers found in storm, shipwreck and desert-island – this is clearly unfeigned. And yet, in the very next breath, she was compelled to deny it!

> Will it be thought to proceed from a spirit of contradiction if we remark, that these species of reading should not early be chosen for boys of an enterprising temper, unless they are intended for a seafaring life, or for the army? The taste for adventure is absolutely incompatible with sober perseverance necessary to success in any other liberal professions. To girls this species of reading cannot be as dangerous as it is to boys; girl must very soon perceive the

impossibility of their rambling about the world in quest of adventures; and where there appears an obvious impossibility in gratifying any wish, it is not likely to become, or at least to continue, a torment to the imagination. When a young man deliberates upon what course of life he shall follow, the patient drudgery of a trade, the laborious mental exertions requisite to prepare him for a profession, must appear to him in a formidable light, compared with the alluring prospects presented by an adventuring imagination. [An unwitting slur on James Cook, who burnt the midnight oil in Whitby, extending his knowledge of navigation!] The histories of realities written in an entertaining manner appear not only better suited to the purposes of education, but also more agreeable to young people than improbable fiction.[50]

There is something rather defeating in all this, and indeed defeated. As for the last sentence, Maria seems to have forgotten that wishing it so does not make it so: indeed the whole argument is shot through with its own brand of Edgeworthian fantasy. As for the hypercensorious division of books into sheep and goats, the danger is, as Mrs Trimmer discovered, that if you don't know where to stop, you end up with very few sheep, if any at all.

At the age of fifteen, Maria had admitted to a friend: 'I am as fond of novels as you can be,' but added: 'I am afraid they act on the constitution of the mind as Drams do on that of the body.' Nearly twenty years later in the Advertisement to her novel, *Belinda*, she declared: ''The following work is offered to the public as a Moral Tale – the author not wishing to acknowledge a Novel.' The distinction that she was anxious to have noted was indeed recognized and respected by many earnest, and perhaps slightly self-deceivingly virtuous, readers: in her 'moral tale', *The Metamorphoses*, Mary Hughes confirmed and endorsed Maria's moral acceptability:

'Look, we have got a book, which I am persuaded thou wouldst have great pleasure in reading. It is Maria

Edgeworth's new novel, for so I suppose we must be obliged to call her stories, though they are so different from the generality of that class of publication.' 'What! a quaker read a novel! (exclaimed Julia.) Oh! then I have found out the reason of your being here so early this morning. You are come to read here what you would be afraid of your father seeing you read at home.'

'No! (replied Mary Ann, with a look of dignity very unlike the usual expression of her gentle countenance.) Thou art mistaken if thou supposest that I am come here for the purpose of cheating my father. He is too good and too reasonable to object to any innocent source of amusement; and, as I have promised that I will never read a novel without his permission, he is too kind to make any unnecessary objections, and puts Maria Edgeworth's works into my hand without even the precaution of looking at them himself first; convinced that I shall find nothing there inimical to the purest virtue. Let me advise, thee, therefore, to stay and read this *Patronage* with us.'[51]

Jane Austen, of course, could be said to speak for those with a less emphatically virtuous public view of what novel-reading is about. But to the modern reader, as to Jane Austen, the question that arises in reading Maria's fiction is not in any sense a moral one in the terms that she herself invited such admirers as Mary Hughes to invoke; it is rather a question of the fictive integrity of her writing – the question that Stewart clearly disturbed her with. It is disconcerting to meet her recurrent footnotes which hasten to assure the reader that there is an actual factual basis for some of the more outlandish or improbable characters and events in her narrative: In *Harrington*, a short novel, there are eight such footnotes, each of which is a distraction. Such appeals to 'reality' tend to strike us as a betrayal of the 'truth' of the imagination, for they break into, and rupture, our belief: the effect of these factual endorsements is that she is unable to trust us to believe her dissembled world, and therefore, willy-nilly, our imaginative commitment is severely undermined: we fluctuate in and out of the fiction, to the detriment of its coherence and integrity.

Ironically, her father criticized her on this very score, even though it was clearly his doing that her relationship with imagination was so nervous: 'My father continues to think Olivia and Leonora flat and spiritless and stuffed with morality – but he says it will be recommended by Governesses and read by Misses. . . .'[52] But it remains paramount that Maria's primary concern in her life was to win, then retain, the love of her father: their relationship, in its intensity and insistences, was as remarkable, as problematic and teasing, as that of Wordsworth and his sister. Even after Edgeworth's death in 1817, when Maria was almost fifty, she continued to need to satisfy his internalized demands: so she gritted her teeth in order to complete *Harry and Lucy*, taking it further into the field of scientific and technological education. She confessed to Scott that her part had been 'merely to spread amusement through it, while he [Edgeworth] furnished the solid knowledge and accurate principles of science'. But she had to complete it alone, and admitted that 'the toil, difficulty, mortification I have gone through in finishing these last volumes without him is not to be described. . . . I have no science; and as to accuracy, can compare myself only to the sailor "who would never quarrel for a handful of degrees".'[53]

Ever since the difficult adolescent years, during which she had paid the price of submission, and had learned to reshape her mind until it was more royalist than the king himself, she had engaged cheerfully and indefatigably in doing work that aimed to satisfy, or, rather, appease her strenuous conscience. But it is possible that, in her final work on *Harry and Lucy*, her own untamed spirit had the last word, and almost a poetic one! It had been planned that Harry and Lucy – Edgeworth and Maria, Science and Art – should perambulate instructively through a landscape that showed off all the great achievements of the industrial revolution, i.e. of the Lunar Society. Harry, predictably, admired the remarkable masterpieces of the great engineers, and both he and Lucy were struck, like many another traveller, by the nocturnal flaming and roaring of the furnaces of the Black Country. But when they saw the same landscape by the sober light of day, Lucy – Maria – perceived, as James Nasmyth had observed, that 'Vulcan had driven out Ceres'. What then were the first fruits of the triumph of science? What had the exercise of reason in the service of utility brought them to?

> They saw only a black dreary waste, with half burning, half smothering heaps of dross, coal and cinders. Clouds of smoke . . . darkening the air; the prospect they could not see, for there was none. It was a dead flat, the atmosphere laden with the smell of coal and smoke. The grass, the hedges, the trees, all blackened. The hands and faces of every man, woman and child they met, begrimed with soot! The very sheep blackened! Not a lamb even with a lock of white wool, or a clean face. Lucy said that it was the most frightful country she had ever beheld.

NOTES AND REFERENCES

1 *Émile, ou de l'Éducation*, 4 vols (Amsterdam: Jean Néaulme, 1762), trans. (by William Kenrick) as *Emilius and Sophia: or, A New System of Education*, 4 vols (London: R. Griffiths, T. Becket & P.A. de Hondt, 1762, 1763).
2 *Emilius and Sophia*, vol, I (1762), pp. 2–3.
3 ibid., p. vi.
4 ibid., pp. xiii–xiv.
5 ibid., p. 168.
6 ibid., pp. 167–8.
7 Wordsworth's early reading included an English equivalent, Gay's *Fables*.
8 *Emilius and Sophia*, vol. I (1762), p. 185.
9 ibid., p. 192.
10 ibid., p. 196.
11 ibid., p. 197.
12 Op. cit., vol. II (1762), pp. 61–2.
13 On the various interpretations of *Robinson Crusoe*, see the

Introduction in J.D. Crowley's edition (London and New York: Oxford University Press, 1981), pp. x–xii.

14 Some of the excesses of Rousseau's more fervent disciples verged on sheer lunacy. See the account of R.L. Edgeworth's son, below, p. 119. And cf. David Williams's account of a thirteen-year-old boy reared on Rousseauesque principles: 'a little emaciated figure; his countenance betraying marks of premature decay, or depraved passions; his teeth discoloured, and his hearing almost gone' (*Lectures on Education*, London, 1789, vol. III, p. 5). This catalogue of symptoms closely resembles those attributed to the effects of masturbation in the child-rearing manuals of the time. Cf. Wordsworth, *The Excursion*, bk 8, ll. 400 ff., and bk 9, ll. 303 ff.

15 Laurence Sterne, *The Life and Opinions of Tristram Shandy*, 9 vols (York, later London: 1760–7), vol. V, ch. XLII.

16 The most judiciously sympathetic account of Edgeworth is offered by Marilyn Butler, *Maria Edgeworth: A Literary Biography* (London: Oxford University Press, 1972). For a chilly account of his vanity and self-puffing, see *The Quarterly Review*, vol. XLVI, p. 510. The liveliest account of Edgeworth is that of Sydney Smith. See 'Edgeworth on Bulls', *Edinburgh Review* (1803): 'He is fuddled with animal spirits, giddy with constitutional joy. . . . A discharge of ink was an evacuation absolutely necessary, to avoid fatal and plethoric congestion.'

17 Erasmus Darwin, one of its members, remarked that 'the milk of science flowed in redundant streams from their learned lunations'. See E. Robinson, *The Bicentenary Exhibition of the Lunar Society* (Birmingham: City Art Gallery and Museum, 1965).

18 *The Parent's Assistant* (London: J. Johnson, 1796), Preface.

19 R.L. and Maria Edgeworth, *Practical Education*, 2 vols (London: J. Johnson, 1798), vol. I, p. vi.

20 Thomas Reid, *Essay on the Intellectual Powers of Man* (1785 edn), quoted in *The Parent's Assistant* (Preface) and in *Practical Education* (Appendix).

21 Letter to Mrs Barbauld, quoted in Butler, op.cit., p. 61.

22 ibid., p. 63.

23 ibid., p. 65.

24 See the Appendix to *Practical Education*.

25 R.L. Edgeworth, *Memoirs of Richard Lovell Edgeworth . . . begun by himself, and concluded by his daughter* 2 vols (London, 1820), vol. I, p. 10.

26 Op.cit., p. xii.

27 ibid., p. xii.
28 ibid., p. xvi.
29 *Rambler*, no. 96 (16 February 1751): *The Works of Samuel Johnson*, vol. 4 (New Haven, Conn., and London: Yale University Press, 1958), p. 152.
30 'Leaves from a Note-Book', *Essays*, ed. T. Pinney (London: Routledge & Kegan Paul, 1963), p. 444.
31 Op.cit., p. xix.
32 ibid., p. xxv.
33 ibid., p. xxvi.
34 Mrs Thrale's *Anecdotes of the Late Dr Samuel Johnson* (1786) were so popular that they went through four printings within a year.
35 *Practical Education*, ch. XXII. In her essay on Akenside's poem, prefixed to Cadell and Davies's 1814 edition, Mrs Barbauld noted its indebtedness to Addison and remarked:

> The exemplification of the love of novelty in the audience of the village matron, who tells of *witching rhymes and evil spirits*, is highly wrought. . . . It may be doubted, however, whether the attraction which is felt towards these kinds of sensations when they rise to terror, can be fairly referred to the love of novelty. It seems rather to depend on that charm . . . which is attached to every thing that strongly stirs and agitates the mind.

36 Butler, op.cit., p. 209.
37 ibid., p. 248.
38 For example, her *Parental Monitor*, vol. 2.
39 *Natural History of Selborne*, letter XXVIII.
40 *Practical Education*, vol. 1, p. 311.
41 ibid., p. 317.
42 ibid., p. 320.
43 Butler, op.cit., p. 232.
44 ibid., p. 267.
45 ibid., p. 261.
46 ibid., p. 262.
47 See below, Chapter Six, and n. 3.
48 *Practical Education*, vol. 1, p. 335. The explorer Matthew Flinders ran away to sea after reading *Robinson Crusoe*. (*Post hoc = Propter hoc?*). After suffering many severe privations, he died young: on his death-bed, he asked for a copy of *Crusoe*.
49 'In imitation of the savages in Robinson Crusoe . . . often in a morning I set off stark naked across the fell, where I was joined by some associates, who, in a like manner, ran about. . . .' (*A*

Memoir of Thomas Bewick, written by himself, Newcastle upon Tyne, 1862, p. 15).

50 Op.cit., pp. 335–8.
51 Mary (Robson) Hughes, *The Metamorphoses, or, Effects of Education. A Tale* (London: William Darton, Jr, 1818).
52 Butler, op.cit., p. 295.
53 Letter dated April 1825, from *Private Letterbooks of Sir Walter Scott*, ed. W. Partington (London: Hodder & Stoughton, 1930), p. 269.

CHAPTER FIVE

REFRACTIONS OF THE LIGHT OF DAY

I had a talent for absurdity; and you don't throw
away any of your talents.
(Saul Bellow, *Humboldt's Gift*, 1975)
There was a sort of theoretical impulse behind
this grotesqueness too.
(ibid.)

1

In her devastating demolition of the pious tuft-hunting poet, Edward Young, George Eliot suggested that 'minds which are predominantly didactic, are deficient in sympathetic emotion. A man who is perpetually thinking in monitory apothegms, who has an unintermittent flux of rebuke, can have little energy left for simple feeling.' Following the precedent of Ruskin's 'pathetic fallacy', she dubbed this bent of mind the 'pedagogic fallacy'.[1] It could have been invented for characterizing Thomas Day, for he was one of its most incorrigible exponents.

The passion for moral reform and renewal that swept over England in the late eighteenth century left few people untouched: issues were often construed in such extreme terms as either to gain immoderate support from those anxious to repair the social fabric or reclaim older and severer pieties, or to provoke the more sophisticated into almost a habit of raillery (one thinks of that great deflater, Sydney Smith) and the sceptical into a state of wonder and amazement. Moral reform, in the name of sobriety, seriousness, austerity and the regulation of the passions, had to start, many argued, with 'the great', 'the Fashionable World', the powerful. Hannah More, William Wilberforce and Wordsworth all saw eye to eye on this, and used their influential energies in various ways to promote a reform of morals. And at a more modest level young people agonized over such questions as the morality of novel-reading: James Hay Beattie, the favourite son of the philosopher-poet, projected an essay on 'the pernicious effects of novel-reading, even where the novel is not profligate'. Because young James earnestly detested card-playing, he fell in with his father's suggestion that he should read *Tom Jones*, only to conclude that 'the time spent in reading it was lost; and there was more danger from the indelicacy of particular passages, than hope of its doing good by the satire, the moral sentiments, or the distributive justice dispensed in winding up the catastrophe.'[2]

The most effective way to initiate moral reform was perhaps to start from the ground up, so to speak, with the education of children: they were still malleable enough to be impressed, in Locke's sense, with proper moral principles, and decent manners. 'Manners are what vex or soothe, corrupt or purify, exalt or debase, barbarize or refine us, by a constant, steady, uniform, and insensible operation, like that of the air we breathe in,' wrote Edmund Burke.[3] Like Wordsworth, he approved of the 'wisdom of unlettered men', and constantly appealed to the 'common feelings', the 'natural feelings'. But there were those, also, who were too impatient, too passionate to wait for the slow and invisible operation of moral influences as subtle and insubstantial as air; who were determined to make moral education as overt and insistent as possible. Thomas Day was perhaps the most egregiously insistent of these, and succeeded in transmogrifying perfectly decent moral and political aspirations into something stiff-necked, uncompromising and intolerant, not to say ridiculous.

James Keir, the distinguished chemist, who came to know Day through their attendance at meetings of the Lunar Society, has left us a vivid account of the man's uncompromising temper, which was already very much in evidence at an early age:

An anecdote is told of him by his relations, which refers to a very early age, and which indicated the marked decision of his character in general, and particularly the perseverance with which he investigated truth and knowledge. When he was yet a child in petticoats and had just learnt to read, he was particularly pleased with the striking decriptions contained in the book of Revelations, and finding there many things not very intelligible, he asked more explanations from his friends than they could easily give. Being puzzled . . . to know who the whore of Babylon is, he asked his mother, and she, to evade the question, said she did not know, but that he might ask the rector when he should come next to the house, not conceiving that the child would think any more of the matter. However, some considerable time afterwards when the clergyman was present along with a good deal of other company, the little boy stood before him in the middle of the room and called out, 'Sir, I want to know who the whore of Babylon is.' The parson, surprised and somewhat embarrassed at being so peremptorily cate-chized, said, after some hesitation, 'My dear, that is allegorical.' The explanation, as sometimes happens, being more perplexing than the original difficulty: 'Allegorical!' the boy replied, 'I do not understand that word.' Then after some consideration, he threw a look of contempt on the parson, and running up to his mother, whispered to her, 'He knows nothing about it.'[4]

When Day, at the age of eighteen, met Edgeworth, they formed a close friendship which lasted until Day's early death. At times, they were inseparable, and they clearly reinforced each other's reformist aspirations: in the early years of their friendship, their most important moral and ideological bond seems to have been a shared discipleship of Rousseau. Day became committed to an extreme form of moral integrity, compounded of an intense idealism and a complementary contempt for polite society and its conventions, offering us a model of adolescent intransigence that has become very much part of 'modern' tradition. These tendencies were reinforced by his being in possession of sufficient wealth to make compromise in such matters unnecessary: he could afford not to toe the line. He had no need to dress fashionably or display orthodox manners, for he had no need to please the world. But his studiedly uncouth manners and his tatty appearance did make for difficulties when he set out to find for himself an acceptable wife, for he was an embodiment of Sidney's 'moral philosopher':

> Step forth the moral philosophers whom, methinketh, I see coming towards me with a sullen gravity, as though they could not abide vice by daylight, rudely clothed for to witness outwardly their contempt of outward things, with books in their hands against glory, whereto they set their names. . . .

A useful example against which to judge Day's social solecisms is offered by Chesterfield, in his account of 'odd tricks, ill habits, and awkwardnesses':

> When an awkward fellow first comes into a room, it is highly probable that his sword gets between his legs, and throws him down, or makes him stumble at least. . . . If he drinks tea or coffee, he certainly scalds his mouth, and lets either the cup or the saucer fall, and spills the tea or coffee in his breeches. . . . He eats with his knife to the great danger of his mouth, picks his teeth with his fork, · and puts his spoon, which has been in his throat twenty times, into the dishes again. . . . Besides all this, he has strange tricks and gestures; such as snuffing up his nose, making faces, putting his fingers in his nose, or blowing it and looking afterwards in his handkerchief, so as to make the company sick. . . .[5]

I am not claiming that Day habitually did all these things, but it is clear that many people found his style either repulsive or ridiculous. His manner evidently corresponded to that of Chesterfield's 'absent man': one with a mind so affected 'that it would be supposed to be wholly engrossed by, and directed to, some very great and important objects'. Chesterfield conceded the right to such odd manners to only 'five or six since the creation of the world' – Sir Isaac Newton, for instance, and Mr Locke – on the grounds of the 'intense thought' that their intellectual life demanded. In a word, Day was 'crotté' – crusted with maladroitness, singularity and gaucheness; he was as one who 'snarled at Pleasure, like a stoic, and preached against it, like a parson',[6] and was a 'preaching missionary of abstemiousness and sobriety'.[7]

In 1768, Day went to stay with Edgeworth in Ireland. There he met his friend's sister, Margaret, and paid her court. Neither was entirely satisfied with the other, and when he left, it was on the understanding that she would work to improve her grasp of moral philosophy and metaphysics, while he, quid pro quo, was to make an effort to soften his manners. But by early 1769 she acknowledged her misgivings and wrote to terminate the arrangement. When, many years later, Étienne Dumont, Maria's friend, read the *Memoir* of Edgeworth, with its account of Day, he told Maria that 'he could not bear that sort of man, who had such pride and misanthropies about trifles, raising a great theory of morals upon an *amour blessé*.'[8] In a similar spirit, in 1818, Maria wrote to her step-mother, after hearing that Lady Lansdowne had expressed enthusiasm for the integrity of Day as portrayed in the *Memoir*: 'Had she seen him, she would not have endured his manners however twenty-four hours.'[9]

While Edgeworth applied Rousseau's education of Émile to the mis-rearing of Richard, junior, Day took to heart Rousseau's Book V, the chapters devoted to Sophia: 'It is not good for man to be alone; and Emilius is now a man: we have promised him also a companion, who must, therefore, now be given him. This companion is Sophia. But, in what asylum is she to be found?'

2

Day seems to have taken Rousseau's question at its face value, and he set off in search of her. At this point, it is worth remarking that those who, for any conceivable reason, are sympathetic to Day, or keen to defend his posthumous reputation, gloss over the next part of his life rather disingenuously, on the grounds that it is so well-known that the story does not need to be repeated. But without it we cannot form a proper estimate of the strength of his commitment to Rousseau's visionary ideals. Keir did his level best to excuse Day for having fallen under such a spell. He adduced 'a youthful and active mind inflamed with the enthusiasm of virtue', but noted that Day had fallen prey 'to some of those delusions created by heated imagination' and had been overcome by Rousseau's 'seductive eloquence'. Keir argued quite reasonably that Rousseau's scheme of education was absurd and impracticable, since education is for life in society and must therefore be a socializing process, but he made as much allowance as he possibly could for Day's uncritical discipleship:

> Rousseau has so artfully interwoven with his wild system many just and ingenious remarks, that although they may have been found to be chiefly borrowed from Montaigne and Locke, they not only seem by their connection to have the merit of originality, but they also throw upon his whole assemblage of opinions on this subject a speciousness, which unguarded minds may easily take for the light of truth; whereas it is in fact but an *ignis fatuus* of the fancy, fanned by the breath of an eloquence peculiarly persuasive.[10]

Under Rousseau's spell, and moved by an extreme desire for a perfectly uncorrupted wife, Day then proposed to 'unite the purity of female virtue with the fortitude and hardiness of constitution of a Spartan virgin.'[11] Like his master, Day found that 'civilized' women had succumbed to 'frivolous vanities, effeminate manners, and a taste for dissipated pleasures' – singularly displeasing to a man whose austere disposition now possessed a plausible rationalization.

Truth being stranger than fiction, Day then went with his friend, John Bicknell, to Shrewsbury Orphanage and chose an attractive eleven-year-old girl, whom he renamed Sabrina, in honour of the River Severn, and gave her the surname of Sidney, in honour, not of Sir Philip Sidney, but of Algernon Sidney, the political martyr who had died rather than relinquish his republican politics. To meet the legal requirements of the case, Day had to bind Sabrina apprentice to a married man, and Edgeworth, without his knowledge or consent, was nominated for this role. He later wrote: 'I had such well-merited confidence in Mr Day that I felt no objection to his being entrusted with the care of a girl who had thus been placed under my protection.' But to double his experiment's chances of success, Day then went to the Foundling Hospital in London: easing the negotiations with a donation of £50 and thus automatically becoming a governor, he then acquired a second girl. With perfect seriousness, and no trace of any awareness of irony, he named her Lucretia. His plan was that at the end of a year the less satisfactory of the two girls should be bound apprentice to some worthy tradeswoman, Day providing £400 for her keep. The other girl would be educated by Day with a view to forming for him a satisfactory wife: if she, however, also failed to measure up to his needs, he would place her with a respectable family with £500 for her marriage portion.

If the Rousseauesque experiment were to have any chance of success, it was clearly crucial that the girls' relatively unformed minds and characters should remain uncorrupted by the conversation of persons already steeped in the ways of the world. What better, for this purpose, than to place them in a situation where they could communicate with no one but their single-minded tutor? So Day took them off to France, and they were thus effectually insulated, encapsulated, in a little world over which Day could exercise exclusive control: in France, he could also observe polite manners – the French provided the best model in these – and so confirm his low opinion of them.

The girls, to their credit, proved to be rather a handful; they quarreled with each other incessantly, and caused Day a great deal of confusion. When they caught small-pox, he had to wait on them hand and foot. In a letter to Edgeworth, he claimed that he had so effectively trained them that he had 'made them . . . two such girls as . . . have never been seen at the same age.' But when he returned with them to England in the spring of 1770, his nerves were badly frayed by their interminable squabbles, and Lucretia's mind was proving to be a severe disappointment. At the end of the twelve-month trial period, he packed her off to a London milliner.

He then took Sabrina with him to live near Lichfield, for he was keen to see more of Erasmus Darwin who was also actively interested in the education of girls. Thus he was introduced to Lichfield society where he met, among others, Anna Seward, the celebrated poetess. She took Sabrina under her wing, and was struck by Day's 'meditative and melancholy air' and his combination of 'awkwardness and dignity'. Through Darwin, Day also met the painter Joseph Wright, who painted his portrait – an image of pseudo-Roman earnestness and dignity: an echo of 'Rome, the seat of glory and virtue, if ever they had place on earth'![12]

Within a matter of months, interesting affairs of the heart were springing up around the impressive person of Honora Sneyd; Edgeworth came over to spend time at Stowe House, Day's new home, and soon he, Day, and a young Swiss, John André, were all intensely attracted by Honora. André simplified matters by joining the army; Edgeworth was already married – to a wife who bored him; so Day seized his chance and proposed to Honora, with Sabrina in the wings as a marital insurance-policy, so to speak, should Honora reject him. The terms of his proposal, which laid heavy moral stress on the virtues of retiring from the frivolities of fashionable society, provoked Honora into making a spirited reply, which amounted to a categorical rejection. But soon her sister, Elizabeth, appeared to offer a satisfactory alternative. To Day's unfashionable eyes, indeed, she had conspicuous virtues: although she had a livelier sense of humour than Honora, she had 'less personal grace; she walked heavily and danced indifferently'.[13] Such disadvantages obviously recommended her to the contrary taste of Day, and he was not slow to propose. Elizabeth did not reject him outright. as her sister had done, but said that she could not think of accepting him, until he had improved his manners. She managed to convince him 'that he could not with propriety abuse and ridicule talents in which he was obviously deficient'; and she stressed that 'she could not be satisfied with the abhorrence, which upon all occasions he expressed, of accomplishments which he had not been able to attain'. Rousseau himself, it is worth noting, approved of singing and dancing, and criticized that 'severe' form of Christianity which 'by prohibiting songs, dancings, and other worldly amusements' had rendered home-life 'heavy and morose'.[14]

Accordingly, in the autumn of 1771 Day went off to France again, this time with Edgeworth and young Richard. In 1772 he returned to Lichfield, where with his incongruous cosmetic French *politesse* he succeeded in cutting a ridiculous figure.[15] He had worked hard to acquire the skills of fencing and dancing, but good deportment sat very uneasily on his inherent maladroit gracelessness: he even submitted to painful experiments to cure his knock-knees, and had his head shaved to make room for a fashionable wig, but all to no good. He was grotesque. Elizabeth, who had a nice sense of humour, could do no other than reject his proposal.

Again, he took himself off to France, to nurse his injured self-esteem; and there he displayed 'an indifference to all human affairs, an aversion to restraint and engagement and embarrassment'. Abandoning all the pretences that he had donned for Elizabeth, he reverted to his old unregenerate self, thinking himself, no doubt, quite a noble savage. In Paris, he was infatuated by a brilliant witty young woman, by the name of Panckcoucke, paid her court, and was once more rejected. As in 1769, four years and three rejections earlier, he retired to the west of England to lick his wounds, and then accompanied Edgeworth once more to Lichfield. Edgeworth, suddenly widowed, immediately proposed to Honora, and was accepted. So the salt must have been rubbed into Day's wounds.

3

Day then returned to the mentorial task of educating Sabrina, who was now sixteen and not developing altogether in accordance with Day's hopes. An essential element of Rousseau's teaching was his stress on an almost Spartan austerity: girls' clothes should be perfectly plain and loose, and totally unaffected by the vagaries of fashion – 'Sophia is a stranger to what colours are in fashion. . . . No young lady seems to have bestowed less thought about dress.'[16] Furthermore, Day clearly embraced Rousseau's view that 'All the ideas of women should be directed to the study of men, and to the attainment of agreeable accomplishments.'[17] So Day returned to the task of forming in Sabrina 'a complete character'[18] and put her through a series of tests. He dropped hot sealing wax on to her bare arms and fired pistols off at her petticoats, to see if she had achieved a Spartan state of indifference to pain.[19] Alas, she flinched as badly as any normal and sane mortal would have done.[20] The last straw came when he discovered her taking a depraved interest in millinery, and so he packed her off to a boarding-school in Sutton Coldfield. Eight years later, in 1781, Day's friend Bicknell married her, and when he died three years later she went to work as housekeeper for Fanny Burney's brother, Charles.

Meanwhile, in 1773, Bicknell and Day won fame with an undistinguished poem, 'The Dying Negro', which captured, and capitalized on, the growing ferment of indignation and reformist zeal provoked in benevolent minds by the slave-trade. The poem was an inert piece of well-timed literary embroidery, in lumpish couplets, and drenched in the self-conscious compassionating of the true Man of Feeling. It went quickly into three editions, and caught the uneasy and prudential nerve of its decade, with an appropriate dressing of nobility and sublimity.

Five years later, in 1778, Day finally met a woman who not only struck him as worthy of his austere ideals, but also failed to find him preposterous. William Small, a fellow 'Lunatic' concerned about Day's matrimonial failures, had dug her out, and pronounced her to be 'a woman capable of appreciating his merit, and treating the small defects in his appearance and manners as trifles beneath her serious consideration'. Although Esther Milnes was rich, Day succeeded in quelling his reservations about marrying wealth, on the grounds that she also was egregiously virtuous and admired him unreservedly. After the marriage, they lived a life of extreme frugality and of retreat – almost of a *de contemptu mundi* extreme. She was completely under his thumb, gave him 'the most complete matrimonial obedience' and submitted to his meanness of spirit. Although she loved music, she learned to live without it, because he told her that 'we have no right to luxuries while the poor want bread'; and he forbade her ever to see her parents again lest they should dilute her virtue.

The year after Day's marriage to Esther, Edgeworth and Honora were embarking on the first part of their plan to produce a series of instructional books for children (see above, pp. 122–3). Maria later recalled the occasion in her *Memoirs* of her father: Edgeworth

> intended to carry on the *History of Harry and Lucy*, through every stage of childhood. Mr Day, who was very pleased with my father's plan, offered to assist him, and with this intention began *Sandford and Merton*, which was first designed for a short story to be inserted in *Harry and Lucy*. The illness of Mrs Honora Edgeworth inter-

FRONTISPIECE

A large Snake on a fudden ftarted up from amongft fome long grafs and
coiled itfelf round little Tommy's leg.

Publifhed March 28, 1786, by John Stockdale Piccadilly.

The History of Sandford and Merton

THE

HISTORY

OF

SANDFORD AND MERTON,

A WORK

Intended for the Ufe of CHILDREN.

" SUFFER THE LITTLE CHILDREN TO COME
UNTO ME, AND FORBID THEM NOT."

IN THREE VOLUMES.

VOL. I.

THE SEVENTH EDITION CORRECTED.

EMBELLISHED WITH FRONTISPIECES.

LONDON:

PRINTED FOR JOHN STOCKDALE, PICCADILLY.

1795.

rupted the progress of that little volume and, after her death, the ideas associated with it were so painful to my father that it was not at the time continued.[21]

Day's avowed intention, in going on to write *The History of Sandford and Merton*, was to counteract 'effeminacy of manners', the 'infection of ostentatious luxury', and the neglect of 'fortitude, patience, and self-control'. His strategy was, therefore, antinomian; his fiction's values, those of the fashionable turned upside down.

Harry Sandford, Day's hero, was, in Keir's words,

> a young peasant, whose body is hardened by toil, who is enured to patience by the fatigues and abstinence of a laborious country life; whose fortitude is confirmed by the habit of exertion; whose appetite whetted by hunger prefers the plainest food to the incitements of luxury.[22]

So naturally virtuous was this young noble savage that 'humanity, forgiveness of injuries, and generosity flow from his breast without effort'. In a phrase, he was too good to be true. Like Fielding's Master Blifil in *Tom Jones*, he was 'sober, discreet, and pious beyond his age'. But Fielding had the intelligence to insist that 'Tom Jones, bad as he is, must serve for the hero of this History',[23] and not the virtuous Blifil. But such human and humorous ironies lay beyond Day's ken. And predictably he made Harry's countertype an effete, vain, spoiled, over-dressed, selfish young brat: Tommy Merton, the son of a wealthy plantation-owner.

The two boys are taken under the tutelage of the Reverend Mr Barlow, a boring, sententious, droning parson, who turns every experience, however trivial, into either a moral lesson or an opportunity for dispensing massive doses of his apparently inexhaustible reserves of 'useful' knowledge. Like William Godwin and Day himself, Barlow manages to express decent principles in such a way as to inspire the reader's revulsion or weariness. In such hands, the virtues of earnest reformers, ostensibly benign, come across as miserably lack-lustre, dull, humourless, priggish, even malign: if one could get a word in edgeways, one would ask, 'Dost think because thou'rt virtuous, there'll be no more cakes or ale?' Or music, dancing, cheerfulness, fun, human weakness, silliness, amusement, or irony?

Tommy Merton, the rich brat, is of course converted by the philanthropic exertions of Harry, and by the dire prosings of Mr Barlow, and rushes off to remove all his splendid clothes: he combs the powder out of his locks, just as Day had done after being rejected by Elizabeth Sneyd, demolishes the complex elegance of his *coiffure*, and – one is tempted to anticipate – puts on sack-cloth and ashes. Then he delivers a virtuous little speech (Newbery's term for such performances was 'pretty'): 'From this time, I shall apply myself to the study of nothing but reason and philosophy; and therefore I bid adieu to dress and finery for ever.'

Years later, just as Lamb and Coleridge misremembered *Goody Two-Shoes*, so Leigh Hunt offered a distorted account of *Sandford and Merton*:

> Books for children during the latter part of the eighteenth century had been in a bad way, with sordid and merely plodding morals – ethics that were necessary perhaps for a certain stage in the progress of commerce and for its greatest ultimate purposes . . . but which thwarted healthy and large views of society for the time being. They were the consequences of an altogether unintellectual state of trade, aided and abetted by such helps to morality as Hogarth's pictures of the Good and Bad Apprentice, which identified virtue with prosperity. . . .
>
> The children's books in those days were Hogarth's pictures taken in their most literal acceptation. Every good boy was to ride in his coach, and be a lord mayor; and every bad boy was to be hung or eaten by lions. . . . But the first counteraction came, as it ought, in the shape of a new book for children. The pool of mercenary and time-serving ethics was first blown over by the fresh

country breeze of Mr Day's *Sandford and Merton* – a production that I well remember, and shall ever be grateful to. It came in aid of my mother's perplexities between delicacy and hardihood, between courage and conscientiousness. It assisted the cheerfulness I inherited from my father; showed me that circumstances were not to crush a healthy gaiety, or the most masculine self-respect; and helped to supply me with the resolution of standing by a principle, not merely as a point of lowly or lofty sacrifice, but as a matter of common sense and duty, and a simple co-operation with the elements of natural warfare.[24]

With all its confusions and hardly concealed vanity and self-regard, this is an extraordinarily revealing appreciation, for it offers, as if in a mirror, a synopsis of the affinities between Day and Hunt: affinities that are echoed in the fact that they both subsequently inspired Dickens's genius for ridicule.[25]

The History of Sandford and Merton appeared in three volumes (1783–9); it was an immediate success, and remained one of the most popular books with parents for over a hundred years. But Day did not live to enjoy any of its glory, for he had made the mistake of training a colt on Rousseauesque principles and, in October 1789, it threw him and then kicked him. He died almost immediately. Esther, who by this time had become almost exclusively devoted to his needs, especially since he had cut her off from her parents, died less than two years later, 'a victim', in the words of *The Gentleman's Magazine*, of 'conjugal affection'.

4

At the time of Day's death, the Edgeworth household was preoccupied with Honora, the talented and beautiful daughter of Edgeworth's second marriage. Born in 1774, she was dying of her mother's fatal illness, tuberculosis. It was not, therefore, until after her demise that Maria could turn her attention reflectively to the man who had in fact played a significant part in her life. Not only had she seen a great deal of Day when he visited her father's house, but she had on occasions stayed with him and Esther in their spartan home, twice in 1781. Day dosed her with tar-water, and 'the lofty nature of his mind, his romantic character, his metaphysical enquiries, and eloquent discussions, took her into another world'.[26] But it was Day who, in 1783, persuaded Edgeworth not to allow, let alone encourage, Maria to become a writer. She only turned to writing after Day's death and, ironically, her first publication was *Letters for Literary Ladies*, published anonymously in 1795, which in part took up the question of whether women should or should not write. She then made up for lost time with a vengeance, for by 1801 she had created two fictional portraits of Day.

In her *Moral Tales* he appears as Forester, in the tale of the same name, a vivid representation of adolescent intemperateness and crass idealism – one of the first concentrated and sharply focused accounts of adolescence, as such, in our literature.[27] In the words of Edgeworth's Preface, it was

> the picture of an eccentric character – a young man who scorns the common forms and dependencies of civilized society; and who, full of visionary schemes of benevolence and happiness, might, by improper management, or unlucky circumstances, have become a fanatic and a criminal.

In these words, Edgeworth was not only disowning the more extravagant follies of his own early years, but delivering a retrospective judgement, even a rebuke, of the stern and intemperate – fanatical? – moralist who had been his own boon companion for over twenty years.

Forester is an unmistakable portrait of Day: 'taught to dislike politeness so much, that the common forms of society appeared to him either odious or ridiculous'. he was so stiff-necked in his virtue that, as with Day, 'his sincerity was

seldom restrained by any attention to the feelings of others'.
Through a series of misfortunes – brought about by his own
obstinacy – Forester is taught to see the errors of his ways, and
as a token of reformation he agrees to have his unkempt hair
trimmed and to put on some respectable clothes. 'Why,' he
asks, 'Why should I fight the world for trifles?' So his
appearance, like his social bearing, was 'brought into decent
order'. The series of disillusionments through which he is
brought to accept common-sense are handled with a liveliness
of deflationary humour, a savour of ironic pleasure, that
reminds one of Jane Austen; but the plot's twists and turns are
sometimes too contrived to be altogether plausible, alas.

5

It was in her much more ambitious *Belinda* that Maria
returned again to Day, and in this case explored in detail his
experiment in the education of Sabrina. In the Advertisement
to *Belinda* she wrote:

> The following work is offered to the public as a Moral
> Tale, the author not wishing to acknowledge a Novel . . .
> it is hoped the wish to assume another title will be
> attributed to feelings that are laudable, and not fas-
> tidious.

In 1812, in conversation with Henry Crabb Robinson, Mrs
Charles Aikin was 'willing to find in Miss Edgeworth's work
every excellence', but Robinson 'disputed her power of
interesting in a long connected tale, and her possession of
poetical imagination'. His considered opinion was that 'the
tendency of her writings to check enthusiasm of every kind is
of very problematical value.'[28] To which one might add the
rider that some kinds of enthusiasm are more properly and
usefully checked than others. In *Belinda*, Maria's 'laudable
feelings' are certainly in evidence, in nailing folly and vice, but
the energy and momentum of her narrative are here beyond

dispute: they owe a great deal not to her heroine, Belinda, on whose social education and voyage to matrimony the plot turns, but rather to Lady Delacour, who takes her education in hand. This formidable woman is an undeniable triumph, very brightly rendered and occasionally almost Falstaffian, and she is a triumph of imagination rather than of didactic intention. Almost inexhaustibly interesting, in terms of the reader's expectations and uncertainties – will this prodigious character end up well or badly? – she possesses a genuine ambiguity and resonance of character. If indeed she got out of hand, and it seems that she probably did, the novel gains from her unpredictable temper, her caustic wit, and her ferocious sallies: she is a potent focus of energy, and transcends any suspicion of didacticism. She is undeniably egocentric and vain, foolish and cynical, and yet she has a weird knack of possessing the reader, and of obliterating one's moralistic reservations. Even when, in a fit of remorse, she becomes infatuated with a specially virulent form of Methodism, yet she still retains one's sympathies. Maria has her punctuate her conversation with numerous references to fairy-tales and the *Thousand and One Nights*, as if to underline her irrationality; the effect is simply to add yet another resonant dimension to an already fascinating woman.

The sensible and rational characters in the tale express various forms of disapproval of romances and novels, especially of the undesirable effects of early novel-reading, and there are also demeaning references to fairy-tales, but these are offered not by the authorial voice but by individuals speaking in character, in consistent relation to their functions in the story. It is instructive, nevertheless, to compare Steele's cameo (see above, pp. 33–5) – in which pleasant children, in a sensitive, intelligent home, were delighting in romance and fairy-tales – with *Belinda*'s counterpart of 1801 clearly endorsed by the author. In Chapter XVI Belinda moves from the hurly-burly of the city to the benign peace and order of Oakly Park, the country home of Lady Anne Percival and her husband. The title of the chapter is 'Domestic Happiness', and it offers a foil to the social perturbations and schemings of the town: Belinda's 'tranquillity of mind' is gradually restored by the Percivals' society. Between husband and wife there was 'a union of interests, occupations, taste, and affection'. The children were 'treated neither as slaves nor as playthings, but as reasonable creatures', and 'without force or any factitious excitements, the taste for knowledge, and the habits of application, were induced by example, and confirmed by sympathy'. Their father, who doubtless represents an ideal portrait of Edgeworth, was 'a man of science and literature' and his 'daily pursuits and general conversation were in the happiest manner instructive and interesting to his family'. One of his virtues was that 'from the merest trifles he could lead to some scientific fact, some happy literary allusion, or philosophical investigation'. His wife was also an Edgeworthian model for she had 'without any pedantry or ostentation much accurate knowledge . . .' and 'the daily sense of her success in the education of their children inspired her husband with a degree of happy social energy, unknown to the selfish votaries of avarice and ambition'. As for their children, one of the boys was fond of chemistry, another of gardening; one of the daughters had a talent for painting, another for music. This arcadian account of domestic felicity is followed by the observation that some readers will perhaps find it 'visionary and romantic', while those whose tastes have been 'vitiated by the stimulus of dissipation' might find it insipid. But, although these reflections may well be symptoms of a touch of authorial nerves, the crucial point is to be found elsewhere: the account is itself vitiated by the 'platitude of statement'; we are told that it was so, but it is not realized; we have to take it on trust. Lady Anne possessed, we are told, 'much accurate knowledge' and even this could presumably be made to 'tell' in some way; but it does not do so. The effect, then, is one of a rather credulous naïvety on the part of the author. The 'accurate knowledge' is offered, to be accepted at its face value, but it fails in any way to come alive: it remains inanimate and unanimating.

Belinda needed the rational tranquillity of Oakly Park in order to compose her mind: for three hundred pages she had been increasingly drawn into the complex social relationships of a group of sophisticated fashionable people, and her own particular tensions arose from Lady Delacour's suspicion that Belinda was waiting for her to die in order to marry her husband, while Belinda's preoccupation is with the mysteries of Clarence Hervey's matrimonial intentions. Hervey is the 'Day' figure: he 'affected singularity, in order to establish his claims to genius' and 'adopted in liberal rotation every possible absurdity'. In Chapter V he teases Lady Delacour with the notion that 'he might, as men of genius sometimes do, look forward to the idea of forming a country novice for a wife', and he is characterized by 'moralité à la glace'. Maria plays a neat little joke on her readers when she has Clarence Hervey praise 'The Dying Negro' and the author, Mr Day, whom he offers as 'an instance that genuine eloquence must spring from the heart'. In his travels in France before the Revolution, Hervey came to believe that 'women who were full of vanity, affectation, and artifice . . . were equally incapable of conferring or enjoying real happiness', and 'whilst this conviction was full in his mind, he read the works of Rousseau'. And as Keir had said of Day, so Maria wrote of Hervey: Rousseau's 'declamations produced more than their just effect upon an imagination naturally ardent'. Three-quarters of the way through the novel, Hervey's secret is made known: for some time, he has been suspected of keeping a mistress in Windsor; but the woman in Windsor is no such thing. She is the victim, the Sabrina, of his matrimonial experiment. He had accidentaly discovered a girl with the requisite Rousseauesque characteristics, a Sophia:

> simplicity without vulgarity, ingenuity without cunning, ignorance without prejudice; an understanding totally uncultivated, yet likely to reward the labour of late instruction; a heart wholly unpractised, yet full of sensibility, capable of all the enthusiasm of passion, the

delicacy of sentiment, and the firmness of rational constancy.

He had found her in the New Forest, in a state of nature, a pastoral idyll, in 'a terrestrial paradise', and soon adopted her, placing her in the care of Mrs Ormond, a benign old widow, first renaming her Virginia St Pierre, in honour of St Pierre's romantic Robinsonnade, *Paul et Virginie*.

But, as with Day's meetings with Honora and Elizabeth Sneyd, Hervey discovered, on meeting Belinda, that Virginia's virtues were purely negative and she then 'appeared to him but an insipid, though innocent, child'; her virtues 'sprang from sentiment; those of Belinda from reason'. As Hervey came to know a real woman, his attempt to create a 'Sophia' for himself, 'his pupil or his plaything', lost its attractions; moreover, poor Virginia has by this time become a pathetic victim of her isolation. Apart from Hervey's occasional visits, the only person whose society she had been allowed was the widow, Mrs Ormond, who had encouraged the poor girl to pass her time in reading romances, including the sentimental and over-heated *Paul and Virginia* (presumably in Helen Maria Williams's translation of 1795!). The effect of this reading on Virginia allowed Maria to express her views on the relationship between life, literature, and the imagination of an adolescent. It seems that she had detected an erotic undertone – undeniably there – in Rousseau's account of Sophia, and this she also tackled.

'Virginia's mind was either perfectly indolent, or *exalted* by romantic views, and visionary ideas of happiness', and she confessed to Mrs Ormond: 'I have only confused ideas floating in my imagination from the books I have been reading. I do not distinctly know my own feelings.' As a result of her reading she was inspired with 'the most exalted notions of female delicacy and honour, but from her perfect ignorance, these were rather vague ideas than principles of conduct'. She lurched into a state of adolescent confusion and distress, intensified by the discrepancy between 'romance' and 'reality', and the most vivid symptom was her dreams. She confessed to Mrs Ormond that she did not wish to marry Hervey, and the following night had an extraordinary nightmare: it began as a dream of erotic romance, and ended with her lover killing Hervey who ended up, 'weltering in his blood' and accusing Virginia of ingratitude and responsibility for his death.

From that time on, her sexual awakening built a barrier between her and Hervey – she 'could neither meet his eyes nor speak to him without a degree of embarrassment'. She became subject to 'fits of melancholy', and Hervey saw 'her bloom fading daily, her spirits depressed, her existence a burden to her'. He was now convinced that he loved only Belinda, but what was the honourable thing to do with Virginia, and her 'disease of the imagination'? As Mrs Ormond told Hervey, 'We have used this girl cruelly amongst us'. Mercifully, they were both relieved by the next twist in the plot, which allowed the discovery of Virginia's father, and the reunion of father and daughter. Hervey's conclusion was one that Day never came near: 'I have no right to blame any one so much as myself. All this has arisen from my own presumption and imprudence. Nothing could be more absurd than my scheme of educating a woman in solitude to make her fit for society': which is entirely in agreement with what Keir had written of Day in 1791. Lady Delacour provided the closing lines of the story:

> Our *tale* contains a moral; and no doubt,
> You all have wit enough to find it out.

In Keats's words, this world is 'a vale of soul-making'.[29] In *Belinda*, Maria offered a variety of ways in which character, if not soul – not a conspicuous part of the Edgeworth vocabulary – could be formed or deformed. The function of the Percivals' domestic happiness was to show how it could be done well; and the trials and tribulations of Belinda herself demonstrated how good sense and reason could survive, indeed learn from, the subtle slings and arrows of initiation into fashionable society: Virginia exemplified the way of folly, devised by enthusiasm and a ruling passion, to the denial of sound reason and good sense. Robinson's charge, in 1812, that she lacked 'poetical imagination', was one that sporadically bothered Maria, and her final novel, *Helen*, published in 1834 was testimony to that concern.

6

When Maria started work on *Helen*, around 1830, her father had been dead for about twelve years, and she herself was about sixty-two. If, then, it was not a novel written in decline or enfeeblement, it may be seen as her major demonstration of artistic maturity and autonomy. Most critics agree that it is, in fact, the latter; and although the writing of it was strenuous and demanding, little of that effort is apparent in the prose. Briefly, its themes are honour, trust, friendship and marriage. Helen, an orphan on the edge of womanhood, goes to live with her friend Cecilia, newly married to General Clarendon. Cecilia's mother, Lady Davenant, also spends much of her time in the Clarendon household. Beauclerc, an attractive but impulsive man, falls in love with Helen, and vice versa. Cecilia, who assured her husband that she had not had a lover before he met her, becomes involved in a desperate effort to conceal a previous affair with a disreputable character: there are letters of a compromising nature. She persuades Helen to pretend that it was she, Helen, who was the woman in the case. In the ensuing scandal, Helen suffers a great deal of grief and distress; when the truth comes out, the General leaves Cecilia, but Lady Davenant, a dying woman, effects their reconciliation, and Helen and Beauclerc are reunited.

What do we know of others? How do we know others? What parts do reason, judgement, intuition, imagination, play in the formation of such knowledge? These questions constitute the psychological sub-text of *Helen*, but are incorporated in such a way that they do not, on the whole, obtrude explicitly to the detriment of the story. The novel displays, or even could be said to betray, Maria's preoccupation with the role of the imagination. There are no fewer than twenty-five explicit references to it, and some of the novel's crucial conversations are devoted to it. In *Forester* and *Belinda* 'imagination' was almost a bug-bear, associated intimately with *un*reason, self-indulgent fantasy, and moral or mental aberration. *Helen* represents a marked shift from that turn-of-the-century position: but how far has the word been rehabilitated? As one might expect, it is used in various ways. When the verb – to imagine – is used, it can carry the conventional meaning as in 'I can't imagine what you mean', although it generally occurs when some misunderstanding is involved – 'No, not so easy as you imagine'. In such instances it carries an emphasis of *mis*conceiving, misjudging, or jumping to conclusions: in general it is the characters that we are implicitly invited to disapprove of, that go in for this sort of imagining.

'Imagination' occurs in various forms. '. . . her imagination was caught': she became preoccupied with the matter, and had to speculate and surmise. 'Riding off on your imagination': a rebuke – going beyond the verifiable facts. 'False, and perhaps vain imaginations, certainly premature, therefore unbecoming': used for Cecilia who is compulsively dishonest. 'Romantic love, love nursed by imagination more than by hope': wishful thinking induced by self-gratification. 'The wonder-loving imagination of the credulous English public': obviously deplorable, not to say vulgar. 'The imagination, to which we are, all of us, more or less, dupes': spoken, self-indulgently, by Cecilia, in a spirit of self-justification and bravado. 'Temporary derangement of the reasoning powers which results from being what is called bit [*sic*] by a fancy': used for a sudden, urgent enthusiasm for a new scheme. '. . . bright in his imagination': used of Beauclerc, a man of generous impulse, but over-quixotic, and inclined to rush in. 'Those who tell us that it is unnatural to recollect poetry or eloquence at times of powerful emotion are much mistaken; they have not strong feelings or strong imaginations': spoken by Lady Davenant, the repository of mature wisdom in the novel, but given to a rather heavy sententiousness. 'It was all Helen's imagination': she was deluded and mistaken. 'An imaginary necessity': spurious and unfounded. 'How much Helen slept may be left to the judgment of those who have any imagination': this is Maria's way of ending Chapter 35, and it is clear from the preceding events that Helen is unlikely to sleep well, if at all. 'You see my fault was having too much imagination': spoken by Beauclerc, when he confesses to having been duped.

On balance, judging by these cases, 'imagination' comes off very badly: it seems to be a 'faculty' which not only can be misused and so lead to error or folly, but which, rather, is *inherently* inclined to error. But let us consider one of the key conversations in which 'imagination' is the topic: Lady Davenant has been expressing envy of Beauclerc's capacity for losing himself in a book. She attributes her own incapacity to her advancing years:

> The fact is, that not only does the imagination cool and weaken as we grow older, but we become, as we live on in this world, too much engrossed by the real business and cares of life, to have feeling or time for factitious, imaginary interests. But why do I say factitious? While they last, the imaginative interests are as real as any others.

'Thank you', said Beauclerc, 'for doing justice to poor imagination, whose pleasures are surely, after all, the highest, the most real, that we have, unwarrantably as they have been decried both by metaphysicians and physicians' (Chapter 16). Helen is attracted more by this 'romantic enthusiasm' than she is by 'wit or fashion', just as she had been charmed by his passionate defence of theatrical illusion and of all 'those blessed illusions, which make the real happiness of life'. His rhetoric is itself rather theatrical: 'Yes, sooner would I believe in all the fables of the Talmud than be without the ecstasy of veneration.[30] It is the curse of age to be thus miserably disenchanted; to outlive our illusions, all our hopes.' He is determined to resist such 'premature ossification of the heart' (Chapter 12). But he is undeniably confused: on the one hand he delights in a rural landscape precisely because it has so far remained untouched by 'the petty uses of mankind' – business and commerce – while in the very next breath he is rhapsodizing about 'education and the diffusion of knowledge'. It is difficult to determine with any degree of certainty whether Maria is deliberately offering us a representation of confusion and self-contradiction, all floating on the swell of enthusiasm, or whether she herself is confused and self-contradictory.

As for the status of the imagination, of the poetic, in this, her last novel, it seems – despite the overt and rather 'staged' assertions of Lady Davenant and of Beauclerc, to be rather low. As for didacticism, Beauclerc waxes lyrical in praise of Walter Scott, the 'great and good Enchanter'. He merits special praise, we are told, because 'His morality is not in purple patches, ostentatiously obtrusive, but woven in through the very texture of the stuff. . . . Without our well knowing how, the whole tone of our minds is raised' (Chapter 12). One could, by analogy, see Beauclerc's defence of imagination as 'ostentatiously obtrusive', while, 'without our well knowing how', at the end of the novel we are left with the sense that the imagination has in effect been demeaned.

NOTES AND REFERENCES

1 'Worldliness and Other-Worldliness: the Poet Young', *Westminster Review*, vol. LXVII (January 1857), p. 1; reprinted in *Essays*, ed. T. Pinney (London: Routledge & Kegan Paul, 1963), p. 335.
2 James Beattie, *An Account of James Hay Beattie, his Life and Character* (London, 1799), p. 54. Cf. Ruskin's essay, written at the age of sixteen: 'Does the Perusal of Works of Fiction Act Favourably or Unfavourably on the Moral Character?' – a spirited reply to the narrowly pious spirit of the Reverend Thomas Dale's *The Student's Guide (Works, ed. E. T. Cooke and A. Wedderburn, London: George Allen, 1903, vol. 1, p. 357).

3 'Letters on a regicide peace'. On Burke and chap-book tales, see
   Margaret Spufford, *Small Books and Pleasant Histories* (London: Methuen, 1981), p.75.
4 James Keir, *An Account of the Life and Writings of Thomas Day,
   Esq.* (1791), p.25.
5 Letter of July 1741.
6 Letter of March 1747.
7 ibid.
8 Emily Lawless, *Maria Edgeworth* (London: Macmillan, 1904),
   p.148.
9 Marilyn Butler, *Maria Edgeworth: A Literary Biography*
   (London: Oxford University Press, 1972), p.442.
10 Keir, op.cit., p.26.
11 ibid., p.25.
12 Rousseau, *Emilius and Sophia: or, A New System of Education*, 4
   vols (London: R. Griffiths, T. Becket & P.A. de Hondt, 1762,
   1763), vol.III,p.243.
13 R.L. Edgeworth, *Memoirs of Richard Lovell Edgeworth . . .
   begun by himself, and concluded by his daughter*, 2 vols (London,
   1820), vol.I,p.253.
14 Rousseau, op.cit., vol.III,p.203.
15 Anna Seward, *Memoirs of the Life of Dr Darwin* (London,
   1804).
16 Rousseau, op.cit., vol.III,p.251.
17 ibid., vol.III,p.233.
18 ibid., vol.III,p.251.
19 Cf. Tom Wedgwood: R.B. Litchfield observes of his unpublished educational writings, 'I have not detected the smallest
   sign of humour in the mature philosopher. His methods remind
   us of another child of the revolution, Thomas Day . . .' (*Tom
   Wedgwood, the First Photographer*, London: Duckworth, 1903,
   p.209). In order to teach a child the virtue of fearlessness,
   Wedgwood suggests:

   > The parent might invite the attack of a fierce bull, stand
   > with perfect composure until the animal be within two or
   > three paces of him, then suddenly open an umbrella, hold
   > his hat before his face [the bull's or the parent's?), or
   > somehow contrive to amuse and terrify the foe, whilst his
   > child, on the other side of the stile, shall witness his
   > intrepidity, and by degrees practise the same feat in
   > company with his parent.

   Of the early years of Charlotte Brontë, Mrs Gaskell observed:

The ideas of Rousseau and Mr Day on education had filtered down through many classes, and spread themselves widely out. I imagine, Mr Brontë must have formed some of his opinions on the management of children from these two theorists. His practice was not half so wild or extraordinary as that to which an aunt of mine was subjected by a disciple of Mr Day's. She had been taken by this gentleman and his wife, to live with them as their adopted child, perhaps about five-and-twenty years before the time of which I am writing. They were wealthy people and kind hearted, but her food and clothing were of the very simplest and rudest description, on Spartan principles. A health merry child, she did not much care for dress or eating; but the treatment which she felt as a real cruelty was this. They had a carriage, in which she and the favourite dog were taken an airing on alternate days; the creature whose turn it was to be left at home being tossed in a blanket – an operation which my aunt especially dreaded. Her affright at the tossing was probably the reason why it was presevered in. Dressed-up ghosts had become common, and she did not care for them, so the blanket exercise was to be the next mode of hardening her nerves. (*The Life of Charlotte Brontë*, London, Smith, Elder & Co., 1857, ch. III)

20 The parallel between Day's treatment of his orphans and the dominating habits of Mary Wollstonecraft's heroine, Mrs Mason, is strikingly close, both in tone and detail.

21 Edgeworth, op.cit., vol. II, p. 335.

22 Cf. Chapter Four, n. 14.

23 *Tom Jones*, bk III, ch. 2.

24 *The Autobiography of Leigh Hunt*, J.E. Morpurgo (London: Cresset Press, 1949), p. 50.

25 See Dickens's 'Mr Barlow' for an eloquent expression of the novelist's contempt for Day (in *The Uncommercial Traveller*, ch. XXXIV). Barlow is also the target for a celebrated broad burlesque, F.C. Burnand's *The New History of Sandford and Merton* (London: Bradbury, Evans & Co., 1872). Some readers have detected Leigh Hunt in the figure of Skimpole in *Bleak House*, but William Godwin may also have served as a model: see Claire Tomalin, *The Life and Death of Mary Wollstonecraft* (Harmondsworth: Penguin Books, 1977), p. 291.

26 Edgeworth, op.cit., vol. I, p. 12.

27 Cf. Chapter Nine, n. 49.

28 Henry Crabb Robinson, *Diary*, ed. T. Sadler, 3 vols (London, 1869), vol. 1, p. 399.
29 Keats, *Letters*, ed. Robert Gittings (London: Oxford University Press, 1970), p. 249.
30 CF. Wordsworth, *The Excursion*, bk 4, ll. 611–30.

CHAPTER SIX

HUFFING, PUFFING, AND PAUSING FOR THOUGHT

Questions of child development
were desperate, dire, mortal.
(Saul Bellow, *Humboldt's Gift*, 1975)

. . . ah, Mr Huffcap would kick the bottom of
the Pulpit out with Passion – would tear off the
sleave of his Gown, & set his wig on fire & throw
it at the people; hed cry & stamp & kick & sweat
and all for the good of their souls.
(William Blake, *An Island in the Moon*, ?1784)

1

When social, moral or intellectual values are dissolving or
solvent; when magisterial authority in such matters is on the
wane; when an orthodoxy is felt to be old-fashioned, obsoles-
cent or constricting – at such moments of transition, the
dialectic of response seems to go in one of two ways. Some
minds will push, nudge or kick the issues emphatically toward
a state of greater fluidity, dissolving the conventional wisdom
even further; while minds of an opposite temper will rally
round to protect what they see as absolute and eternal verities
from the presumptions of impiety, and counter-attack with
what Lawrence Stone has characterized as a 'siege-
mentality'.[1]

Maurice Morgann, Joseph Pott and William Scolfield offer
three late eighteenth-century minds which exemplify, in
various ways, the tendency to dissolution. Mrs Sarah Trimmer, conversely, exemplifies the 'siege-mentality', which, in

Stone's words, 'saw everywhere a conspiracy of evil, planning the satanic capture of the world'.[2]

By the 1770s there was quite clearly a shift of attitude, in many prescient minds, to the relationship between reason and judgement, on the one hand, and imagination and fancy, on the other; and, in some cases, to the related question of taste, class and cultural subordination.

Some examples, chosen almost at random, may serve to show the veerings of the wind:

[1755] We who live in the days of writing by rule, are apt to try every composition by those laws which we have been taught to think the sole criteria of excellence. . . . Spenser did not live in an age of planning.

(Thomas Warton, *Observations on the Fairie Queene*)

[1756] A clear idea is another name for a little idea. . . . No work of art can be great but as it deceives.

(Burke, *On the Sublime and Beautiful*)

[1756] Milton's mention of places remarkably romantic, the supposed habitation of Druids, bards, and wizards, is far more pleasing to the imagination than Pope's obvious introduction of Cam and Isis as seats of the Muses.

(Joseph Warton, *Essay on Pope*)

[1759] A Genius differs from a good Understanding as a Magician from a good Architect. . . . In the Fairyland of Fancy, Genius may wander wild; there it has creative power, and may reign arbitrarily over its own empire of Chimeras. . . . To the neglect of Learning, Genius sometimes owes its greater Glory.

(E. Young, *Conjectures on Original Composition*)

[1759] All power of fancy over reason is a degree of insanity.

(Samuel Johnson, *Rasselas*)

[1760] Had Shakespeare crept by modern rules,
We'd lost his Witches, Fairies, Fools;
Instead of all that wild creation,
He'd formed a regular plantation.

(R. Lloyd, *Shakespeare*)

[1761] *Addison*: 'What can the ruins of Kenilworth
call to mind but the memory of barbarous
manners and a despotic government?'
Arbuthnot: 'The Gothic tilts and tournaments
exceeded, both in use and elegance even, the
Greecian gymnastics. . . . I consider the legends of ancient chivalry in a very serious
light.' (Richard Hurd, *Moral and Political
Dialogues*)

[1761] Gray thought it an advantage to Dante to have
been produced in a rude age of strong and uncontrolled
passions, when the muse was not checked by refinement
and the fear of criticism.

(N. Nichols, *Reminiscences of Gray*)

[1762] 'May there not be something in the Gothic
Romance peculiarly suited to the views of a genius, and to
the ends of poetry?'
'What we have gotten, you will say, is a great deal of
good sense. What we have lost, is a world of fine fabling;
the illusion of which is so grateful to the Charmed Spirit.'

(Hurd, *Letters on Chivalry and Romance*)

[1763] Imagination dwelt many hundred years ago in
all her pomp on the cold and barren mountains of
Scotland.

(Thomas Gray)

[1765] . . . blend the wonderful of old stories with the
natural of modern novels.
(Horace Walpole, Preface to *The Castle of Otranto*)

[1767] Creative Imagination is the distinguishing

characteristic of true Genius . . . which proceeds from
the copious effusions of a plastic imagination.

(W. Duff, *Essay on Original Genius*)

[1773] The old Gothic Romance and Eastern Tale,
however a refined critic may censure them as absurd and
extravagant, will ever retain a most powerful influence on
the mind.

(Mrs Barbauld, *On the Pleasure Derived from Objects of
Terror*)

[1777] The Chronicle, the Novel, or the Ballad; the
King, or the beggar, the hero, the madman, the sot or the
fool; it is all one; nothing is worse, nothing is better: The
same genius pervades and is equally admirable in all.

(Maurice Morgann, *Falstaff*)

[1778] Verses which, a few years past, were thought
worthy the attention of children only, or of the lowest and
rudest orders, are now admired for that artless simplicity
which once obtained the name of coarseness and
vulgarity.

(Vicesimus Knox, *On the Prevailing Taste for the Old
English Poets*)

[1779] It is hardly possible to put stones together with
that air of wild and magnificent disorder which they are
sure to acquire by falling of their own accord.

(William Cowper)

[1779] . . . ever despise those opinions that are formed
by rules.

(Fanny Burney)

[1789] Read Sinbad the Sailor's Voyages and you will
be sick of Aeneas. . . .

(Horace Walpole, *Letters*)

[1791] More than four times the number of books are
sold now than were sold twenty years since. The poorer

sort of farmers, and even the poor country people in general, who before that period spent their winter evenings in relating stories of witches, ghosts, hobgoblins, etc., now shorten the winter nights by hearing their sons and daughters read tales, romances, etc., and, on entering their houses, you may see *Tom Jones, Roderick Random*, and other entertaining books stuck up on their bacon racks. . . .

(Joseph Lackington, *Memoirs*)

For those who were finding satisfaction of a deeper and less stringently rational kind in the experiences that art offered, Maurice Morgann was a particularly eloquent spokesman. In his extraordinary essay, 'On the Dramatic Character of Sir John Falstaff',[3] published in 1777, he breaks off suddenly – impulsively, indeed – to offer his views on what we would now call the psychology of art. Like Locke's *Thoughts*, the essay was published only on the insistence of friends, but unlike the *Thoughts*, Morgann's essay provoked a great deal of incredulity; indeed, some of his readers suspected him of indulging in an elaborate joke. Attached to older Augustan orthodoxies they were unprepared for the mercurial motions and the deeper reach of his mind.

Commitment to reason and judgement was based on the assumption that one's best self was always in control of one's experience, standing – so to speak – always to attention. Morgann, with unconcealed enthusiasm, turns this orthodoxy upside down: in the first place, he argues, the real phenomenon, which we may subsequently talk about in a perfectly reasonable way, is *not* an objective event, but an internal happening: 'the impression is the fact'; and 'it is safer to say, on many occasions, that we are possessed by Shakespeare, than that we possess him'. As audience, we are not in the event critically conscious, not exercising our reasonable power of judgement: on the contrary, 'we are rapt in ignorant admiration.'[4] Shakespeare's art, in particular, is so 'exquisite' that 'whilst every woman and every child shall feel the whole effect, his learned Editors and Commentators should yet so very frequently mistake or seem ignorant of the cause'.

His view of Shakespeare, as artist, is as of a magician: 'with what a Magic hand does he prepare and scatter his spells! The Understanding must, in the first place, be subdued; and lo! how the rooted prejudices of the child spring up to confound the man!'[5] And so much of our experience of Shakespeare is beyond the bounds of urbane civilized rational sense, that we cannot continue to praise him for his 'truth to nature' – the orthodox eighteenth-century yardstick – invoking, or appealing to, nature as for the previous fifty years, as representing that publicly shared 'reality' about which there can be no epistemological disagreement. Morgann, being 'convinced' by everything in the plays – *Macbeth* offers a good case – everything that either transcends or denies such 'nature', therfore insists: 'I see that a more compendious *nature* may be obtained; a nature of *effects* only, to which neither the relations of place, or continuity of time, are always essential.' The conventional version of 'nature' was so rule-bound and so emphatically coherent that it had 'drawn through human life a regular chain of visible causes and effects.' And such a 'nature' in no way corresponds to the *felt* truth of Shakespeare's plays: for 'Poetry delights in surprise, conceals her steps, seizes at once upon the heart, and obtains the Sublime of things without betraying the rounds of her ascent.' Morgann's whole drift here is anti-reductive: an extraordinary effort to release the energies of his own experience, of the impressions that he had felt, from the diminishing constraints, the pre-emptive limits, set by reason and judgement. We must, he argues, be prepared to accept the fact that poetry, true poetry, is not susceptible of cool appraisal: 'True Poesy is *magic*, not nature; an effect from causes hidden or unknown. To the Magician I prescribed no laws; his law and his power are one; his power is his law.' And the means whereby the poetic imagination achieves its effects are 'most perfect and most admirable when most concealed'.

At this point he pulls himself up – 'But whither am I going!'

– and returns to his account of his experience of Falstaff. But in a footnote, he allows himself to pursue the subject of poetic magic a little further; where Goldsmith's notion of magic in poetry is merely a perfunctory way of accounting for the transforming function of metaphor, Morgann's is richly suggestive, expressive of a very different sensibility, with many more of its pores open, many more antennae quivering and responding. 'A felt propriety, or truth of art, from an unseen, tho' supposed adequate cause, we call *nature*.' Conversely,

> a like feeling of propriety and truth, supposed without a cause, or as seeming to be derived from causes inadequate, fantastic, and absurd, – such as wands, circles, incantations, and so forth, – we call by the general name *magic*, including all the train of superstition, witches, ghosts, fairies, and the rest.

The inherent limitation of reason is that it is 'confined to the line of visible existence'; whereas 'our *passions* and our *fancy* extend far beyond into the *obscure*; but however lawless their operations may seem, the images they so wildly form have yet a relation to truth, and are the shadows at least, however fantastic, of reality.' Most of Shakespeare's 'preternatural beings' are in fact 'images of *effects* only, and cannot subsist but in a surrounding atmosphere of those passions from which they are derived': the witches in *Macbeth*, for instance, are called up by the passions that we know to be in Macbeth's own soul: a bodying forth, a visible correlative, and a manifestation. But, alas, the urbane eighteenth-century audience, misconstruing the nature of this 'nature', 'now laughs in some places where it ought to shudder'.

Morgann's view that 'the images of *effects*' cannot exist except in an atmosphere informed by 'those passions from which they are derived' helps to clarify for us the relationship between monster and terror; giant and superhuman courage, following on fear; exotic landscape and an impulse to explore; all such relationships are, of course, perfectly 'sensible' and coherent to the child reading a tale. But, more inclusively, Morgann's insight helps us to understand better the peculiar fascination of such tales for young readers. For the tales themselves, as 'gestalts', are inherently 'images of effects' for they provide an external, dramatic, narrative correlative to the 'passions' in the young reader, and can be said to derive from such passions: the effect, indeed, is as if the child had actually made up the story, so well does it 'fit' and express the child's own internal needs, desires, anxieties, and fantasies. Or, as Charles Lamb was soon to say, 'the archetypes are within us'.[6]

Addison had offered his early eighteenth-century readers a rationale of the imagination by appealing to the great, the uncommon and the beautiful, and had legitimized these by arguing that in some mysterious way they 'matched' the mind. Subsequently, it was difficult to open a magazine without encountering an essay on the prior claims of reason, the need for judgement, and the various aberrations that the fancy or imagination were prey to. The *Rambler*, no. 89,[7] for instance, offered a melancholy, not to say gloomy account of fancy, construed as a kind of solipsistic day-dreaming, an 'invisible riot of the mind', for which the best cures are exercise and 'free and easy conversation'. No. 96[8] offered a rather laboured allegory in which Truth is the daughter of Jupiter and Wisdom, while Falsehood is the progeny of Folly, impregnated by the wind. In the struggle between them, Truth obstructs her own progress by her own too severe aspect, while Falsehood wins men's support because she always suffers herself to be dressed and painted by Desire. So the muses weave an attractive robe for Truth; 'with this they invested Truth, and named her Fiction'.

Morgann's admission of his experience of 'being possessed'; his sense of the power of fiction as being beyond the analytic scrutiny of reason; his perfectly sane notion of 'magic' – all of these signal a new sensibility – one that will be very ready to understand and sympathize with the ways in which preposterous tales of marvels and wonders can possess the mind of a young reader.

2

Where Morgann is mercurial, serendipitous and vivacious, the Reverend Joseph Pott is quiet, subtle and judicious. He advances his argument with steady care, but it is no less interesting, in its own way, than Morgann's. In 1787 he published his essay, 'The sallies of a Juvenile imagination to be checked rather than suppressed':[9] by this time, virtually every publisher had climbed on to what was for many a lucrative bandwagon: the production of didactic juvenilia, written mostly by poorly paid hacks; all tending to foster or reinforce infantine rationality, precocious prudence and a deep mistrust of fancy.

Pott first offers the orthodox, 'reasonable' view of the relationship between 'romance' and young readers: such reading offers an illusory experience of people 'elevated above the wants of life, its coarser inconveniences, its sullen irksome hours, its attendant troubles and diseases'. Such fictive illusions 'give but a false draught of the state of man'. As Hester Chapone insisted, such 'fictitious stories' mostly tend to 'inflame the passions of youth, whilst the chief purpose of education should be to moderate and restrain them'.[10] The result of such reading is, alas, an 'expectation of extraordinary adventures – which seldom ever happen to the sober and prudent part of mankind'. Fictions simply arouse 'the admiration of extravagant passions and absurd conduct'. Thus Chapone, and most of her contemporaries; but Pott is not content to leave the matter there. What, essentially, are these romances? He suggests in a pregnant and suggestive trope that they are perhaps 'broken rays of lost perfection' – vestiges of a prelapsarian bliss, an unconditional state of blessedness. They are 'the emanations of minds whose early purity is yet untainted by the common ordinary objects and pursuits, the passions and engagements of real life, disfigured as it is'.[11] Such a view of romance is clearly radically at odds with the conventional wisdom, which sees it as the product of a diseased or inflamed imagination.

What, then, is the relationship between such 'romantic' views of life and the 'disfigured' actuality of 'real life'? How do they interact? Pott argues that, as the mind moves from fiction into actual experience, the romantic views are quickly 'contradicted by experience, by real images, by daily documents, by repeated and inevitable truth'. Overwhelmed by the combined pressures of actuality, and reason, the banalities and tensions of ordinary daily life and the critical scrutiny of the reasoning mind, then romance will simply yield: the mind will 'grow up', will submit to the process that Piaget was to label 'accommodation'. Life, it will concede, is like that, or, rather, is not like that. That has all the appearances of a sensible and realistic conclusion, quite unexceptionably so. Most of Pott's contemporaries would there have rested their case, if indeed they had exercised their minds as far as this. But Pott takes it yet further and asserts that 'reason should not assume too much applause in shaking off these vain and empty notions'.

At this point, readers such as Hester Chapone would have consigned Pott to outer perdition; and wittier readers would probably have assumed – as Morgann's had of the Falstaff essay – that the author was not altogether serious, was playing with paradoxes. But Pott is perfectly in earnest. What happens, he asks, when these 'vain and empty notions' are indeed shaken off? Reason *seems* to 'rise superior to them' – but does it? On the contrary, too often it sinks *below* them: 'the selfish reasoner and worldly monitor, in banishing these phantoms, do not always substitute more noble emulations'. They do indeed 'pluck away the weeds and the wild flowers' but in their stead they 'sow tares at last'.

In the name of reason, and with the unquestioned authority that reason is to be accorded, they merely 'chill the warmth of untramelled and disinterested minds'; they 'fasten impudence by precept upon honest natures'; in a word, they foster worldliness, in the name of 'advantage, expedience, and necessity' – the mercantile values purveyed by Newbery and his ilk. In the name of reason and usefulness, they 'plunge themselves and others into selfish sordid habits and opinions, in order to avoid the folly or the inconvenience of those which are selfish or imaginary: they put away airy pleasures and speculations, to addict themselves to actual grossness'. But, the reader may feel impelled to interpose, the fact that young people lapse into a cynical or calculating materialistic worldliness is surely not a sufficient or necessary reason for allowing them to continue to 'live' in a fictive world of romantic visions and delusions?

Pott anticipates this objection: 'But can we continue the dreams of fancy to the ends of our lives?' And his answer is perfectly unswerving: 'No more than we can the games and amusements of children'. The world, the 'real' world, calls us to do its work, and 'we must learn to harden ourselves against the true climate in which we are to live' for 'the land of experience will pluck away our soft and glittering robes; the sun will vanish from our landcape; the leaves will drop from our shrubs'.

What then is left to us of that ideal world, that paradisal garden, that golden age? 'Some traces of delight from those fantastic images of youth, remain for recollection; we acknowledge them as true sources of pleasure, but we cannot recur to them.'[12] No regression, no backsliding, is possible for the mature mind: it must abandon the pleasure-principle, and accept the demands and constraints of adult reality and the requisite exercise of reason: 'Reason compounds her judgments of different materials' – different from the 'fantastic images', the 'dreams of fancy', the 'childish or imaginary' notions. The rule of reason forces us to recognize that 'whatever is unnatural cannot please or edify' the rational mind. 'It cannot please, because the sober mind can only be interested by truth', and it cannot 'edify, because so little of it can apply to ourselves or others'. Romance simply fails to fit the exigencies, the constraints of adult, public life.

But even when this is conceded, even when the reality-principle is allowed its due demands, it has to be admitted that the principle is enforced or 'applied by selfish and worldly men' and therefore 'does *not* improve the mind'. On the contrary, it rather 'injures and contracts it'.

How then does this perversion, this perversely distorted realization, of a legitimate principle of growth come about? How is it that a positive ideal of intellectual and emotional emancipation is, in its outcome, a negative deprivation and depravation? Pott contends that the process is characterized by a form of reductive and selfish cynicism: 'the ridicule thrown upon false pleasures and ideal amusements leads the way to real sensuality' – gratifications of the senses to the exclusion of the mind and spirit – and the fear of being deluded or imposed on 'first abates the warmth of true benevolence, and, at last, excuses churlishness and avarice'. What, then, are the fruits of worldly men's 'boasted experience . . . sagacity, and emancipation'? They are nothing more than 'suspicious hearts, narrow minds, gross ideas instead of fanciful ones, real errors, genuine arrogance, and substantial ambition': in sum, a pusillanimous kind of materialism.

Practical men, versed in the ways of the world and determined to succeed in the world of hard-headed realities, will 'deride all eminent degrees of virtue as romantic and impracticable'. If, then, you speak to them of 'tenderness, of charity, and zeal, they will demonstrate to you how unfit they [i.e. these virtues] are for the purposes of life'.

At this point, Pott pushes his case further, and offers his most important paradox: we accept that the 'juvenile and silly inexperience of a warm imagination' is indeed well suplanted by the contrary attachments of 'real life': but what if 'the real, the substantial, and immediate fruition' of the exercise of pragmatic sense is, in the event, more of an illusion, a fantasy, a notion, than the fancy that we have discarded? What if this material fruition 'hurts us more; is more a shadow; more a dream; and has an issue infinitely worse, a sum of covenanted ills, of woes'? What then? Certainly, there will be 'little scope remaining for complacency, and still less expectation of better habits to succeed'.

For almost a century, the conventional wisdom had argued, both on moral and evolutionary grounds, that such a development – from fancy to reason, from illusion to reality, from romance to business – was the path of wisdom and good sense. But what, in effect, did it amount to? Pott sees it as 'a shift only from the pleasures and chimeras of imagination to the pursuits of appetite', whereby 'keen desires' and 'real nakedness' replace the 'sports and masquerade of fancy'. And such a change is hardly flattering: on the contrary, it is a matter 'rather of disgrace than gratulation, that we are subject, in our chosen pleasures, to the rule and caprice of present things; the fund and objects of the senses'.

By this stage in his argument it is possible for Pott to offer his legitimation of fantasy. Consider again the young person's inclination to follow 'imaginary pursuits', 'wild and empty notions'. Such a temper of mind will be more open to receive 'what is truly excellent' and more easily 'converted into right and lively impressions of what is really desirable and eminent' than will the mind which is 'well-compacted . . . confirmed by solid enjoyment . . . by the real fruits of worldly prudence, of temporal acquisitions, temporal gratifications, or temporal distinctions'. For the tendency of youthful fantasy is toward a spiritual ideal: the 'wild conceits and speculations of the young disclose a taste for some superior kinds of pleasure, which is supported by the fancy before it finds a truer foundation'. There is, therefore, a close bond of affinity between a susceptibility to the blandishments and beguilings of romance on the one hand and a sensitivity to the spiritual and transcendent ideals of religion on the other.

The task of education is to 'lift the heart, and raise the front of man' to perceive and cherish ideals above and beyond the 'dead and worthless prizes' of worldly success, above and beyond the fluctuations and 'shifting hues of all things' that constitute our material world. The task then is to 'furnish scenes analogous to those which fancy trod before' but with this difference: that the scenes be 'opened to the steadfast eyes of reason and of hope, revealed to calm and salutary speculation, and ensured in their reversion', and to trace out prospects 'far more ravishing than all the pages of romance could feign' – prospects 'neither inaccessible nor visionary, but properly and truly such as may concern and interest us, and may be our inheritance and our portion'. As for our uniquely human talents, the 'purest faculties, the noblest energies of intellect, the powers and compass of the soul', our task is to keep these 'exalted and ascendant, elevated high above the transient and embarrassed scene of temporal vicissitudes and exigencies'.

Ten years later, Anna Barbauld was to write:

> each mind
> Of finer mould, acute and delicate,
> In its high progress to eternal truth
> Rests for a space, in fairy bowers entranced.[13]

And Coleridge offered this image of the child's growing consciousness:

> Fancy is the power
> That first unsensualises the dark mind,
> Giving it new delights; and bids it swell
> With wild activity; and peopling air,
> By obscure fears of Beings invisible,
> Emancipates it from the grosser thrall
> Of the present impulse, teaching Self-control,
> Till Superstition with unconscious hand
> Seat Reason on her throne.[14]

Pott's achievement was to frame his defence of fancy, which has a great deal in common with both Anna Barbauld and Coleridge, in the context of a larger cultural critique. He knew the City of London well, and his diagnosis of the spiritual atrophy and philistinism that may dog the footsteps of those who commit their energies to the pursuit of wealth is a fitting comment on a century that saw the centre of real power shift

from the court to the City. His essay also provides a perfectly
level-headed answer to the questions of such as the Sceptic in
Wordsworth's *Excursion* (ll. 768–9):

> Love, Hope, and Admiration – are they not
> Mad Fancy's favourite vassals?

And not the least of Pott's achievements is unwittingly to have
made the Wordsworth of *The Prelude* look less revolutionary,
less eccentric, less startling.[15]

3

When Sarah Kirby[16] married, and took her husband's
name, Trimmer, she misled the world, for there was never
anyone less capable of trimming. Sydney Smith, in a celebrated essay for the *Edinburgh Review*, in 1806,[17] characterized her as

> a lady who has gained considerable reputation at the
> corner of St Paul's Churchyard; who flames in the van of
> Mr Newberry's [*sic*] shop; and is, upon the whole, dearer
> to mothers and to aunts than any other author who pours
> the milk of science into the mouths of babes and
> sucklings.

She struck him as 'a lady of respectable opinions, and very
ordinary talents; defending what is right without judgment,
and believing what is holy without charity'. Smith also hit her
off, judiciously, when they quarrelled over the respective
claims of Bell and Lancaster in pioneering cheap schooling;
but he erred on the side of charity. Of all the morally shrill
women active in the late eighteenth and early nineteenth
centuries, she was probably the shrillest. Unbalanced, fren-
etic, paranoid, she may have been, but no one could deny her
energy and perseverance in defending the souls of the children
of England from the assaults of the devil.

Samuel Johnson met her when she was a young girl of

fifteen, at the house of her father's friend, Sir Joshua Reynolds. Johnson and Reynolds were having an argument about *Paradise Lost*; Sarah resolved it, like a magician, by pulling a copy of the poem from her pocket. Johnson was duly impressed, and invited her to visit him next day: he then presented her with a copy of the *Rambler* – the Great Cham at his gravest and most grandiloquent. It perhaps served as a disastrous model in the development of her prose style, for she went on to out-circumlocute even Johnson.

By the time she came to write her *Fabulous Histories* in the 1780s, she had evolved a prose remarkable for its convoluted neo-classicisms, dangling periodicities, and prodigious periphrases. The sun makes its appearance as 'that bright luminary'; the sky is 'the arch of heaven'; the lark is 'the herald of the morn'; he does not sing, but 'modulates his delightful pipe'; the nightingale offers not bird-song, but 'an enchanting lay': the inflationary prose-equivalent of Young's more pretentious verse. *The History of the Robins*[18] – the title by which her *Fabulous Histories* came to be known – is based on the good idea, derived perhaps from *Gulliver's Travels*, of having a family of birds make observations on a human family, and vice versa. The result could be a fascinating interplay of perspectives – the reader perceiving familiar realities as if for the first time. But the effect is spoiled by the abominable prose and by interminable moralizings.

Mrs Benson, the mother – human counterpart of Mrs Redbreast – proses on in exactly the same way as the Reverend Mr Barlow, doling out cliché-ridden homilies at the drop of a feather. But perhaps something fresh is offered when the perspective shifts and we see the world through the eyes of the birds? Not at all: Mr and Mrs Redbreast also deliver frequent lectures on prudence and good sense. The effect is of a series of repetitious, cameo-like set-pieces, illustrating various forms of folly and vice; the virtuous submissiveness of Miss Harriet Benson is almost beyond enduring; and Mrs Trimmer betrays a rather dubious, even perverse, tendency to dwell on the more vividly painful details of cruelty to animals:

Some people will flay eels alive, then put them without their skins into a pail of cold water, and afterwards cut them in pieces, and throw them into a fryingpan of boiling fat, where sometimes every separate piece will writhe about in agony.

Or: 'the blackbird hopped too near the edge, and fell to the ground, where he was snapped up by a dog, and torn to pieces in an instant.'

Her pedestrian narrative acquires a spark of nervous energy only when the sadistic Master Jenkins in Chapter VI gives a richly savoured account of all his acts of cruelty to animals. Mrs Trimmer's quill becomes noticeably animated in recording this detailed catalogue of ingenious atrocities, and in the neat moral scheme of the story, the vile boy receives his just deserts when, like Thomas Day in real life, he is thrown by his horse, and killed on the spot. Throughout the story, it is clear that Mrs Trimmer's mind is never on mere story-telling: always her sights are set on higher things.

When a young bird, a Redstart, is blasted out of the sky by a skilled marksman, it falls bleeding to the ground, and as if in a melodramatic scene in a bad opera, it manages a death-bed cry of regret: 'Oh! my dear father, why did I not listen to your kind admonitions, which I now find, too late, were the dictates of tenderness!' And when ambulatory children pause to admire the ordered life of a beehive, Mrs Benson seizes the chance to deliver a lecture on bees and politics:

> There is something very wonderful in the strong attach-
> ment these little creatures have to their sovereign, and
> very instructive too. I wish our good king could see all his
> subjects as closely united in his interest! What say you,
> Frederick, would you fight for your king? . . . I beg you
> will remember what I now tell you as long as you live, that
> it is your duty to love your king, for he is to be considered
> as the father of his country.

This gives rise to a moment of unconscious humour when the

tiresome child points out that 'it is the Queen that the bees love', but Mrs Benson immediately steers the conversation into rational, dutiful, patriotic sense: 'Her Majesty is much honoured and beloved, but it is the King who is at the head of the nation.' And, of course, she cannot leave the beehive without reminding them of the 'pretty hymn' that they have learnt: Isaac Watt's 'How doth the little busy Bee/Improve each shining hour. . . .'

Mr Redbreast, lecturing his son, Robin, on the proper regulation of the passions, tells him that 'peace and tranquillity are the most valuable things you can possess', but Sarah Trimmer was not made to enjoy much of either. She bore twelve children, and became actively involved in the Sunday School movement and in establishing schools of industry. For eleven years she ran the *Family Magazine* (1778–89), which aimed to counteract the pernicious influence of immoral books; and, from 1802 to 1806, her even more determined and tight-lipped *Guardian of Education*. By 1802, she was both unresting and relentless in her campaign to expose and root out the forces of Anti-Christ; in her view, they were led by Voltaire, Frederick of Prussia, D'Alembert and Diderot, not to mention Rousseau. But as every witch-hunt in history has shown, once you start to look for witches, it is difficult to know where to draw the line. For Sarah Trimmer, no one was above suspicion, and no book, however ostensibly innocent, could escape her needle-eyed scrutiny. As for philosophers, she simply divided them into sheep and goats, i.e. Christians and Infidels.

Her introduction to volume I, no. 1,[19] of the *Guardian* strikes the characteristic hyperbolic note: 'There never has been a time since the creation of the world, when the important business of education was more an object of general concern in any civilized country, than it is at the present day in our own.' This all-embracing cosmic claim, however, pales into relative moderation when set against the conspiratorial world-view she offers when she gets into her stride:

young children to learn to read, for which purpose the words are divided into syllables, and the embellishment of prints is added. We rank it with interesting and innocent books, which is all that an author can aim at in publications for infants.

ART. VIII.—*Presents for good Girls.* Price 1s. Tabart. 1804.

We conceive this little book to have been the production of the same amusing pen as the preceding article. We agree with the writer in approving of *dolls* and other toys of what may be called a *domestic nature,* as exciting a taste for feminine employments.

ART. IX.—*Presents for good Boys; or, the Toy Shop.* Adorned with beautiful Engravings. Price 1s. Tabart. 1804.

WE have here a book of the same class as the last, but adapted to children of the other sex. The work is apparently of the same author. To these three articles no objection we think can be made but to the price of them. The expensiveness of children's books is a growing evil!

ART. X.—*The Comic Adventures of old Mother Hubbard and her Dog.* Price 6d. Harris. 1805.

THIS little book, the poetry of which is of ancient date, comes forth in this *edition* as we must call it, with uncommon attraction. In the first place it has the following engraved dedication :

" *To J. B. Esq. M. P. County of —— at whose suggestion, and at whose house* these notable sketches were designed, *this volume is with all suitable deference* dedicated by his humble servant,

S. M. C.''

We consider as a *jeu d'esprit,* the designs for the Prints in which Mrs. Hubbard and her Dog, are very respectably represented to the eye in every situation described by the

poetic

Many people, who for want of obervation and reading, are ignorant of what is going on in the world, will be apt to consider us in the light of alarmists, if we talk of a conspiracy against CHRISTIANITY and all SOCIAL ORDER, which is at this time carrying on in the world by various means; one of which is, endeavouring to infect the minds of the rising generation, through the medium of books of Education and Children's Books; but that such a conspiracy does actually exist has been proved by undeniable authority (as we shall shew in the course of our work). Admitting this to be the case, how anxious, how vigilant, should parents be to secure their children from the dangers that threaten them! This can only be done by impressing upon their hearts from their earliest infancy, the PRINCIPLES OF CHRISTIANITY; we shall therefore, in defiance of the censure of modern philosophers, venture to recommend the commencement of a CHRISTIAN EDUCATION from the very cradle, and shall endeavour to point out by what means it may be conducted, so as to prove, with the divine blessing, the most powerful antidote against the increasing corruption of the age.

Her puritanism, like that of Thomas Day, abhors the 'artificial refinements' of polite society, and she is keen to promote 'simplicity of manners'. But where Day learned his rationale for his peculiar severities from Rousseau, Mrs Trimmer sees Rousseau as not merely false, but as actively injurious:

The greatest injury the youth of this nation ever received, was from the introduction of Rousseau's system . . . which proposed to banish Christianity from the nursery and the school, to make room for a *false* Philosophy, which has no foundation in truth or reason. . . . In consequence . . . many individuals have grown up from childhood to maturity without any knowledge of religion; and have remained throughout life totally indifferent to the concerns of eternity, and professed infidels.

How then did the Edgeworths fare at Mrs Trimmer's hands? Were they 'professed infidels' or unprofessed, covert and therefore possibly even more dangerous? There had after all been no mention of religion, of Christianity, let alone Mrs Trimmer's evangelicalism, in the pages of *Practical Education*. Could such an omission be allowed to pass? She concedes that the book is a 'very ingenious composition', offering many valuable hints, but she insists that it would be inconsistent with 'the object of our present undertaking, to express ourselves satisfied with a book on Education from which RELIGION is totally excluded'. There is, indeed, a system of education which can meet all our needs, she avers, and it is founded 'upon the rock of ages'. It must be defended against 'innovation' because we 'know it to be agreeable to the will of GOD, that the members of the Church of Christ should be educated in the principles of the Christian Religion', i.e. the Church of England. 'Fanciful systems' devised by mere mortals will not answer, however clearly they may be 'enlightened by philosophical research, or distinguished by the brilliancy of their wit and the variety of their accomplishments'.

Edgeworth had stressed the *utility* of his methods, and had repeated almost *ad nauseam* that they aimed to diffuse *useful* knowledge. Very well, replies Mrs Trimmer, if it is utility you want, I will tell you where to find it:

> If Religion is to be considered as an essential part of Education, and real utility is to be consulted in respect to their other acquirements, there is nothing to study but what is already known; no hidden paths to explore: all that is necessary is, to follow an old and beaten track, which has conducted many of the human race to eminent distinction among their fellow mortals; and led multitudes, it is to be hoped, to eternal glory and happiness.

The Edgeworths, she argues, made far too much of science, which is a discipline which most people would never have occasion to use. Not only does their promotion of science drive out religion – the first need of 'a being created for eternity' – but scientific education is 'in these days carried so far, as to injure the bud of reason by premature expansion, instead of assisting its gradual growth by gentle culture': this metaphor is not only uncharacteristic in its stress on gentleness, but is also one of the recurring commonplaces of educational thought at this time, and one that the Edgeworths themselves had used with a wealth of specific detail in their advice on early reading.

Mrs Trimmer concedes that the Edgeworths' technique of teaching by conversation is sound, but insists that it is applicable to 'a higher purpose than that to which they apparently confine it – to the very highest; for RELIGION and VIRTUE may be as easily taught to children as Chemistry, Mechanics, etc.' What is one to make of such an assertion? Is it anything more than a rather crass equating of religious education and catechizing? Is Mrs Trimmer here displaying an incurable spiritual vulgarity? As Lionel Trilling remarked, 'It is beyond human ingenuity to define what we mean by vulgarity, but . . . it has these elements: smallness of mind, insufficiency of awareness, assertive self-esteem, and the wish to devalue, especially to devalue the human worth of other people.'[20] Mrs Trimmer qualifies on all four counts: both 'smallness of mind' and 'insufficiency of awareness' are displayed in her attitude to the claims of the imagination. Here she achieves a severe narrowness and dismissiveness akin to that of the puritans of the seventeenth century, and following 'an old and beaten track' she digs up the noxious weeds of fantasy and even makes public confession of contrition over her own earlier permissiveness or tolerance.

In a survey of eighteenth-century children's books, she recalls her own childhood pleasure in Perrault, 'Esop' (sic), Gay's Fables and Sarah Fielding's The Governess. She deplores the recent growth of circulating libraries, which have allowed novels to reach the eyes of young people, and concludes with an unexceptionable judgement. The children's books of her early years, she thought, were in general of 'a very harmless nature'. But she does enter the reservation that they were 'mostly calculated to entertain the imagination, rather than to improve the heart, or cultivate the understanding'. In an unguarded moment of weak and irrational nostalgia, she recalls her juvenile delight in fairy-tales, but these now fall under her newly sharpened axe, for they are 'only fit to fill the heads of children with confused notions of wonderful and supernatural events, brought about by the agency of imaginary beings'. In Pott's terms, Mrs Trimmer emerges, ironically, as a sensualist. *The Governess* must be discarded, for it is in some ways 'very exceptionable' – not because its fairy-tales are tedious, factitious and feeble, but simply because they *are* fairy-tales.[21] As for *Robinson Crusoe*, established by now as a children's favourite, and spawning innumerable imitations, it is to be kept out of children's hands on the grounds that it will promote 'an early taste for a rambling life, and a desire of adventures',[22] when our first duty is to keep to the place and station to which God and his mysterious Providence have seen fit to call us. Clearly, what Mrs Trimmer wanted, at a time of social and political perturbations, was a theocentric conservatism, a firm stability.

When she comes to review Lucy Aikin's *Poetry for Children* (1801), she is pleased to notice that

> in a Dialogue, with which this instructive volume closes, the principles of the new school, as it is called, are weighed against those of Christianity, by their probable effects on the lives of mankind; and by the comforts they respectively offer in the closing scene of moral existence.

It is hardly surprising that Mrs Trimmer should have reserved her approval for *Poetry for Children*, for Lucy Aikin conceives of poetry in almost exclusively moral and didactic terms: it calms the passions, 'enforces sentiments of piety, humanity and tenderness', soothes the soul to tranquillity, rouses it to 'honourable exertion', and fires it with 'virtuous indignation'. Conversely, 'dragons and fairies, giants and witches', which have happily 'vanished from our nurseries before the wand of reason', are pernicious, for they excite 'a wild and exalted fancy'; as for the 'novel-like tales now written for the amusement of youth', they are even worse, for their 'romantic sensibilty' gives a 'false picture of the real world'. One can see Mrs Trimmer nodding her approval of such immaculate opinions.

In common with both Sarah Trimmer and Lucy Aikin, Maria Hack and the anonymous author of *Buds of Genius* are both to be found casting a shuddering backward glance over their shoulders at the unredeemed state of children's books before the brooms of reason and high moral tone had swept out all the fanciful rubbish. Maria Hack stands for the 'realities of life' and expresses the characteristic evangelical view that fiction can enfeeble the character, even that of Samuel Johnson:

> How far the supernatural tales that delighted his infant ear, had a tendency to check the progress of his vigorous mind, by shading it with the gloom of superstition, this is not the place to enquire. Stories of giants and castles do not accord with the taste of the present day; but surely there is much truth and good sense in the remark of the learned doctor, that children like to be told 'of somewhat which can stretch and stimulate their little minds' – something which may open a wider and more elevated range of thought, than can possibly be afforded by the best-written stories for children. Some of these are admirable in their kind; but perhaps it may be doubted whether habituating children to seek amusement, almost exclusively, in fictitious narrative, has not a direct tendency to weaken the mental powers. These tales are the novels of childhood; and it is much to be feared that an

unlimited perusal of them will exhaust the sensibility, and produce the same listless indifference to the realities of life, observable in older persons who devote their time to this kind of reading. The dose is weaker; but let it be remembered, that it is proportioned to the age of the patient. . . .[23]

It is doubtless no coincidence that at this time books on child-rearing included a discreet section, usually in Latin, on the dangers of masturbation, which is essentially the bodily counterpart of an indulgence in fiction, and leads to the same end – apathy, enfeeblement and moral depravity. And both are 'unnatural'.

Buds of Genius[24] – a collection of exemplary lives and the childhoods of great men – knows exactly where it stands in this matter:

> The reign of unnatural fiction is past; truth is not now deemed incompatible with amusement; the imagination of children is no longer powerfully excited at the expense of the understanding and the heart. To blend entertainment with instruction, has been a principal design in the execution of this little work.

Here is a typical dialogue from *Buds*: the subject is the famous blue-stocking, Hester Chapone, who, like Mrs Trimmer and Hannah More, learned and confessed the errors of her earlier unredeemed ways:

> *Mamma:* It is to be regretted that her young mind was so impressed and delighted with works of fiction.
> *Henry:* Such as novels and romances, I suppose. I wonder such reading could afford her pleasure, for you have often told us that it is very injurious; and, indeed, if a book were given to me that I knew to be untrue, I believe I should feel no interest in it.
> *Louisa:* I am quite of the same opinion; for I always like to read accounts that *really did happen.*

Mamma: Romances appear to have been the favourite
reading of females at that period; and it is not to be
wondered at, that this young lady, influenced by the
example of those around her, should have read, with
avidity, works so alluring in their composition, though
so little instructive in their tendency. The children of
the present day have great advantages: there are now so
many interesting and valuable juvenile publications,
that they need never be at a loss to spend a leisure hour
improvingly; but in the beginning of the last century, it
was not so much the aim of authors to imbue the minds
of the young with just sentiments, as to amuse them
with marvellous and ridiculous stories; and the histories of Tom Thumb, and Jack the Giant-killer, and
Mother Bunch's Fairy Tales, were the favourite books
of children. . . . At nine years of age, she herself
composed a romance . . . her good understanding did
not suffer to be long seduced by the absurdities of
works of fancy. She soon turned with disgust from
these unprofitable pursuits, and eagerly sought every
opportunity of cultivating and improving her
mind. . . .[25]

Such opposing distinctions between the life of the imagination and the regulated discipline of heart and mind are
perfectly characteristic of the late eighteenth century's moral
psychology: they were conceived of as separate faculties by the
orthodox wisdom of the time; therefore they were felt to be
separate; as Wordsworth observed:

> we create distinctions, then
> Deem that our puny boundaries are things
> Which we perceive, and not which we have made.[26]

It is on this issue that Mrs Trimmer's position – the morality
of her psychology, so to speak, and the psychology of her
morality – is seen at its worst. The occasion is her review of

William Scolfield's *Bible Stories* (1802).[27] Like many another writer for children, Scolfield was provoked into authorship by his dissatisfaction with the books currently in fashion: of those published between 1780 and 1800, he found not one 'which he could with complete satisfaction put into the hands of his own children'.

What, then, was so very wrong with them?

> There is a style now in fashion, which more or less infects every book for children . . . stamped with the ultimate refinements of a high civilization, and full of abstract terms and universal propositions. Why should we debauch the taste of our children by presenting this as the first object of their attention and admiration?

Not only are these books excessively abstract in their level of discourse, but they are crammed with an unattractive moralizing: he finds them

> much more encumbered with abstract and general propositions. The meanest narratives formerly written for the use of children, had at least the merit of going straight forward, and of stating in every sentence some fact to keep alive attention; or some picture to engage *imagination*. They did not stop at every turn to moralize in language which no child's understanding can comprehend, and no child's temper relish.

Outside Wordsworth, Scolfield offers the most coherent and radical critique of 'moral' literature, much more so than either Coleridge or Lamb. He puts his finger precisely on an essential paradox: that the old vulgar romances, for all their extravagant fantasizing, had created credible, authentic human characters whose trials, tribulations and successes aroused and powerfully engaged the 'sympathetic imagination'.

> The old books described the real temper and passions of human beings. Their scenes were supernatural and

impossible, but their personages were of our own species. The modern books, on the other hand, abound in real scenes, but impossible personages. They would not for the world astonish the child's mind with a giant, a dragon, or a fairy; but their young people are all so good, and their old people so sober, so demure, so rational, that no genuine interest can be felt for their adventures. No two things can be more unlike than the real inhabitants of the world, and these wonderful personages; their proceedings are destitute of the firmness and vigour of a healthy mind, and their records are artificial, repulsive and insipid.

There is the central contradiction: that the didactic realists, committed to the fabrication of an ostensibly 'real world', had actually produced an anaemic figment, for which one could feel absolutely no genuine heart-felt interest, whereas the chap-books had generated a vivid and compelling sense of human reality. How, then, had the new writers, so strenuously committed to a no-nonsense actuality, to public and sensible realities, failed so lamentably to represent them in ways that would arouse 'genuine interest'? In a word, their failure was a failure of imagination:

The modern improvers have left out of their system that most essential branch of human nature, the imagination. Our youth, according to the most recent systems of education, will be excellent geographers, natural historians, and mechanics; they will tell you from what part of the globe you receive every article of your furniture, and will explain the process in manufacturing a carpet, converting metals into the utensils of life, and clay into the cups of your tea-table, and the ornaments of your chimney; in a word, they are exactly informed about all those things, which, if a man or woman were to live and die without knowing, neither man or woman would be an atom the worse.

The charge, then, is a charge against the Aikin of *Evenings at Home*, and against the Edgeworth of *Harry and Lucy*; not to mention the prosy informations of Mr Barlow and Mrs Benson. And it is a Wordsworthian charge, virtually identical with that of *The Prelude*, book V. Scholfield's final counter-blast is also distinctly Wordsworthian:

> Every thing is studied and attended to, except those things which open the heart, which insensibly initiate the learner, in the relations and generous offices of society and enable him to put himself in imagination in the place of his neighbour, to feel his feelings, and to wish his wishes.

The failure of late eighteenth-century didacticism lay in its infatuation with a pseudo-fiction which had relentless a priori designs on its young readers' heads and hearts. The story was not to be told for its own sake. 'What is the best way of telling a story?' George Eliot was to ask in her note-books.[28] For simple 'primitive' stories, she offered the compelling analogy of the Jack-in-the-box: 'The presence of the Jack in the box affects every child: it is the more reflective lad, the miniature philosopher, who wants to know how he got there.' The mistake of the didacts was many-sided: it was to consign Jack to the outer darkness of discarded superstitions; to insist on telling the child, even when it preferred not to know, how and why Jack got there in the first place, and how the mechanism of his body operated – the mechanical principles involved, and of how such principles were applied in 'useful' manufactories – thus dispelling all 'magic'; to impose a superstructure of adult moral interpretations on Jack, who would thus be transformed into a boring 'example'.

But George Eliot can be pressed into service to offer a more crucial gloss on this question of didactic failure: for, as Scolfield perceived, the failure was there in the nature of their very language – a language that would have earned the approval of the Royal Society or of any respectable empiricist or utilitarian; a language cleansed of resonances and purged of suggestiveness; a language without 'poetry' and free of any personal expressiveness. It was a perfectly serviceable language for science, technology, business or commerce, but for story-telling purposes, it was mere juiceless chaff: 'Suppose, then,' George Eliot wrote,

> Suppose that the effort which has been again and again made to construct a universal language on a rational basis has at length succeeded, and that you have a language which has no uncertainty, no whims of idiom, no cumbrous forms, no fitful shimmer of many-hued significance, no hoary archaisms . . . a patent deodorised and non-resonant lanuage, which effects the purpose of communication as perfectly and rapidly as algebraic signs.[29]

A perfect language for utilitarian purposes, and not unlike the ideal of Bentham; but she goes on:

> Your language may be a perfect medium of expression to science, but will never express *life*, which is a great deal more than science. With the anomalies and inconveniences of historical language, you will have parted with its music and its passion, with its vital qualities as an expression of individual character, with its subtle capabilities of wit, with everything that gives it power over the imagination.

Her conclusion is that 'the sensory and motor nerves that run in the same sheath, are scarcely bound together by a more necessary and delicate union than that which binds men's affections, imagination, wit, and humour, with the subtle ramifications of historical language'.

Scolfield's affirmation of the claims of the imagination proceeds in much the same way: a perfect language for science will be the language of a well-regulated machine, and the same is true of that limited range of mental operations that the associationist psychologists had laid bare. But, like 'poetry', as characterized by Wordsworth's *Essay* of 1815, Scolfield is 'passionate for the instruction of reason', and insists:

Imagination is the ground-plot upon which the edifice of a sound morality must be erected. Without imagination we may have a certain cold, arid, circle of principles, but we cannot have sentiments: we may learn by rote a catalogue of rules, and repeat our lesson with the exactness of a parrot, or play over our tricks with the docility of a monkey; but we can neither ourselves love, nor be fitted to excite the love of others.

Finally, Scolfield demonstrates that he already possesses insights that others had to wait to learn from Wordsworth: one is reminded especially of De Quincey's celebrated essay on the poetry of Pope:

Imagination is the characteristic of man. The dexterities of logic, or of mathematical deduction, belong rather to a well-regulated machine; they do not contain in them the living principle of nature. It is the heart which most deserves to be cultivated, not the rules which may serve us in the nature of a compass to steer us through the difficulties of life; but the pulses which beat with sympathy, and qualify us for the habits of charity, reverence, and attachment. The intellectual faculty in the mind of youth is fully intitled to the attention of parents and instructors; but parents and instructors will perform their office amiss, if they assign the first place to that which is only intitled to the second.

In 1823, Robert Fellowes, in a posthumous tribute to Vicesimus Knox, could look back and observe that 'those who lived, and lived to reason, between the years 1793 and 1803, must have felt that Mr Pitt's domination was almost as much a reign of terror, as that of Danton or Robespierre'.[30] It is entirely characteristic of that mean, repressive, pusillanimous, illiberal and reactionary decade that Mrs Trimmer's voice was more clearly heard than that of such as Scolfield. But it would be a nice piece of historical justice, and irony, if she were to be remembered as the critic who woefully failed to measure up to Scolfield, and who in so failing revealed her philistine, adamantine coarseness of spirit. She must, of course, be allowed the last word. Here is her response to Scolfield's defence of the imagination:

> That this is the language of modern philosophy we scarcely need observe, and we hope every parent who has not unfortunately imbibed its principles . . . will discern the folly, as well as wickedness, of leaving children to form their own principles, and regulate their own manners, without lesson or rule, as the wild flights of an unbridled imagination shall direct; instead of teaching them the *lessons* given to mankind by DIVINE WISDOM, and the *Rules* prescribed by DIVINE AUTHORITY − for *bringing every thought into captivity to the obedience of* CHRIST. . . . How the heart is to be cultivated by the force of *imagination* only, is to us inconceivable? [*sic*] − We are told by GOD himself, that *the imagination of the heart of man is evil from his youth*, and we are persuaded that this will be fully exemplified in those who have been accustomed in their earliest days to be led by it.

There are none so deaf as those who will not hear.

NOTES AND REFERENCES

1 Lawrence Stone, *The Family, Sex and Marriage in England, 1500–1800* (Harmondsworth: Penguin Books, 1979), p. 176.
2 ibid.
3 See Maurice Morgann, *Shakespearean Criticism*, ed. D.A. Fineman (Oxford: Clarendon Press, 1972).
4 'admiration': for Ruskin this was one of the key Wordsworthian values.
5 Johann Gottfried Herder in 1772 argued that neither Hurd nor Johnson had evolved an aesthetic capable of giving an adequate account of Shakespeare. See his 'Shakespeare' in *Von der Urpoesie der Völker* (Stuttgart: Reclam, 1972).
6 See below, p. 262
7 22 January 1751.
8 16 February 1751.
9 In *Olla Podrida*, no. 24 (25 August 1787).

10 *Letters on the Improvement of the Mind*, new edn (1793), p. 193.
11 Cf. Wordsworth, *The Prelude*, bk V, ll. 516–19, where he characterizes the great tellers of tales as being guided by 'a gracious spirit' and who, in their telling, 'care not, know not, think not what they do'.
12 Cf. John Clare, above, p. 61.
13 'Mrs Barbauld to Mr Coleridge' (September 1797), Bristol Public Library, ms B21076.
14 'The Destiny of Nations', ll. 80–8.
15 When George MacDonald published his essay 'The Imagination: Its Functions and its Culture' a century later, his argument bore a strong resemblance to that of Potts; with this difference: that his language was distinctly Wordsworthian. See *A Dish of Orts* (London: Sampson Low & Marston, 1893).
16 Sarah Trimmer, née Kirby, 1741–1810.
17 Sydney Smith found Mrs Trimmer almost as absurd as he found the Methodists, and for similar reasons: see 'Methodism', *Edinburgh Review* (1808), and 'Trimmer and Lancaster', ibid. (1806).
18 First published in 1786, and subsequently one of the most frequently reprinted books of the next hundred years.
19 Published June 1802; see n. 35, p. 112.
20 *The Opposing Self* (London: Secker & Warburg, 1955).
21 Mrs Sherwood later revised *The Governess*, compounding its austerities by omitting the fairy-tales.
22 When the German naturalist and traveller Von Humboldt first stood at the mouth of the Orinoco, he exclaimed, 'Ever since I read *Robinson Crusoe*, it has been my wish to stand here'.
23 Preface to *Winter Evenings; or, Tales of Travellers*, 4 vols (London: Darton, Harvey & Darton, 1818–20).
24 *Buds of Genius; or, Some Account of the Early Lives of Celebrated Characters who were Remarkable in their Childhood. Intended as an Introduction to Biography* (London: Darton, Harvey & Darton, 1816). Despite the rearguard action of such men as Thomas Day, by 1816 the fact of women as writers was firmly established. But what Hazlitt remarked of Joanna Baillie was also true of virtually all women then writing for children: 'her comedy appears to me the perfection of baby-house theatricals. Everything in it has such a do-me-good air, is so insipid. . . . Virtue seems such a pretty playing at make-believe, and vice is such a naughty word' ('On the living poets').
25 *Buds of Genius*, p. 126.
26 *The Prelude*, bk II, ll. 222–4.
27 *Bible Stories, memorable Acts of Ancient Patriarchs, Judges and*

Kings, extracted from their original Historians for the Use of Children by William Scolfield, 2 vols (London: Philips, 1802).

28 'Leaves from a Note-Book', in *Essays*, ed. T. Pinney (London: Routledge & Kegan Paul, 1963), p.437.

29 'The Natural History of German Life', ibid., p.287.

30 Preface to *Winter Evenings: or, Lucubrations on Life and Letters*, 3 vols (London: Charles Dilly, 1788), vol.1.

CHAPTER SEVEN

APOTHEOSIS OF THE CHAP-BOOK

Infancy, fearless, lustful, happy! nestling for
delight
In laps of pleasure. . . .
(William Blake, *Visions of the Daughters of
Albion*, 1793)

1

'I wish I had been born in the Moon,' sighed Tristram
Shandy, in Sterne's novel; and he then offered to dedicate part
of the book, of which he himself was part, in exchange for fifty
guineas, to any nobleman who was in need of a 'tight, genteel
dedication'. The remainder of the book was to be dedicated to
the Moon, 'who . . . has most power to set my book a-going,
and make the world run mad after it.'[1]

Twenty-five years later, in late 1784, William Blake, then
twenty-seven, did indeed 'run mad after it'. Taking hints
from Sterne and Rabelais, he wrote his delectable burlesque,
An Island in the Moon.[2] It is a cunning little drama, packed
with ostensibly inconsequential, seemingly innocent, fun and
nonsense, but cannily contrived to tiptoe neatly across various
serious matters then close to Blake's own concerns.

In 1781, Mrs Barbauld had published her *Hymns in Prose
for Children*; this was, as I hope to show, a crucial text in
Blake's own development. But for the moment let us merely
note that in Hymn XI she posed some earnest cosmic
questions: looking at the planets and the stars, she asked,

> Who can tell the birth and generations of so many
> worlds? Who can relate their histories? Who can describe
> their inhabitants?
> Canst thou measure infinity with a line? Canst thou
> grasp the circle of infinite space?
> Yet all these depend upon God, they hang upon Him as
> a child upon the breast of its mother; He tempereth the
> heat to the inhabitant of Mercury; He provideth re-
> sources against the cold in the frozen orb of Saturn . . .

– a workmanlike pastiche of the *Book of Job*, with variations on
the theme of Divine Providence, stressing the exotic *otherness*
of those far-off other worlds, so as to point up the Deity's
ubiquitous resourcefulness.

In *An Island in the Moon*, Blake took the opposite tack;
Chapter One begins: 'In the Moon is a certain Island . . .
which . . . seems to have some affinity to England, & what is
even more extraordinary the people are so much alike & their
language so much the same that you would think you was
among your friends.' Blake's tone is as reassuring as a trim
booby-trap: his story-drama opens with three Philosophers,
sitting together, 'thinking of nothing' – Suction, the Epicurean; Quid, the Cynic (identified as Blake himself); and
Sipsop, the Pythagorean. Etruscan Column, the Antiquarian
– his name itself a glancing reference to the cult of neo-
classicism in such circles – enters and, being a good didactic,
he 'described something that nobody listend to'. He is
followed by Mrs Gimblet, who *seems* to listen carefully while
Etruscan Column 'seemd to be talking of virtuous cats' – a
popular topic in the moral fables of the time. But the word
'seemd' should have alerted us: in fact, Mrs Gimblet 'was
thinking of the shape of her eyes & mouth' and the distinguished antiquarian was 'thinking of his eternal fame'.

As the three philosophers continue to sit, each laughing at
his own imaginings, Inflammable Gass, the Wind-finder,
enters; or, to give him his proper name, Joseph Priestley,
philosopher, theologian, electrician, chemist, unitarian min-

ister and polymathic member of the Lunar Society. His *Disquisitions Relating to Matter and Spirit* were published in 1777, a second enlarged edition following in 1782, by the radical bookseller, Joseph Johnson, for whom Blake worked as an engraver. Column tells Gass of a 'little outrè fellow' who, on seeing a flock of swallows, had asked him who they all belonged to. Column had called him a fool for asking such a silly question, but Gass solemnly insists that the man was quite properly 'desirous of enquiring into the works of nature', and therefore, as an experimental philosopher, deserved a courteous answer.

Obtuse Angle, the mathematician, enters, and wants to know what exactly is going on. Sipsop's answer is that they are 'endeavoring to incorporate their souls with their bodies', a trim reference to Priestley's *Disquisitions*. The conversation turns to consider the merits or otherwise of Voltaire, and when Column says that he 'was immersed in matter & seems to have understood very little but what he saw before his eyes', Gass – a good associationist and popularizer of Hartleyan psychology – retorts that 'he was the Glory of France – I have got a bottle of air that would spread a Plague'. Priestley's *Experiments and Observations on different kinds of Air* had appeared in 1774:[3] Gass's claim to possess a bottle of air that 'would spread a Plague', following hard on Voltaire's heels, is a neat case of collocation, for orthodox English opinion saw Votaire's views as a moral plague. It was indeed to counteract the spread of such a plague that Priestley's house in Birmingham was to be attacked and burnt by the Church and King mob, the authorities turning a blind eye, only seven years later.

Chapter Two enlarges the cast of Blake's farce: the entire chapter consists of:

> Tilly Lally, the Siptippidist, Aradobo, the dean of Morocco, Miss Gittipin, Mrs Nannicantipot, Mrs Sistagatist, Gibble Gabble the wife of Inflammable Gass – & Little Scopprell enter'd the room.

(If I have not presented you with every character in the piece, call me Ass.)

In Chapter Three, which is slightly longer, Aradobo appears as a pedagogue's vision of the dutifully enquiring child: his role is to feed questions, as in the didactic dialogues of children's books, to whoever is likely to have Useful Knowledge to dispense; Obtuse Angle for example, tells him that Phoebus was 'the God of Physic, Painting Perspective geometry Geography Astronomy, Cookery Chymistry Mechanics, Tactics Pathology Phraseology Theology Mythology Astrology Osteology, Somatology . . .', a fair parody of the age's mania for polymathy; Angle also delivers a characteristically pedagogical rebuke – 'you should always think before you speak' – and poor Aradobo ends the chapter duly chastened: 'Here Aradobo sucked his under lip.'

Chapter Four involves the company in a discussion of profanity and religious orthodoxy. With unwittingly prescient irony, Blake has Gass admit that, 'If I had not a place of profit that forces me to go to church . . . Id see the parsons all hangd; a parcel of lying –.' Mrs Sistagatist recalls her own girlhood church-going with odd relish, and the chapter ends with a sprightly Shandyesque trick: 'Then Mr Inflammable Gass ran & shovd his head into the fire & set his hair all in a flame & ran about the room – No no he did not, I was only making a fool of you' [i.e. the reader].

In Chapter Five, poor Aradobo continues to ask his dutiful infantine questions, but only succeeds in getting into deeper water for his pains:

> 'Pray . . . is Chatterton a Mathematician?' 'No' said Obtuse Angle 'how can you be so foolish as to think he was?' 'Oh I did not think he was; I only askd . . .' 'How could you think he was not, & ask if he was?' 'Oh no Sir I did think he was before you told me but afterwards I thought he was not.' '. . . in the first place you thought he was & then afterwards when I said he was not you thought he was not! Why I know that –' 'Oh no sir I

thought that he was not but I asked to know whether he
was. −'

Everyone who can recall a smart teacher from their early years
will recognize the truth of that encounter, which peels away all
the layers of cant that overlay the dialogues in most children's
books of the time. When the three philosophers return, and
'lowring darkness hoverd oer the assembly', Aradobo decides
to show off the useful knowledge that he has acquired: his
performance is a delightful parody of an infantine display of
knowledge:

> In the first place I think I think in the first place that
> Chatterton was clever at Fissic Follogy, Pistinology,
> Aridology, Arography, Transmography Phizography
> Hagamy Hatomy, & hall that but in the first place he eat
> wery little wickly that is he slept very little which he
> brought into a consumsion, & what was that that he took
> Fisic or somethink & so died.[4]

Sipsop is nevertheless − or therefore − optimistic about
Aradobo's mental development, and so is Quid, who, in the
next chapter, dismisses Plutarch as 'a nasty ignorant puppy
. . . theres Aradobo in ten or twelve years will be a far superior
genius'. Sipsop agrees: 'Aradabo will make a very clever
fellow'. Indeed, Quid continues, 'I think that any natural fool
would make a clever fellow if he was properly brought up' − a
case of Locke being stretched to absurd extremes. Suction
will have none of this: 'Ah hang your reasoning . . . I hate
reasoning. I do everything by my feelings.' Thus the man of
feeling is also allowed to make his voice heard in the midst of
all the pother about the proper formation of the mind!

There follows a satire on surgery as an experimental science
− no one is safe − and Hunter, the distinguished surgeon,
enters, as Jack Tearguts. As for benevolence of motive, or
utility, in such a calling, Sipsop confesses cheerfully: 'When I
think of Surgery − I dont know, I do it because I like it. My
father does what he likes & so do I.' Nothing, it seems, is safe
from Blake's light-hearted iconoclasm!

Suction's defence of feeling, or 'sensibility', continues throughout Chapter Seven, and he cries out 'Hang Philosophy . . . do all by your feelings and never think at all about it.' Chapter Eight finds the artist, Flaxman, disguised as Steelyard the Lawgiver, gloomily taking extracts from Hervey's *Meditations among the Tombs* and Young's *Night Thoughts*, and hoping that he will live to see 'The wreck of matter & the crush of worlds', a forerunner of Lady Delancour's observation, in Maria Edgeworth's *Belinda*: 'Here she is – what doing I know not – studying Hervey's Meditation on the Tombs, I should guess, by the sanctification of her looks.'[5]

Scopprell, nosing about, misreads 'An Easy of Huming Understanding by John Lookye Gent' and much singing ensues, though 'felicity does not last long'. In Chapter Ten we are offered a hilarious scene of confusion that reads like a farcical parody of Joseph Wright's 'Experiment on a Bird in the Air Pump' of 1769: experimental philosophy domesticated with a vengeance!

> 'Come Flammable,' said Gibble Gabble, '& lets enjoy ourselves; bring the Puppets.' 'Hay Hay!' said he, 'you sho. why ya ya. *H*ow can you be so foolish – Ha Ha Ha she calls the experiments puppets!' Then he went up stairs & loaded the maid with glasses, & brass tubes, and magic pictures. . . .
> While Tilly Lally & Scopprell were pumping at the air pump Smack went the glass – 'Hang!' said Tilly Lally. Inflammable Gass turnd short round & threw down the table & Glasses & Pictures & broke the bottles of wind & let out the Pestilence. He saw the Pestilence fly out of the bottle & cried out while he ran out of the room, 'come out come out we are putrified, we are corrupted, our lungs are destroyd with the Flogiston this will spread a plague all thro the Island.' *He* was down the stairs the very first; on the back of him came all the others in a heap.
> So they need not bidding go.

The Edgeworths, Mrs Marcet and Jeremiah Joyce, in their popularization of scientific enquiry, never let it be known that it could be so perilously hilarious, so humanly fallible, so very comical. The remainder of the surviving text, which was never published during Blake's lifetime, is mostly devoted to lively sessions of singing. Among the songs performed are nursery-rhymes, Newbery-style ABCs, and three of Blake's own songs that we know better in the context of *Songs of Innocence* (1789). It would be contrary to the spirit of *An Island* to read it solemnly, but there is, nevertheless, much point in Blake's burlesque. He was keenly attentive to the intellectual and pedagogical currents of radical, dissenting and scientific thought that flowed – sometimes it must have been a torrent – through Joseph Johnson's shop, which was as much a talk-shop as a book-shop.[6] Implicit in all the farce, nonsense and Shandysim is a clear view of the influence and fashions to which the late eighteenth century mind was exposed: mechanistic notions of consciousness, a utilitarian view of what was worth knowing, a fashion for moralizing cant, the spread of an infantine proto-science, a largely prudential moral ortho-doxy, the enthusiasm of the Man of the Feeling, the encyclo-paedic aspirations of dutiful children – all are poured into Blake's topsy-turvy lunar world, and given a good shaking.

2

Towards the end of *An Island*, Tilly Lally sings a song of execrable doggerel, a banal parody of a moral tale in verse:

> O I say you Joe,
> Throw us the ball.
> Ive a good mind to go
> And leave you all.[7]

If such fustian can be said to hit off the miserable doggerel that passed for verse in such books as Newbery's, did *Songs of Innocence* spring fully formed from Blake's idiosyncratic genius? Did they in any way follow precedent? What, if any, were Blake's precedents? Isaac Watts, assuredly. Blake's 'Cradle Song' – 'Sweet dreams form a shade' – clearly owed something to Watts's 'Cradle Hymn', one of the few almost tender hymns from his pen; 'A Dream' – 'Once a dream did weave a shade' – owed something to Watts's 'The Ant, or Emmet', as well as to the traditional nursery rhyme, 'Ladybird, ladybird, fly away home'; and one of Watts's *Horae Lyricae* poems lies behind Blake's 'Little Black Boy'.

Two closer influences are to be found in eighteenth-century hymns, as John Holloway has shown,[8] and in Mrs Barbauld's *Hymns in Prose for Children* of 1781. Dr Johnson observed that, for children, Watts 'condescended to lay aside the scholar, the philosopher, the wit, to write little poems of devotion'.[9] In general, though, Johnson would have been grateful for 'a greater measure of sprightliness and vigour' – a nice understatement. Mrs Barbauld echoed Johnson's words: 'The author is deservedly honoured for the condescension of his Muse, which was very able to take a loftier flight.' Then she straightway entered a reservation: 'It may well be doubted whether poetry ought to be lowered to the capacities of children.' Poetry should be kept from them, she argued, until they are capable of relishing 'good verse': nursery rhymes, or folk-songs, are implicitly, *not* good verse, for 'the very essence of poetry is an elevation in thought and style above the common standard'. For such reasons, she decided to write her hymns in prose! They were written, moreover, to be committed to memory, and recited: she had a much less ironic view of children's memorizings than Blake had. Her larger, or higher, aim was to 'impress devotional feelings as early as possible on the infant mind' – the verb is Locke's, but the sentiment could embrace both deism and evangelicalism: hence, the extraordinary success of Mrs Barbauld's volume. 'They cannot be impressed too soon . . . a child ought never to remember the time when he had no such idea.' And such ideas are to be firmly impressed 'by connecting religion with a variety of sensible [i.e. perceived] objects, with all that he sees, all he hears'. The law of the association of ideas will do the rest. Here are her lambs:

> The lambs just dropped are in the field, they totter by the side of their dams, their young limbs can hardly support their weight. If you fall, little lambs, you will not be hurt; there is spread under you a carpet of soft grass; it is spread on purpose to receive you.

And here is her village green:

> Look at that spreading oak, the pride of the village green: its trunk is massy, its branches are strong. Its roots, like crooked fangs [an inept association!] strike deep into the soil, and support its huge bulk. . . . The old men point it out to their children [sic], but they themselves remember its growth.

Having abandoned, or forsworn, lyricism, and not having a story to tell, Mrs Barbauld sailed perilously close to the stupefying wind of explanation. Indeed, her village green echoes, not with song and laughter, but with the voice of the tutor or governess: as she insisted towards the end of her hymn, 'Instruction is the food of the mind; it is like the dew and the rain and the rich soil.' The itch to instruct proved too strong: it is difficult to believe, or to remind oneself, that this *is* a hymn. And yet there are many moments of genuine delicacy and tenderness in the hymns, and it seems that they both touched and provoked or vexed Blake at various points, for many of his *Songs* either alight on the same subject or feeling or, conversely, counteract or contradict Mrs Barbauld, in a kind of dialectic. Let us see how they correlate:

Songs	*Hymns*
'The Shepherd' – protective shepherd and lambs	Hymn III – protective shepherd and lambs

'Infant Joy'	Hymn III – baby gives mother joy
'A Cradle Song'	Hymn V – God protects sleeping children
'Laughing Song' – 'the green woods laugh with the voice of joy'	Hymn VI–cheerful forest Hymn VII–the trees have no voice, but we have: to praise God
'The Little Black Boy'	Hymn VIII – a black woman slave, with sick child: God hears her weeping and pities her

There is also a debt here to Isaac Watts's 'Grace Shining' in the *Horae Lyricae*:

'And we are put on earth a little space, That we may learn to bear the beams of love. . . .'	'Nor is my soul refin'd enough To bear the Beaming of his Love, And feel his warmer Smiles. When shall I rest this drooping Head? I love, I love the Sun, and yet I want the Shade'
'The Ecchoing Green'	Hymn X – oak tree on village green, with old men and children
'Nurse's Song' (This appears in *An Island*, where Mrs Nannicantipot introduces it as 'my mother's song')	Hymn V – Sunset and rest: 'no sound of children at play'
'Holy Thursday'	Hymn VII – 'Can we raise our voices up to the high heaven?'

'On Another's Sorrow'	Hymn VIII – 'If one is sick they mourn together; and if one is happy they rejoice together'
'Spring'	Hymns IX and XIV – spring
'The Schoolboy' 'If buds are nipped, And blossoms blown away . . . How shall the summer arise in joy? Or how shall we . . . bless the mellowing year, When the blasts of winter appear?'	Hymn IX – 'Who preserveth [flowers] alive through the cold winter . . . when the sharp frost bites on the plain? Hymn XII – 'O Nature . . . why dost thou sit mourning and desolate [in winter]?'
'The Lamb'	Hymn II – lamb
'Little lamb, who made thee?'	Hymn IV – 'He that made the lion is stronger than he'
'Night'	Hymns XII—XV – night, death and an after-life

The extent and proximity of these correspondences of subject-matter suggest that the relationship between Mrs Barbauld's *Hymns* and Blake's *Songs* is much more than a matter of coincidence, or of both drawing on the appropriate parts of the Bible. And this is confirmed by the evidence of the *Songs of Experience* (1794), some of which were written during the same period – the late 1780s. The most obvious are these:

'My Pretty Rose Tree'	Hymn IV – 'Come and I will show you . . . a rose fully blown' Hymn XV – 'The rose is sweet, but it is surrounded with thorns'

'The Lilly' – 'The modest Rose . . . the Lilly white'	Hymn IX – 'How doth the rose draw its crimson from the dark brown earth, or the lily its shining white?'
'The Tyger'[10]	Hymn IV – 'The lion is strong, but He that made the lion is stronger than he: His anger is terrible' Hymn VI – 'Did thy heart feel no terror but of the thunderbolt? Was there nothing bright and terrible but the lightning? . . . His terrors were abroad, and did not thine heart acknowledge Him?'

Mrs Barbauld's *Hymns* are sung, if that is the right word, in praise of a benevolent Divine Providence, and they assert the presence, in nature and human life, of winter, slavery, decay, death and suffering – they are, therefore, *not* innocent; they do not represent human life and nature through the unclouded eye of innocence. Blake's *Songs*, on the contrary, do just that: they are not songs *about* innocence, or songs written for innocent readers, but songs sung, as it were, *by* innocence. In *Songs of Innocence*, the 'of' signifies 'from' or 'belonging to' or 'expressing', rather than 'about'. Mrs Barbauld's *Hymns*, being providential, embrace aspects of 'experience', such as slavery and illness, and resolve them easily by placing them within the *reconciling* framework of a divine plan, which is to be accepted by the reader. Blake's *Songs of Innocence* do not even attend to the darker aspects of the world because the child who makes the song is simply not aware of such aspects: he is still innocent of them. The *Songs of Experience*, conversely, speak with the knowledge of the pain, suffering and evil, but offer no reconciliation, no harmonious resolution.

Thus, we can see Blake's creative energy working in two ways: it is as if he began by writing *Songs of Innocence* – a chapbook of poems or hymns for young children – in order to prove Mrs Barbauld wrong, i.e. to prove that it *was* possible to write poetry for children. But even as he worked on the repertoire of Innocence, that he had drawn from the *Hymns* and elsewhere, its contrary, Experience, insisted on being given a hearing, too. So the creative dialectic threw up two contradictory and irreconcilable perceptions of the same range of subjects. Declining to meet Mrs Barbauld on her comfortable, providential and reconciling ground, he side-stepped her to both left and right: towards an innocence which had no need of providential rationalization and towards an experience which could not be providentially rationalized.

In themselves, the *Songs of Innocence* are totally successful poems for children: fresh, alert, lyrical and simple: quite free of the trammels of serious, or solemn, significance that renders the hymns of John Wesley, Christopher Smart[11] and Mrs Barbauld so unsympathetic and uneven. But since Blake, in 1794, brought them into intimate and inevitable relationship with their contraries in *Song of Innocence and Experience*, the consequences are, for the reader, similarly unavoidable. Whilst children may continue to find joy and delight in the *Songs of Innocence*, the adult reader must face up to the tensions, the intimate contradictions, of the *Songs of Innocence and Experience*, accepting what Blake explicitly offers: 'the Two Contrary States of the Human Soul'. As he wrote in his unpublished Motto:

> The Good are attracted by Mens perceptions
> And Think not for themselves
> Till Experience teaches them to catch
> And to Cage the Fairies & Elves.[12]

Once we have caught and caged the Fairies and Elves, we cannot pretend not to have done so, cannot reclaim Innocence and deny Experience. The adult reader, therefore, unlike the child, is not free to read the *Songs of Innocence* alone, exclusively, as if the *Songs of Experience* did not exist, or could be put aside or forgotten. For the adult reader, they must be accepted as inseparable.

Two examples may suffice to show that to ignore this inseparability can lead to gross misreadings. Both involve the social and economic condition of children in eighteenth-century London, and we can begin by looking at this through the optimistic eyes of Joseph Addison, back in July 1713. He was feeling rather euphoric after the celebrations of the end of the war:

> There was no part of the show on the thanksgiving-day that so much pleased and affected me as the little boys and girls who were ranged with so much order and decency in . . . the Strand. . . . Such a numerous and innocent multitude, clothed in the charity of their benefactors, was a spectacle pleasing both to God and man. . . . Never did a more full and unspotted chorus of human creatures join in a hymn of devotion. The care and tenderness, which appeared in the looks of their several instructors, who were disposed among this little helpless people, could not forbear touching every heart that had any sentiments of humanity. . . . I have always looked on this institution of charity-schools, which of late years has so universally prevailed through the whole nation, as the glory of the age we live in, and the most proper means that can be made use of to recover it out of its present degeneracy and deprivation of manners. It seems to promise us an honest and virtuous posterity. There will be few in the next generation, who will not at least be able to write and read, and have not had an early tincture of religion.[13]

Or, as Vicesimus Knox wrote later, of the 'modern palaces erected for the poor and the afflicted': 'These . . . are the trophies of Christianity. . . . I congratulated myself on being born in an age in which Christian charity never shone in works of allowed public utility with greater lustre.'[14] The Charity

School movement had begun in 1699 as a means of averting, or ameliorating, a national scandal: namely, the remarkable number of orphaned and abandoned children on the streets of London, 'in tattered raggs, cursing and swearing at one another . . . rolling in the dirt and kennels, or pilfering on the Wharffs and Keys'.[15] By 1704, there were over fifty schools with over 2000 pupils; by 1730, these figures were almost trebled.

On the occasion that Addison was so touched, they were placed, in their thousands, on tiers along the Strand, to see the jubilant procession pass along to St Paul's, and to sing an 'Alleluia' chorus in praise of the Queen.

Apart from special occasions such as the thanksgivings of 1713, the usual occasion for the public parade of the charity school children was the first Thursday in May: initiated in 1704, this service of thanks was transferred to St Paul's in 1782. *The Times'* reporter in 1788 gave a glowing account of such an occasion:

> Yesterday being the Anniversary of the Patrons and Subscribers to all the Charity Schools in London, Westminster, and Southwark, the children of the different Charities were assembled in St Paul's Cathedral. . . . The temporary erection is well designed to display the glorious sight of 6000 children, reared up under the humane direction of the worthy Patrons, and supported by the public contributions of well-disposed persons, which must raise the mind to sympathy and brotherly-love . . . – his present Majesty, by affording it his presence, would be aiding to [sic] the nurture of a future generation to fight his battles – carry forward the commerce and manufactories of Great Britain, and assist in maturing infant arts, to the honour and prosperity of the country . . . A most excellent sermon was preached on the occasion, by the Right Hon. Lord Bagot, Bishop of Norwich, who took great pains in a sermon of forty minutes, to explain the tendency of this laudable institution – the great duty required from his young Auditors to show their gratitude to their benefactors.

After the sermon, the children sang the 100th Psalm and 140th Psalm, and the reporter waxed sentimental: 'the artless notes of youthful innocence afforded more pleasing sensation, than the notes of the most celebrated performers. . . .'[16]

That is the 'philanthropic' view of the occasion, fitting neatly into a view of society as decently doing its duty to the deserving poor, and simultaneously making a sound investment, for the pupils emerged from the charity schools well scrubbed and tamed, ready to take their appointed, subordinate place as servants, clerks, apprentices, cabin-boys, and so on. But how did the same occasion appear to the 'innocent' eye?

We know that Hector Berlioz was deeply moved by the spectacle when he saw it in 1851 – a choir of 6500 children could hardly have failed to move such a man: he added a chorus to his *Te Deum* as a result, scored for a modest choir of 600! And George Cruikshank drew the procession for his *Comic Almanack* of 1845, to accompany a serio-comic piece of verse that oddly echoes Blake:

> Oh! 'tis a glorious sight to see
> Those rosy little chaps,
> Decked by the hand of charity,
> In graceful muffin caps.

The writer observes the sad irony of their dress for the occasion:

> The very cap they're doomed to wear,
> Has cruel mockery in it;
> Type of a luxury so rare
> They ne'er can hope to win it.

But the overall tone is closer to Hood at his more ludicrously facetious. What, then, of Blake? Here is his 'innocent' view:

Holy Thursday

Twas on a Holy Thursday their innocent faces clean
The children walking two & two in red & blue & green;

223

Grey headed beadles walkd before with wands as
  white as snow
Till into the high dome of Pauls they like Thames
  waters flow.
Oh what a multitude they seemd these flowers of
  London town!
Seated in companies they sit, with radiance all their
  own.
The hum of multitudes was there but multitudes of
  lambs,
Thousands of little boys & girls raising their innocent
  hands.
Now like a mighty wind they raise to heaven the voice
  of song,
Or like harmonious thunderings the seats of heaven
  among.
Beneath them sit the aged men wise guardians of the
  poor;
Then cherish pity, lest you drive an angel from your
  door.[17]

The vision here is totally innocent and benign, even to the
implicit assumption that 'Thames waters' were clean and
seemly.

> There is a natural beauty in Uniformity which most
> People delight in. It is diverting to the Eye to see children
> well matched, either Boys or Girls, marching two and
> two in good Order; and to have them all whole and tight
> in the same Cloaths and Trimming must add to the
> comeliness of the Sight.

Is that also the voice of innocence? On the contrary, it is from
the cynical Bernard de Mandeville's *Essay on Charity and
Charity Schools* (1723). Charity schools, he argued, pleased
people for all the wrong reasons: inferior people came to
exercise power and authority in them, either as teachers, or as
governors.

In all this there is a shadow of property that tickles every body that has a right to make use of the Words, 'Our Parish Church', 'Our Charity Children', but more especially those who actually contribute and have a great hand in advancing the pious work.

Apart from which, education was wasted on such children: all they were fit for was a 'Laborious, Tiresome, and Painful Station of Life' and the sooner they took their due places the better for all concerned, for 'the more patiently they will submit to it ever after'. In de Mandeville's misanthropic vision, everyone was at fault, no one could do right: the voice of worldly 'wisdom' is corrosively reductive: no one is entitled to compassion. What, then, of Blake's 'Experience's view of the matter?

Holy Thursday

Is this a holy thing to see,
In a rich and fruitful land,
Babes reducd to misery,
Fed with cold and usurous hand?

Is that trembling cry a song?
Can it be a song of joy?
And so many children poor?
It is a land of poverty!

And their sun does never shine,
And their fields are bleak and bare,
And their ways are fill'd with thorns:
It is eternal winter there.

For where-e'er the sun does shine,
And where-e'er the rain does fall:
Babe can never hunger there,
Nor poverty the mind appall.

The sharp, penetrating, eye of 'Experience' effects a startling transformation: the benevolent, philanthropic hand, holding out the bread of charity, is seen to be 'cold and usurous': for the children's care is seen as a good investment: the interest will serve, in the words of *The Times*, to 'carry forward the commerce and manufactories of Great Britain . . . to the greater prosperity of the country'. The innocent eye saw the 'joy', the cheerfulness, the awesome solemnity, as Berlioz was to see them in 1851; the eye of experience sees a form of exploitation, but it withholds any providentially benign interpretation: there is none to be had.

A similar dialectic is offered by Blake's poems on the chimney-sweep. Jonas Hanway had first attempted to rouse the conscience of the nation about child-sweeps in 1773: as Vicesimus Knox wrote,

> Who ever ventured to appear the public advocate of the chimney-sweeper but Jonas Hanway? The poor infant of five or six years old, without shoes or stockings, almost naked, almost starved, driven up the narrow flue of a high chimney, driven by the menaces and scourges of an imperious master, and sometimes terrified with flames! think of this, ye mothers who caress your infants in your laps . . . and, at the same time, exert your interest and abilities, like Jonas Hanway, in preventing the employment of babes in a work under which the hardened veteran might sink with pain, terror, and fatigue.[18]

The legislation inspired by Hanway lacked teeth, alas, and it was only after Charles Kingsley published his odd, confused and powerful book, *The Water Babies*, in 1863, that an effective law was enacted in 1875. Kingsley's use of transformation through water seems to owe something to Blake's Song of Innocence:

The Chimney Sweeper

When my mother died I was very young,
And my father sold me while yet my tongue,
Could scarcely cry 'weep weep, weep weep,'
So your chimneys I sweep & in soot I sleep.
Theres little Tom Dacre, who cried when his head

That curl'd like a lambs back, was shav'd, so I said:
'Hush Tom never mind it, for when your head's bare,
You know that the soot cannot spoil your white hair.'

And so he was quiet, & that very night,
As Tom was a sleeping he had such a sight,
That thousands of sweepers Dick, Joe Ned & Jack
Were all of them lock'd up in coffins of black,

And by came an Angel who had a bright key,
And he open'd the coffins & set them all free.
Then down a green plain leaping laughing they run
And wash in a river and shine in the Sun.

Then naked & white, all their bags left behind,
They rise upon clouds, and sport in the wind.
And the Angel told Tom if he'd be a good boy,
He'd have God for his father & never want joy.

And so Tom awoke and we rose in the dark
And got with our bags & our brushes to work.
Tho' the morning was cold, Tom was happy & warm.
So if all do their duty, they need not fear harm.

Ingeniously, Blake slips Tom into a dream-world which is probably the only place in which the boy could plausibly be presented enjoying himself. And the last line is not so much the voice of innocence itself, as the innocent voice, the voice of the child, ingenuously repeating what it has been told by someone who subscribes to a providential scheme of rewards and punishments. The social historians Pinchbeck and Hewitt misconstrued the poem badly, and commented:

> The degree to which . . . self-delusion [on the part of those who exploited children] was possible . . . emerges from contemporary literature. Blake, for example, wrote a well-known poem, about a chimney-sweep. . . . For Blake, the chimney-sweep's salvation lay in resignation, not legislative reform.[19]

That comment exemplifies the kind of misapprehension that

can arise when adults read the *Songs of Innocence* in isolation; they should also have read the 'contrary' poem of Experience:

The Chimney Sweeper

A little black thing among the snow:
Crying '*weep, weep,*' in notes of woe!
'Where are thy father & mother? say?'
'They are both gone up to the church to pray.

'Because I was happy upon the heath
And smil'd among the winters snow:
They clothed me in the clothes of death,
And taught me to sing the notes of woe.

'And because I am happy & dance and sing,
They think they have done me no injury:
And are gone to praise God & his Priest & King
Who make up a heaven of our misery.'

Blake in the late 1780s was radical, even revolutionary, and his insistence here that the Establishment's 'heaven' is in effect a sanction for social and economic injustice can hardly be construed as an expression of 'resignation'; it is indeed antinomian, even blasphemous, by the lights of orthodoxy. An acceptance of the tensions that he sets up between Innocence and Experience is a condition of 'growing up', a provocation of spiritual and even of political growth; it is also a counterblast aimed against what he perceived as deformative influences, such as the prudential and providential morality of the mercantile classes, well summed up for young readers in the worldly little proverbs of Newbery's *Little Pretty Pocket Book*. In the event, Blake himself produced, in his *Marriage of Heaven and Hell*, an ironic parody of the frontispiece to Newbery's *Pocket Book*, and of didactic primers in general:[20] and his *Proverbs of Hell* offered a direct and lively rebuttal, not only of the commercial platitudes of Newbery's proverbs but also of Mary Wollstonecraft's 'enlightened' and bullying moral severities. 'Prudence is a rich ugly old maid courted by Incapacity'; 'Damn braces: Bless relaxes'.[21] It was entirely characteristic of Blake that, while polite eighteenth-century opinion deplored the 'vulgar' proverbs of oral tradition, he should make them very much his own. It was also typical of the man that, while deeply sympathetic to Mary Wollstone-craft's fierce political and social indignations, he should see her 'answer' as itself deeply wrong-headed and wrong-hearted.

3

Mary Wollstonecraft's *Original Stories from Real Life; with Conversations, calculated to regulate the affections and form the mind to truth and goodness* was published by Joseph Johnson in 1788, and reissued in 1791 with illustrations drawn and engraved by Blake, who also engraved the illustrations for Mary's translation of Salzmann's *Elements of Morality*, published by Johnson in 1790. As Blake was working on his *Songs*, he thus had occasion simultaneously to give some close attention to the work of a thorough-going radical spokes-woman for the cause of rational education.

Original Stories has a strong claim to be the most sinister, ugly, overbearing book for children ever published.[22] It is permeated by a grim, humourless, tyrannical spirit of hector-ing and unswerving spiritual and mental rectitude – all in the name of healthy growth: a dream of reason producing, indeed, a veritable monster in the form of Mrs Mason, the book's equivalent of Day's Barlow and Trimmer's Mrs Benson. 'I will give you a moral for your dream', writes Lady Fenn in 1789;[23] but Mrs Mason, relentless, severe, preoccupied with the 'regulation of appetites' in her two young charges, Mary and Caroline, gives them morals for their waking nightmares. Mrs Barbauld's God is primarily protective toward sleeping children; 'His hand is always stretched out over us' and 'You may close your eyes in safety, for His eye is always open', not to spy, but 'to protect you' (Hymn V). But poor Mary is reduced to nervous insomnia by Mrs 'Nobodaddy' Mason:[24]

'I declare I cannot go to sleep. I am afraid of Mrs Mason's eyes.'
Like the pinder in Wordsworth's *Prelude*,[25] Mrs Mason is
always on the look-out for any untoward display of irrational
impulse, any merely human aberration, any show of freedom
of spirit, and quickly blusters in to quell it, and so confine the
girls within the pinfold of her own conceit.

It is hardly surprising that Blake was repelled and even
horrified by her: when he came to illustrate the book, he
turned his gaze away from her, and could not bring himself to
draw her likeness. But she reappears in the *Songs of Experience*
as the killjoy, disenchanted nurse of the 'Nurses Song' . . .,
who tells the children:

> Your spring & your day are wasted in play
> And your winter and night in disguise.

'Disguise' here is a shorthand term for 'make-believe' or
'pretending'. Story-telling is traditionally associated with
winter evenings, just as 'pretend-games' are the child's way of
redeeming the fact of being sent to bed early. The intimate
relationship between Mrs Mason and the life-denying nurse
of Blake's song is underlined by the fact that the drawing that
frames the 'Nurses Song' is a direct and unequivocal parody
of the frontispiece that Blake had provided for *Original
Stories*. As for Mrs Mason's manic preoccupation with the
rational economy of the mind, her severe preoccupation with
the unrelenting denial of natural feeling, Blake's own position
was perfectly clear:

> I was angry with my friend;
> I told my wrath, my wrath did end.
> I was angry with my foe;
> I told it not, my wrath did grow.[26]

By the early 1790s Blake was clearly reacting against the
ostensibly very different values of such as Newbery, on the
mercantile side, and Wollstonecraft, on the 'radical' rationalist side. He found them both wanting, and for the same reason:
their moral psychology was wrong, falsifying, damaging,

Blake. del & sc.

Look what a fine morning it is.—Insects,
Birds, & Animals, are all enjoying existence.

Published by J. Johnson. Sept.r 1.st 1791.

Original Stories from Real Life

deformatory. His own position was by this time deeply ironic and ready to embrace paradox: 'without contraries is no progression'. And he was beginning to form clear, sharp and uncompromising alternatives to both the philistine mealy-mouthed didactics such as Newbery, and to the arid arithmetical ultra-rationalism of the stridently enlightened. His alternatives were passionate, intuitive and antinomian, and they were richly fed and sustained by his wide autodidactic reading in philosophy and theology. They centred on an uncompromising and insouciant acceptance of Eros, of desire, of impulse and of natural unrationalized feeling.

The tragedy was that he chose to publish his alternatives in such a form that they had little or no chance of creating the taste whereby they could be appreciated.[27] It is a curious irony of the time that Wordsworth's *Prelude*, which also grew out of the moral, intellectual and social ferment of the 1790s, and also offered a radical and passionate counteraction, was also to be kept – at least for fifty years – from the larger reading public.

4

Blake's works for children were not yet complete. He had one more offering for them, and it was as far removed from the prevailing rage for Lilliputian rationality as could be imagined; it seems to have been designed indeed to countervail both in form and content the conventions of explicitness and enlightenment through overt instruction.

In general, the didactic fashion in books for children had drawn on two rather jaded traditions: the fable, which offered examples of virtue and vice in action; and the emblem, which presented an object for contemplation, the allegorical or anagogical significance being carefully disentangled and explained. By Blake's time, both had developed, or degenerated, to a point where no room was left at all for the play of pre-critical, preconceptual, intuitive understanding: no room left for 'poetic' meaning because the writers were committed to guiding by explanation, taking the young readers by the elbow or the scruff of the neck, to make sure that they did not miss the 'point'. Quite the opposite of the subtle uncalculating art of the traditional tale; as Walter Benjamin said,

It is half the art of story-telling to keep a story free from explanation. . . . The most extraordinary things, marvellous things, are related with the greatest accuracy, but the psychological connection of the events is not forced on the reader. It is left up to him to interpret things the way he understands them, and thus the narrative achieves an amplitude that information lacks.[28]

David Erdman has shown us, in his exploration of Blake's *Notebook*,[29] that Blake was familiar with both the older emblem-books, such as that of Francis Quarles (1635), and the more recent ones, such as Wynne's of 1772. In their prime, they had provided an occasion for the contemplation of sacred mysteries, and exemplified what Benjamin observed of story – they had 'achieved an amplitude that information lacks'; but they had gradually and irrevocably lapsed into the business of tendering advice on how to get through life with the minimum of distress or trouble: a process of secularization, or prophanation, had overtaken them. By the time Blake turned his mind to them they were already on the way out: when, in the 1790s, John Aikin and Mrs Barbauld produced *Evenings at Home*, they put the following words into Cecilia's mouth: 'Pray, papa, what is an emblem? I have met with the word in my lesson today, and I do not quite understand it.'

Blake decisively rejected the secularized, explicatable, eighteenth-century form, and his reason for doing so involved a fundamental insight: 'The Last Judgment', he wrote in his *Notebook*, 'is not Fable or Allegory but Vision. Fable or Allegory are a totally distinct & inferior kind of Poetry.'[30] He recognized, however, that even though they were degenerate, they might still possess vestigial powers: 'Note here that Fable or Allegory is seldom without some Vision. Pilgrim's Progress is full of it.' But he acknowledged that there was a 'Mighty difference' between 'Allegoric Fable & Spiritual Mystery'. He had, then, arrived at a rejection of the 'knowing' analytic, step-counting orthodoxies of the rationalists and of the conventional forms of moral instruction. He was later to write: 'The Learned, who strive to ascend into Heaven by means of learning, appear to Children like dead horses, when repelled by the celestial spheres'; and 'the Beauty of the Bible is that the most Ignorant and Simple Minds Understand it Best' – not unlike Morgann's perception of women and children drinking in Shakespeare while the scholars knitted their heavy brows!

Could Blake, then, speak directly to children, and effectively address his vision to their pre-critical minds or souls? *Songs of Innocence* is triumphant proof that he could do so. But could he subvert or side-step the operations of the consciously cognitive mind even further by addressing them virtually *without words*, by emblem alone? As Auden has remarked, 'the significance of an emblem is not, like a simile, self-evident. The artist who uses one must either assume that his audience already knows the symbolic association – it is a legend of the culture to which he belongs – or, if it is his own invention, he must explain it.'[31] Was it possible to get round these conditions, and to create a new repertoire of emblems, that would speak for themselves?

This was the task that Blake set himself in the late 1780s. The various stages that his emblems went through have been scrupulously charted by David Erdman so that we can now see the way in which 'Ideas of Good and Evil' eventually became *The Gates of Paradise*, a series of seventeen emblems 'For Children' (1793). In the *Songs of Experience*, the sunflower was offered as a 'vision', an enigma, unyielding to the reasoning intellect, offering its meaning in exclusively poetic ways, and completely divested of the 'fable' of Hyperion and Clytie from which it derived. The emblem was left to speak for itself. Similarly, these little pictures are divested of all support, save for a few intriguing minimal captions. Consider, then, the frontispiece: two oak-leaves, one in shade, the other in light. On the first is a caterpillar, or 'worm', that is nibbling away at its supporting leaf. On the second, with its face turned up to the light, is a little swaddled creature, a human infant in chrysalis-form. And beneath the picture, there are three words: 'What is Man!' The Infant, left to itself, will presumably break out of its swaddlings, put out its wings and fly. This may be compared with what Mrs Barbauld had made of similar material, in her Hymn XIV:

I have seen the insect, being come to its full size, languish and refuse to eat: it spun itself a tomb, and was shrouded in the silken cone; it lay without feet, or shape, or power to move. I looked again, it had burst its tomb: it was full of life, and sailed on coloured wings through the soft air; it rejoiced in its new being.

This may well strike us as having a certain charm; but it is set in the context of a series of conventional analogies, all of which are disposed to support her essential – and predictable? – argument: 'Jesus hath conquered death: child of immortality! mourn no longer.' Mrs Barbauld's eyes are seen to be firmly set – as the child-reader's eyes are to be set – on the after-life; and her *Hymns* exemplify the conventional and jaded dichotomies: Good and Evil, Human and Divine, Salvation and Damnation, and Mortal and Immortal.

By the time he came to make *The Gates of Paradise*, Blake was rejecting these conventional Christian beliefs, for the simple reason that for him there was no longer any truth in them, but rather 'Serpent Reasonings of Good & Evil, Virtue & Vice' – 'reasonings' which not only 'entice us' but are drummed into tender minds as the only truth by the Mrs Trimmers, the Mrs Masons and the Mrs Bensons, the monitorial handmaidens of a tyrannical Nobodaddy:

> Why darkness & obscurity
> In all thy words & laws,
> That none dare eat the fruit but from
> The wily serpent's jaws?
> Or is it because Secresy
> Gains females' loud applause?

The neatly schematized doctrines of conventional religion did not correspond with the facts, the personal truths of his own experience. Furthermore, Christian dogma was mediated by those who 'have spent their lives in Curbing & Governing other People's [Passions] by the Various arts of Poverty & Cruelty of all kinds'. Even woman had become the agent of a moral tyranny, 'Prying after Good & Evil', and serving the patriarchy of 'God Almighty [who] comes with a thump on the Head' rather than 'Jesus Christ [who] comes with a balm to heal it'. Lavater had written 'I know not which of those two I should wish to avoid most; the scoffer at virtue and religion . . . OR THE PIETIST, WHO CRAWLS, GROANS, BLUBBERS, AND SECRETLY SAYS TO GOLD, THOU ART my hope! and to his belly, thou art my god!': and Blake wrote in the margin 'I hate crawlers'.[32]

Mrs Barbauld's emblems were conventional, explicated, and as familiar as the iconography of the cross. But, given Blake's free spirit and the autochthonous nature of his spiritual life, was there ever any chance that the emblems of *The Gates of Paradise* would offer a poetic, symbolic alternative to 'debtor and creditor notions of morality' to the children of the 1790s? Did they, indeed, fall into the hands of any appreciable number of children? Or was Blake, in his visionary ingenuousness, over-reaching the limits of his medium, and simply demanding too much?

It is clear that he himself was forced to reconsider the feasibility of his enterprise, for he abandoned his plans for a companion-book, *The Gates of Hell*, and subsequently re-issued *Paradise* for an adult readership – 'For the Sexes' – about twenty-five years later. In the event, he seems to have realized that his little emblems, loaded with meanings, but depending entirely on the relatively obscure image, were too cryptic. So he fell back on words, and on his title-page spelled out his meaning:

> Mutual Forgiveness of each Vice,
> Such are the Gates of Paradise. . . .

The caterpillar of the frontispiece was now glossed:

> The Caterpillar on the Leaf
> Reminds thee of thy Mother's Grief.

He provided keys for all the emblems, and added an Epilogue, addressed to 'the Accuser who is the God of This World'.

'Reason' or 'reasoning' emerges from the sequence as the way of error and illusion; prudential morality as a source of moral perversion and of sorrow, and as the denial of an inherently benign Nature.

Alas, it has to be said that only a very careful reading of Erdman's exhaustive analysis of the *Notebook*, together with a peaceful contemplation of the emblems, is likely to bring most modern readers anywhere near a positive appreciation of this visionary, resonant, idiosyncratic and enigmatic work. The tragedy of *The Gates*, as of Blake's subsequent output, is the growing disconnection between the genius and his public; a growing privacy, and a deepening privation. Political factors clearly exacerbated his own hermetic inclinations: in a decade of severe political repression, he learned to write heresy and treason under the guise of exotic myth. But he never wrote again for children; and the loss is immeasurable, for *Songs of Innocence* was the only work of genius for children, in its century.

NOTES AND REFERENCES

1 Laurence Sterne, *The Life and Opinions of Tristram Shandy*, 9 vols (York, later London, 1760–7), vol. I, chs V and IX.

2 *William Blake's Writings*, ed. G.E. Bentley, Jr, 2 vols (Oxford: Clarendon Press, 1978), vol. II, pp. 875–900. Quotations are from this edition.

3 Through the mediation of enlightened spirits such as Dr Thomas Percival of the Manchester Literary and Philosophical Society such matters entered quickly into the repertoire of young peoples' reading. See below, Chapter Nine, nn. 15 and 18.

4 Stylistically – 'was clever at Fissic Follogy . . .' – this is an acute adumbration of an actual infantine performance in which Blake himself became involved. See below, p. 276.

5 Maria Edgeworth, *Belinda* (1801), ch. 5.

6 Godwin, Priestley, Mary Wollstonecraft, Fuseli and Tom Paine were some of the more celebrated, or notorious, who met there.

7 A characteristic situation, duly moralized, in many children's books of this time.

8 See John Holloway, *Blake: The Lyric Poetry* (London: Edward Arnold, 1968).

9 'Isaac Watts', in *Lives of the English Poets*, 2 vols (London: Oxford University Press, 1961), vol. 2.

10 John Holloway (op.cit., p. 35) is entirely convincing in relating this also to Philip Doddridge's Hymn 100.

11 John Wesley, *Hymns for Children* (1763). Christopher Smart, *Hymns for the Amusement of Children* (1775).

12 *Notebook*, p. 101; in *Writings*, vol. II, p. 974.

13 *The Guardian*, no. 105 (11 July 1713).

14 Vicesimus Knox, *Winter Evenings; or, Lucubrations on Life and Letters*, 3 vols (London: Charles Dilly, 1788), vol. II, pp. 231–2: reprinted in *The British Essayists*, 45 vols (London: T. & J. Allman, 1823), vol. 42, p. 169.

15 Quoted by I. Pinchbeck and M. Hewitt, *Children in English Society*, 2 vols (London: Routledge & Kegan Paul, 1969 and 1973), vol. I, p. 293.

16 *The Times* (6 June 1788).

17 *Songs of Innocence* are quoted from *Writings*, vol. I, pp. 22–61; *Songs of Experience*, ibid., pp. 171–200.

18 Knox, op.cit., vol. II, pp. 233–4; reprinted in *The British Essayists*, vol. 43, p. 128. Cf. Sydney Smith, 'Chimney sweepers', a review of the *Account of the Society for superseding the Necessity of Climbing Boys*, in the *Edinburgh Review* (1819). This inspired James Montgomery to produce his *Chimney-Sweeper's Friend, and Climbing-Boy's Album* (1824). Montgomery included Blake's poem, which had been sent to him by Charles Lamb, who characteristically changed the name 'Tom Dacre' to the Blytonish 'Tom Toddy'.

19 Pinchbeck and Hewitt, op.cit., vol. I, p. 355.

20 Cf. Gary J. Taylor, 'The Structure of *The Marriage*: A Revolutionary Primer', *Studies in Romanticism*, vol. 13, no. 2 (Spring 1974), p. 141; and David Erdman, *The Illuminated Blake* (London: Oxford University Press, 1975), p. 80.

21 *Writings*, vol. I, pp. 81, 83.

22 Claire Tomalin's biography is a remarkable effort at rehabilitation, yet even she admits to finding a sinister note in Mary Wollstonecraft's fiction. The most searching account of Wollstonecraft remains that of Virginia Woolf, in *The Common Reader*, second series (London: Hogarth Press, 1932), pp. 156–63.

23 In *The Fairy Spectator*.

24 Cf. David Erdman's edition of Blake's *Notebook* (Oxford: Clarendon Press, 1973), p. N109, last line.

25 *The Prelude*, bk V, ll. 238–45 and 358–62.
26 'A Poison Tree'.
27 Cf. Robert Fellowes's comment, above, p. 204; Blake's suppression of his *French Revolution* (1791); and Wordsworth's *Excursion*, bk 3, l.827.
28 Walter Benjamin, 'The Storyteller', in *Illuminations* (London: Fontana, 1973), p. 83.
29 See note 24, above.
30 *Notebook*, p. 68.
31 *The Dyer's Hand* (London: Faber & Faber, 1963), p. 301.
32 J.C. Lavater, *Aphorisms* (London: J. Johnson, 1788), p. 25; quoted with Blake's comment, from *Writings*, vol. II, p. 1354.

CHAPTER EIGHT

ETERNAL ARCHETYPES AND TEMPORAL ENERVATIONS: LAMB AND GODWIN

> I am in no hurry to begin my story
> – indeed I have little or none to tell.
> (Charles Lamb, 'Barbara S—',
> in *London Magazine*, 1825)

> I was full of unmastered intimations
> and transitional thoughts. . . .
> (Saul Bellow, *Humboldt's Gift*, 1975)

1

As recently as 1975, Charles Ryskamp characterized Lamb as 'a writer of delightful stories for children';[1] E.V. Lucas, a Lamb-disciple, found them 'charming'. But the judgement of most modern readers, especially young ones, will probably be that if Lamb's stories for children are indeed valued, it is more likely to be by bibliographers, book-auctioneers, and those who would like to put every clock back about 150 years.

By any adequate reckoning, Lamb was incapable of art. His finest achievements are to be found, rather, in certain confessional pages of almost riveting intensity and urgency. As with De Quincey, so with Lamb, creative talent was put to best use in the proto-art of autobiography, and came through most powerfully when stretched to its limits by the irresistible need to confess.

Lamb himself unwittingly offered a way of representing the issue, in his essay, 'Barrenness of the Imaginative Faculty in the Production of Modern Art':

Hogarth excepted, can we produce any one painter within the last fifty years . . . that has treated a story *imaginatively*? . . . upon whom his subject has so acted, that it has seemed to direct *him* – not be arranged by him? Any upon whom its leading or collateral points have impressed themselves so tyrannically, that he dared not treat it otherwise, lest he should falsify a revelation?[2]

This could stand as one way of recognizing Blake's distinctive genius, but it could also offer a way of pointing up Lamb's relative feebleness.

As a result of his now faded 'charm' and his excessive 'sweetness' – qualities that few modern readers find particularly ingratiating – he mostly offers little more than a dilution, a weak parody, of whatever he had learned either from his reading in Burton and the Elizabethan drama, or from the more immediate influence of Wordsworth. Indeed, we can now see him as contributing to influential prototypes of nineteenth-century forms of nostalgia and sentiment, in response to the past: both the larger, historical past, and also the personal, local past of childhood; indeed, he often affected a *persona* which took somewhat perverse pride in being old-fashioned, and this could lead to both complacency and to self-deception: one only has to note the obvious discrepancies between 'The Old and the New Schoolmaster' and the portrait of Boyer in 'Christ's Hospital Five and Thirty Years Ago'.[3]

To descend to the kind of pun which delighted Lamb himself, one might suggest that, as with Goldsmith, his patron saint should have been Saint Francis of a See-saw,[4] for he oscillated uncontrollably between a best self – an honest, even ruthlessly honest best self – and a comedic self, a coy mask, silly, whimsical, naughty-boyish, self-consciously playful and overtly harmless. This second, feebler self may in the event have had its roots, as Hazlitt suggested, in a kind of humility.[5] It may have been a form of self-defence when in the presence of – under pressure from – stronger men. It could have been a carefully contrived prop for helping his sister to cope with 'the variable weather of the mind, the flying vapours of incipient madness'.[6] Or it may have been the manifesto of a failure to achieve selfhood, to become fully and securely mature: how else could one make sense of his tendency not only to snigger at weddings, but to make puns at funerals?

Whatever the causes, this much seems clear: that it was almost invariably Lamb's feebler self that was engaged in the writing of books for children. When he and Mary wrote for the children's market – and market-forces seem to have played an undue part in their enterprise – they chose feeble models and then failed to improve on them. The piecemeal day-by-day apportioning of their respective contributions to their collaborative work is not always clear, but where it is so one has to admit that his work is barely less feeble than that of his sister.

Mrs Leicester's School owes more than a little to Sarah Fielding's *The Governess*; the poetry for children leans heavily on the wretched precedents of Watt's *Divine Songs*,[7] Lucy Aikin's *Poetry for Children* (1801), and the Taylors' *Original Poems*.[8] *Ulysses* has the story-telling power and the rhetorical resourcefulness of neither Homer nor Chapman;[9] and as for the lamentable *Tales from Shakespeare*, perhaps the most appropriate analogy is with the burglar who steals nothing that is of any real value.[10]

How, then, is one to account for such feebleness, such factitious and maladroit stuff, coming as it did, at least in part, from the pen of a man whose letters are characterized by an often deft wit, a lively humour, a vivid sense of the resourcefulness of the English language, and a pioneering responsiveness to the energies of Elizabethan drama? How was it that Lamb allowed himself to follow such vapid models and then to perform at so abysmal a level as story-teller? Is it enough merely to insist that Lamb's talent was not for story-telling, for narrative?

Part of the answer is surely to be found in the circumstances of their composition. It was an ideal way of keeping Mary quietly occupied, even though for Lamb it was 'task-work' coming on top of his day's work at East India House. But above all, the Lambs were singularly unfortunate in their choice – if that is the right word – of publisher. For they wrote these books for William and Mary Jane Godwin, and it is clear that the Godwins' disabling and enervating influence was largely the result of their philistine and grubbily commercial view of the business of publishing books for children.

In most of the recorded moments of the pre-literate oral tradition of story-telling, it is noteworthy that no firm distinction seems to have been enforced between the children and the adults of the audience: they all sat, or stood, commingled and united in a shared experience; the story-tellers had no patronizing or condescending designs on them: there was no 'calculation'. The essential bond, the community of feeling, of shared laughter or apprehension, was not dissevered by any notion of hierarchy. The notion that 'fairy-tales' are suitable only for children is a relatively modern development, and persists today despite the advocacy of such readers as Randall Jarrell and W.H. Auden. It may well be connected with the progressive deferring of maturity that has been so marked a feature of our culture in the last two hundred years.[11] and certainly derives in part from the view that the world-view of the tales is something to be grown out of, to be displaced by something more sensible.

Be that as it may, as soon as the tales of the story-*tellers'* repertoire began to be available in print, we can observe the beginnings of a separation. It was, indeed, such a divorce – of young from old, of child from adult – that Wordsworth quite calmly ignored when he confessed to having written some of his early ballad-poems in the hope that they might circulate in chap-book form. And it was Wordsworth who insisted that 'There is no harm, but, on the contrary, there is benefit in presenting a child with ideas beyond his easy and immediate comprehension', and who was 'absolutely convinced' that 'children will derive most benefit from books which are not unworthy the perusal of persons of any age'.[12] Blake, likewise, saw no need to lower his sights when writing for children.

But such uncompromising and incorruptible spirits ran directly counter to the policies and ambitions of most of the bookseller-publishers. As books for children engaged more and more in social education, in a didacticism of manners and mental improvement, and as they came to be used more specifically in pedagogical settings, whether in the school or in the 'apartment' set aside for child and governess in the genteel household – the separation of culture became quite emphatically a matter of commercial intention and of convenience. So, by the time the Edgeworths wrote *Practical Education* in the 1790s, 'books for children' were clearly defined as a distinct category, and written for, or at, and too often down to, the specific readership of the immature, the unformed, those who were to be formed.

As a result of the growth of this sub-culture and sub-commerce, by the early 1800s most books published for children were quite simply unworthy of the attention of any intelligent adult reader; the adults who had to read them, or had to make sure that the children read them, were usually persons in subordinate roles, i.e. women, and specifically those charged with the early training of good habits, i.e. governesses. Few sane adults would have chosen to read them of their own free will.

Such was the state of the art in 1801, when William Godwin, political philosopher and novelist, married Mary Jane Clairmont. Godwin had been widowed in 1797 by the tragic death of Mary Wollstonecraft, and Mrs Clairmont, so legend has it, endeared herself to him with her very first salutation: 'Do I indeed behold the immortal Godwin?' Lamb, who came to know her at close quarters, described her variously as 'a widow with green spectacles and one child'; 'that bitch'; 'the Professor's Rib'; and 'the Bad Baby'. And he went on to compose a savage portrait of her under the guise of Mrs Pry, in the *Lepus Papers* of 1825.

In 1804 Mary Jane persuaded Godwin that they should try to lift themselves out of severe financial embarrassment by setting up in business as publishers and booksellers, under the name of The Juvenile Library: 'an inferior shop for stationery and children's books' was how Horace Smith characterized their establishment. The business staggered along until 1822, and Godwin was declared bankrupt in 1825. They failed despite the fact that, when they embarked on their business, Godwin was recognized, indeed respected, in rationalist and radical circles, as something of an authority on education in general – his *Enquirer*[13] had appeared in 1797 – and on children's books in particular.

In 1802 William Cole asked him for advice on these matters, and his reply reveals not only signs of Wordsworthian influence, but also a man who was of two minds. Earlier, Wordsworth had fallen under the spell of Godwin's *Political Justice*, an epoch-making nine days' wonder of a book devoted to a thorough-going rationalism in political and social reform; now the tables were turned, and Godwin speaks with echoes of Wordsworth, presumably mediated by the incorrigible monologues of Coleridge, who often dined with Godwin. As for Godwin's two minds, in his letter to Cole he could pay almost rhapsodic tribute to the unconstrained imaginative life of the chap-book romances, but he could also endorse the prosy didacticism of those who were intent on 'forming' children's minds. Such two-sidedness may, of course, be construed as a form of broadminded openness; but it may also be seen less charitably as the shilly-shallying, the hedging, of one who is keen to 'have it both ways', even anxious to back the winning party before it was entirely clear which way the proverbial cat was going to jump. But, if it was broadmindedness, then it was one that involved a deep contradiction, unadmitted and unresolvable. For the necessary consequence of accepting the Wordsworthian position was the impossibility of simultaneously supporting the cohorts of those committed to infantine enlightenment.

Had the wiser part of either Lamb or Godwin learned

anything from Wordsworth or from the Coleridge who busily sat regaling Wordsworth's words? Whatever this influence may have been, for good, it was certainly counteracted by two features of the Lamb-Godwin circumstance. Lamb was irreversibly committed to writing for Godwin, and the erstwhile free spirit of Godwin was rapidly being supplanted or over-ruled by the desperate need to earn cash: as he remarked to Lamb, a publisher or bookseller learns to 'see' books very differently from the way in which authors see them.

Sporadically, both Lamb and Godwin relieved themselves of Wordsworthian sentiments, distant echoes of *The Prelude*; but the sentiments which in Wordsworth's poems and letters compel attention, and carry weight, through their subtle intensity of feeling, the reach of the mind, and the vivid energy of the voice, and which on Coleridge's lips could assume a magisterial or canonical tone of authority – these come, transmuted and diminished, from Lamb and Godwin as the words of men striking a pose, either to be agreeable, as in Lamb, or to express a willed force of character, an uncompromisingly high moral pretension, as in Godwin.

This may seem unfairly put, but let us consider Lamb's famous letter to Coleridge of 23 October 1802:

> Mrs Barbauld's stuff has banished all the old classics of the nursery; . . . at Newbery's . . . Mrs B.'s and Mrs Trimmer's nonsense lay in piles about. Knowledge insignificant and vapid as Mrs B.'s books convey, it seems, must come to a child in the *shape* of *knowledge*, and his empty noddle must be turned with conceit of his own powers when he has learnt that a Horse is an animal, and Billy is better than a Horse, and such like; instead of that beautiful Interest in wild tales which made the child a man, while all the time he suspected himself to be no bigger than a child. Science has succeeded to Poetry no less in the little walks of children than with men. Is there no possibility of averting this sore evil? Think what you

would have been now, if instead of being fed with Tales and old wives' fables in childhood, you had been crammed with geography and natural history?[14]

Lamb is here offering Coleridge an assurance that is in part an echo or mirror-image of Coleridge's own position; there is a hint of preening, too: a whiff of 'Thank God you were not perverted!'; and Lamb also indulges in a fashionable, rather silly contempt for blue-stockings, an attitude that is seen at its most repulsive in Southey, and often indulged in by Coleridge.[15] In this letter Lamb laments: '"Goody Two Shoes" is almost out of print', and exclaims: 'Damn them! – I mean the cursed Barbauld Crew, those Blights and Blasts of all that is Human in man and child.' He thus falls into some odd confusions and misrepresentations; for *Goody Two-Shoes* was a type of the very didacticism that Lamb is attacking![16] As for Mrs Barbauld, had she not written:

Midway the hill of science, after steep
And rugged paths that try th' unpractised feet,
A grove extends; in tangled mazes wrought,
And filled with strange enchantment . . .
With moonbeam rainbows tinted. – Here each mind
Of finer mould, acute and delicate,
In its high progress to eternal truth
Rests for a space, in fairy bowers entranced;
And loves the softened light and tender gloom . . .?[17]

And that in a poem entitled, 'To Mr S.T. Coleridge. 1797'! The inference is irresistible – that Lamb is playing up to Coleridge's prejudices.

Again, consider Godwin's letter to William Cole of 2 March 1802. He refers to the prevailing fashion for the public exhibition of infant prodigies and their grossly lop-sided hypertrophies, at one with the Wordsworth of *Prelude*, book V, in thinking that 'it is a miserable vanity that would sacrifice the wholesome and gradual development of the mind to the desire of exhibiting little monsters of curiosity'. He deplores the age's preoccupation, in the education of children, with 'a miserable minuteness of detail', and argues that such 'minutenesses' – his word – 'freeze up the soul, and give a premature taste for clearness and exactness, which is of the most pernicious consequence'. Again, this is a view that recurs in Wordsworth's poems and letters.[18] What Godwin wishes to promote, rather, is the imagination. And of the books that are 'calculated' – incongruous term! – to 'excite the imagination and quicken the apprehensions of children', he instances *Beauty and the Beast* – 'a little French book' – *Fortunatus, Valentine and Orson, The Seven Champions of Christendom, Robinson Crusoe* – duly 'weeded of its methodism' – the *Arabian Nights*, and the story of the Queen and the country-maid in Fénelon's *Dialogues of the Dead*. For younger children – and here he changes tack – he recommends Mrs Barbauld's 'little books, four in number, admirably adapted, upon the whole, to the capacity and amusement of your children', i.e. the enlarged, revised, four-part edition of *Lessons for Children*, first published in 1778; and Mrs Lovechild's *The Infant's Friend*. Let us put a generous gloss on these recommendations and say that they represent an equilibrist's curriculum – they find room for both animals, the wild and the tamed. Then we might expect Godwin, as publisher, two years later, to maintain something of the same balance: certainly we would not expect him to concentrate almost exclusively on publishing the kinds of books that would depend on, and serve to promote, 'minuteness'.

In the event, most of the books that he published were textbooks, some written by Godwin himself, judiciously[19] disguised behind the pseudonym of 'Edward Baldwin', since his real name was still tinged with disreputable political and downright immoral social attitudes – his disapproval of marriage, for example. His list included *Lessons for Children* by Eliza Fenwick, erstwhile friend of Mary Wollstonecraft, and here an imitator of Mrs Barbauld. (In 1805, Tabart published her representatively titled *Visits to the Juvenile Library; or knowledge proved to be the source of happiness*; and

FABLES

ANCIENT AND MODERN.

ADAPTED FOR THE USE OF CHILDREN.

BY EDWARD BALDWIN, ESQ.

TENTH EDITION.

LONDON: PRINTED FOR M. J. GODWIN AND CO.
AT THE FRENCH AND ENGLISH JUVENILE AND SCHOOL LIBRARY,
195, (ST. CLEMENT'S), STRAND.

1824.

the Godwins also published her misleadingly titled *Rays from the Rainbow*, 1812, 'an easy method for perfecting children in the first principles of grammar'.) The Godwins also produced a grammar by Hazlitt; the books of Charles and Mary Lamb; and Godwin's own *Fables, Ancient and Modern* (1805).

The young William Mulready illustrated the *Fables*; he later confessed to Henry Cole that he had great difficulty in wresting payment from the Godwins, but his illustrations for this book must be numbered among the best of this period: they have a gauche, naïve power, unrefined and raw, unsophisticated and strangely fine. The text exemplified Godwin's avowed aim of 'refining and elevating the circle of juvenile studies', and it was in the same spirit that Godwin also cranked out his *New Guide to the English Tongue* and an *Outline of English Grammar*, which was based on his firm conviction that he had made 'an entirely new discovery as to the way of teaching the English Language',[20] a fairly typical claim or illusion.

It is in the Preface to the *Fables* that we find Godwin most explicitly contradicting the views that he had expressed three years earlier in his letter to William Cole; in the spirit of the more single-minded disciples of John Locke, he asserts: 'I have introduced no leading object without a clear and distinct explanation. By this means the little reader will be accustomed to form clear and distinct ideas.'[21] He concludes: 'I have intended, as far as I was able, that these volumes should surpass most others in forming the mind of the learner to habits of meditation and reflection.' Is there perhaps a hint of modesty in that word, 'most', rather than 'all'? And why no mention at all of the imagination when it had been so important a part of his vocabulary only three years before? As for 'meditation and reflection', one is reminded of Coleridge's observation of 'the cadaverous silence of Godwin's children, quite catacombish'. As for the *Fables* themselves, a brief example should be enough to show how Godwin's didactic itch defeated the disinterested integrity of the mere story-teller:[22]

I have one thing to mention to you for fear of mistakes. Beasts and birds do not talk English; but they have a way of talking that they understand among one another, better than we understand them; and you, if you attend to your dog, or your cat, or your horse, may generally make out what he wants from his voice or his look. I am going sometimes to tell you what an animal says; that is, I am going to put his meaning into English words.

But let me say one thing more. It is not always necessary that a story should be true. Some stories are true, and some are invented; and, if they are very prettily invented, we are much obliged to the people that made them. A lie is what naughty folks say, that they may deceive; like the boy and the wolf. But, if I tell a pretty story of a dog and a fox, or any other animals, I do not mean to deceive, I only mean to tell a pretty story. Now then I begin.

And about time, too! the child presumably exclaims.

An ant is a very wise, though a very little animal, and lays up food in the summer when there is plenty, against the winter, when there is none. He is thoughtful and serious. A grasshopper is the merriest creature in the world; he sings all the summer long; but, when the winter comes, he dies of hunger and cold.[23]

The inevitable moral, and a very ironic one coming from Godwin, who by now was a notorious sponger, is that the industrious cannot be expected to carry those who will not work but sit around all day, singing.

Godwin was by now a man of deep and ridiculous contradictions, not letting his left hand know what his right hand was writing; in effect, he had settled for swimming with the tide: he was reduced, not only to publishing, but also writing, hack-work. The most glaring case is probably his *Life of Chaucer* (1803), which fell into the hands of Walter Scott for review in the *Edinburgh Review* in 1804. Scott found

Godwin's style to be 'uncommonly depraved, exhibiting the opposite defects of meanness and bombast'; much of the book was 'twaddling' and uncommonly 'dull'; and the only gratitude that Scott could summon was for the fact that 'there is no apparent return of that fever of the spirits which alarmed us so much' in the *Political Justice.*

When Godwin tried to persuade Wordsworth to write a versified form of the story of *Beauty and the Beast* for his Juvenile Library, Wordsworth, erstwhile disciple, replied most scrupulously:

> I received your letter and the accompanying Booklet yesterday. Some one recommended to Gainsborough a subject for a picture, it pleased him much, but he immediately said with a sigh, 'What a pity I did not think of it myself'. Had I been as much delighted with the Story . . . as you . . . and as much struck with its fitness for Verse, still your proposal would have occasioned in me a similar regret . . . it is unnecessary to add that, in my opinion, things of this sort cannot be even decently done without great labour, especially in our language.

He then proceeds to try to remedy some of the more glaring deficiencies in Godwin's understanding:

> I confess there is to me something disgusting in the notion of a human being consenting to mate with a beast, however amiable his qualities of heart. . . . I have never seen the Tale in French, but as everybody knows, the word Bête in French conversation perpetually occurs as applied to a stupid, senseless, half-idiotic person – Bétise in like manner stands for stupidity. . . . Brute, metaphorically used, with us designates ill-manners of a coarse kind, or insolent and ferocious cruelty. I make these remarks with a view to the difficulty attending the treatment of this story in our tongue, I mean in verse, where the utmost delicacy, that is, true philosophic permanent delicacy is required.[24]

The pity is that, by this time, such fastidious advice was wasted on Godwin. What, then, of Lamb? Where are we to look for manifestations of his best self? And where, conversely, are the defects of his texts for children most injuriously evident? He achieved his most convincing power as a writer in two places: in his 'Confessions of a Drunkard', and in 'Witches, and other Night-Fears'. The mode in each of these is more nearly confessional than narrative, and the interest that they possess is not so much in the story that is told as in the act of self-revelation. No doubt, a fictive resourcefulness such as Dickens's would have transformed such 'difficult' and tense matter into a compelling fiction: but fictive talent is precisely what was lacking in Lamb. If, for example, one examines the individual 'stories' of *Mrs Leicester's School*, what they do *not* possess is a narrative interest; or, rather, one's expectations of narrative are totally frustrated, for these are undirected, disorientated, inchoate fragments of imperfectly transformed memories: neither autobiography, nor fiction, nor confessional reflection, but a confused stew of all these genres, served up in some indeterminate no man's land. As stories, they go nowhere, because they lack a shaping, formative focus of interest.[25]

In Section VII, for example, 'Maria Howe', we find Lamb reworking material that had first appeared in the drafts of an abortive drama, *John Woodvil* (1798–9), and which later reappeared, expressed with total conviction, in the essay, 'Witches, and other Night-Fears', in the *London Magazine* (October 1821). In the crucial passages, the girl narrator – for Lamb assumes a female persona – speaks of being terrified by the picture of the raising up of Samuel in Stackhouse's *History of the Bible*. She is afraid to go to her old aunt for comfort, for she believes the old woman to be a witch: 'I shrunk back terrified and bewildered to my bed, where I lay in broken sleeps and miserable fancies, till the morning.' The tension within the child's perception of her aunt both as 'good creature who loved me above all the world', and simultaneously as 'a witch . . . who would perhaps destroy me', is resolved very arbitrarily – in fact, is not resolved – by the child's removal to another house. Thus, the 'story' offers an adult's account of childhood crisis and trauma, an account written ostensibly for children but offered in a maladroit fashion, with gross misjudgement, in such a way that the anxiety, the pain, is 'solved' by a *deus ex machina* removal, a mere change of circumstance. The perception of the old aunt as both benign protector (mother-surrogate) and malign witch – this is indeed a rich matter for adult reflection: but it is not imaginatively appropriated in such a way as to render it available to young readers: if indeed such unresolved matter could usefully have been attempted in the first place. As it is, Lamb feels impelled to explain, explain, in order to reassure his young audience.

Similarly, in his Preface to *The Adventures of Ulysses*, he defuses the mysterious mythic power of his story by explaining that 'the agents in this tale, beside men and women, are giants, enchanters, sirens: things which denote external force of internal temptations, the twofold danger which a wise fortitude must expect to encounter in its course through this world.' The potential power of the myth as compelling and terrifying narrative is thus pre-emptively reduced, enervated, by Lamb's demythologizing explanation, despite the fact that Lamb himself was aware of the damaging effects of 'enervation' in writing for children. In his exchange of letters with Godwin, for example, he made his position perfectly clear.

Godwin had read Lamb's *Ulysses* in manuscript, and pleaded with him to tone it down:

> It is strange with what different feelings an author and a bookseller looks at the same manuscript. . . . The author thinks what will conduce to his honour: the bookseller what will cause his commodities to sell.
>
> You, or some other wise man, I have heard to say, 'It is children that read children's books . . . but it is parents that choose them.'[26] The critical thought of the trades-

man puts itself therefore into the place of the parent, and what the parent will condemn. We live in squeamish days.

Godwin pressed Lamb to omit references to cannibalism; to giant's vomit; and to the removal of the giant's eye: his reason was that they would shock 'the female sex'. Lamb's reply did him credit, but also served to point up the fact that Godwin – and perhaps he himself – had painted himself into a corner; for the true power, the dynamic energy, of Homer was not to be truly reconciled, without damage, to the genteel susceptibilities of 'squeamish days', with the forces of the particular market that Godwin was desperately anxious to corner: 'The giant's vomit was perfectly nauseous, and I am glad you pointed it out. I have removed the objection.' As for the rest, Lamb insisted,

> they are lively images of *shocking* things. If you want a book, which is not occasionally to *shock*, you should not have thought of a tale which was so full of anthropophagi and wonders. I cannot alter these things without enervating the book, and I will not alter them if the penalty should be that you and all the London booksellers should refuse it. But speaking as author to author, I must say that I think *the terrible* in those two passages seems to me so much to preponderate over the nauseous, as to make them rather fine than disgusting. . . . I only say that I will not consent to alter such passages, which I know to be some of the best in the book. As an author I say to you, an author, Touch not my work. As to a bookseller I say, Take the work as it is, or refuse it. You are as free to refuse it as when we first talked of it. As to a friend I say, Don't plague yourself and me with nonsensical objections. I assure you I will not alter one more word.[27]

Godwin went on to propose changes in the Preface, so that it would serve to introduce children to Homer – again the itch to instruct – and to explain why they should read him – again the itch to form minds. Lamb replied:

> I have read your letter and am fully of the opinion that
> such a drawling biography as you have chalk'd out is not
> my forte to write. I totally disagree with you; and prefer
> my own preface . . . to any preface a man tells me to write.
> You must take that, or none. I am *sick* absolutely sick of
> that spirit of objection which you constantly shew. . . .[28]

That is the exhilarating and enlivening voice that Lamb
occasionally raised against Godwin; the pity of it is that it
seems to have been raised too infrequently. One may also note
that, on the evidence available, Lamb most strenuously
defended those enterprises in which he alone was involved,
whereas he voiced no hint of intransigence in connection with
the texts on which he collaborated with Mary; it seems that he
was perhaps compromised by his own compassion.

If such ripostes as those letters can be said to show a lively
spirit, so can the following passage, from his 'Dissertation
upon Roast Pig'. One day, when he was a child, he had
received a gift of a plum cake from his Aunt Hetty:

> In my way to school . . . a grey-headed old beggar saluted
> me (I have no doubt at this time of day that he was a
> counterfeit). I had no pence to console him with, and in
> the vanity of self-denial, and the very coxcombry of
> charity, school-boy-like, I made him a present of – the
> whole cake!
>
> I walked on a little, buoyed up, as one is on such
> occasions, with a sweet soothing of self-satisfaction; but
> before I had got to the end of the bridge, my better
> feelings returned . . . and I blamed my impertinent spirit
> of alms-giving . . . and above all I wished never to see the
> face again of that insidious, good-for-nothing, old grey
> imposter.[29]

The point, which became almost a commonplace of
Coleridge's lectures,[30] is nicely made: one is convinced, one's
sympathies are engaged. But it is contradicted, again and
again, in the Lambs' *Poetry for Children*, where frequent calls
are made on the child to exercise, or at least make a display of,

benevolence.[31] As for the qualities of the verse as verse, the tell-tale signs of an amateurish degree of ineptitude are only too obvious: everywhere one finds limp rhythms, forced rhymes, grotesque inversions of word-order for the sake of reaching a rhyme, and overall a generally flaccid tone; nowhere is there any evidence of any deeply compelling energy. It is, indeed, an enervated performance. In Blake's terms, it is 'Insipid' rather than 'Simple'; and 'How wide the Gulf & Unpassable between Simplicity and Insipidity'.

When one actually reads *Tales from Shakespeare* it is difficult to undertand its popularity, unless one recalls that generations of parents, anxious for their children to meet 'high' culture sooner rather than later, have seen it as a stepping-stone, and E.V. Lucas's observation, that its sales in overseas markets have always been higher than at home, also offers a clue: it has found favour with colonial readers, offering as it does a convenient short-cut to mastery of the bard! Godwin's clear admission that the tales had in fact been miconceived followed hard on their first appearance. In the advertisement to the second edition, he wrote:

> The Proprietors of this work willingly pay obedience to the voice of the public. It has been the general sentiment, that the style in which these Tales are written, is not so precisely adapted for the amusement of mere children, as for an acceptable and improving present to young ladies advancing to the state of womanhood.

But he still hedged his bets: 'A few copies have been worked off on the plan of the former impression, for the use of those who rather coincide in the original conception of the writer, than in the opinion above stated.'

Lamb, who had 'written' the tragedies, told Wordsworth that he was very distressed by the 'vulgar' illustrations, which had been supervised by Mrs Godwin. He was also annoyed that Godwin 'cheated me into putting a name to them . . . and then wrote a puff about their *simplicity*, &c., to go with the advertisement as in my name! Enough of this egregious dupery.'[32]

Eight years later Lamb reviewed Wordsworth's *Excursion* for Gifford's *Quarterly Review* (January 1815), and observed of book IV: 'The general tendency of the argument . . . is to abate the pride of the calculating *understanding*, and to reinstate the *imagination* and the affections in those seats from which modern philosophy has laboured but too successfully to expel them.' It is clear that Lamb had grasped one of the essential elements of Wordsworth's poem; yet what is Lamb's Preface to *Ulysses*, if it is not a concession to the claims of 'the calculating understanding'? And perhaps an implicit disavowal of trust in the imagination? Again, in his review of *The Excursion*, he remarked:

> If from a familiar observation of the ways of children, and much more from a retrospect of his own mind when a child, he has gathered more reverential notions of that state than fall to the lot of ordinary observers and . . . has tuned his lyre to the milder utterance of that soft age, his verses shall be censured as infantile by critics who confound poetry 'having children for its subject' with poetry that is 'childish', and who, having themselves perhaps never been children, never having possessed the tenderness and docility of that age, know not what the soul of a child is – how apprehensive! how imaginative! how religious!

At this point one is impelled to cry halt: for Lamb's representation of Wordsworth is veering persistently and softeningly away from Wordsworth, toward an offering of certain features – disabling, weakening, features – of Lamb's potentially regressive sensibility.

If indeed the Victorians inherited and nurtured a sentimental view of childhood, it certainly did not come from Wordsworth; but it may well have incorporated Lamb's tendentious glossing of Wordsworth, just as it owed something to some of Lamb's feebler effusions, such as the pathetic and queasy bachelor's reverie of the 'Dream-Children'.[33]

Such a moment, when Wordsworth's poem is almost reduced to an excuse for Lamb's own reverie, is akin to the

Poetry for Children, offering an abstracted, unlived image of stereotypic children, emblematic of virtue, or of vice, and of Lamb's own sensibility – valetudinarian, soft, self-indulgent, given to a rather pathetic kind of tearful poignancy. Again one wishes that Lamb could have known *The Prelude*, book V, and some real children, as a salutary and tonic corrective. But if such moments offer the feeble, vapid side of Lamb, there is also a much more bracing and potent side to the man. One that he could not share with children.

Like cannibalism, night-fear is a recurrent theme in Lamb, even obsessive. Consider, for example, his objections to John Martin's ambitious painting, *Belshazzar's Feast*; these are presented at length in his essay, 'Barrenness of the Imaginative Faculty . . .', but are also passionately present in a letter to Bernard Barton (11 June 1827): 'Its architectural effect is stupendous; but the human figures, the squalling, contorted little antics that are playing at being frightened, like children at a sham ghost who half know it to be a mask, are detestable.' It is as if only one who knows real fear or terror intimately can object so strongly to images of people merely playing at it. Real terror at an imagined cause is vividly offered in one of his earliest surviving poems, from late 1794, addressed to Mrs Siddons:

> As when a child on some long winter's night
> Affrighted clinging to its Grandam's knees
> With eager wond'ring and perturbed delight
> Listens strange tales of fearful dark decrees
> Muttered to wretch by necromantic spell;
> Or of those hags, who at the witching time
> Of murky midnight ride the air sublime,
> And mingle foul embrace with fiends of Hell:
> Cold Horror drinks its blood![34]

The experience of solitude in the dark was for Lamb clearly bound up with such terrors, and Lamb's nocturnal writings are a record of either deep perturbation or an almost morbid obsession: 'Composed at Midnight', for example, and

'Hypochondriacus. A Conceipt of Diabolical Possession', which he fathered on Robert Burton:

> Fierce Anthropophagi,
> Spectra, Diaboli,
> What scared St Anthony,
> Hobgoblins, Lemures,
> Dreams of Antipodes,
> Night-riding Incubi
> Troubling the fantasy. . . .

This is clearly an exercise in pastiche, which seems in turn to have served as a model for Robert Graves's 'In the Wilderness'. But in the next example there is not only parody, but also a matter that lies much closer to the darker side of Lamb's sensibility: between August 1798 and May 1799 he wrote an Elizabethan-cum-Jacobean pastiche drama, *John Woodvil*, which was published in 1802. One of the passages that he cancelled before the final draft was this:

> I can remember when a child the maids
> Would place me on their lap, as they undrest me,
> As silly women use, and tell me stories
> Of Witches – Make me read 'Glanvil on Witchcraft',
> And in conclusion show me in the Bible,
> The old Family-Bible with the pictures in it,
> The 'graving of the Witch raising up Samuel,
> Which so possest my fancy, being a child,
> That nightly in my dreams an old Hag came
> And sat upon my pillow. . . . Spite of my manhood,
> The Witch is strong upon me every night.[35]

This episode is essentially the same as that which we have met in *Mrs Leicester's School*, of 1808. But it had to wait for Lamb to find his voice as a prose writer before it could achieve its fullest and most telling expression in 'Witches, and other Night-Fears' (1821).[36] It is here that Lamb himself 'dare not treat it otherwise, lest he should falsify a revelation': Lamb 'upon whom his subject has so acted, that it has seemed to direct him – not to be arranged by him'. But, as if in accordance with his own description of the 'sanity of true genius', he also has 'dominion over his subject', and achieves a fullness and coherence that mark the essay off from the whimsical flummery of most of Elia's effusions.

Like Bentham, Dickens and many others, Lamb recalls that he was told many ghost-stories as a child – though he chooses to call them 'witch-stories'. He then tells of his discovery of Stackhouse and, in particular, of the picture of 'the Witch, raising up Samuel, which I wish that I had never seen'. As a child, he says, he was 'dreadfully alive to nervous terrors. The night-time solitude, and the dark, were my hell.' For four years, from the age of four to eight, he knew terror every night; and the worst terror came in the form of the witch he had seen in Stackhouse. Every night he groped and reached out for a friendly arm, but found none, hoped to hear a friendly voice, but heard none.

Then he offers the core of his argument – for he has a case to put, in both senses of the word: 'It is not book, or picture, or the stories of foolish servants, which create these terrors in children.' Whatever form the terror may assume, whatever name we give it – whether Gorgon, Hydra, Chimaera or Witch – the essential truth is this: 'they were there before'. For 'they are transcripts, types – the archetypes are in us, and eternal'. And that, quite simply, is that. It is the high point of Lamb's essay. He goes on to speculate that the answer to this psychic riddle may lie hidden in 'our antemundane condition, and a peep at least into the shadow-land of pre-existence'.[37] And then he lapses into some whimsical thoughts about dreams, and contends that his own are almost exclusively urban in their setting. The tone of the essay pulls back, falls away, and we are back to a kind of chatty amiability, Lamb making himself agreeable. The immediate inspiration for Lamb's momentary transcendence may well have been his love for young Thornton Hunt, Leigh Hunt's child.[38]

He introduces the child as a demonstration of his claim that the terrors of the night are of internal origin, and not derived from external demonstrable causes, such as ghost-stories.

> Dear little T. H., who of all children has been brought up with the most scrupulous exclusion of every taint of superstition – who was never allowed to hear of goblin or apparition, or scarcely to be told of bad men, or to read or hear of any distressing story – finds all this world of fear, from which he has been so rigidly excluded *ab extra*, in his own 'thick-coming fancies'; and from his little midnight pillow, this nurse-child of optimism will start at shapes, unborrowed of tradition, in sweats to which the reveries of the cell-damned murderer are tranquillity.

This, then, was the theme that Lamb returned to time and again, both in verse and prose, the theme that would not let him rest until the essay of 1821 finally seems to have offered an adequate, exorcizing, appeasing, confession. The best of his writing centres on suffering, on vulnerability to pain and fear, and the terrible deprivations of nocturnal loneliness. But when he came to write for children, he always fudged it: his tone is overly didactic or maundering; the narrative is unsure, uncompelling, meandering; his prose often limp, and his verse clumsy. His work for children reminds one of what Jeffrey said of Byron's abortive dramas: 'There is an air of anxiety and labour, and indications, by far too visible, at once of timidity and ambition.'[39]

NOTES AND REFERENCES

1 Preface to *Early Children's Books and their Illustrators* (London: Oxford University Press, 1975), p. xi.

2 *Athenaeum* (January and February 1833); reprinted in *Last Essays of Elia* (1833); E. V. Lucas, *Works of Charles and Mary Lamb*, 7 vols (London: Methuen, 1903–5), vol. II,. p. 226.

3 Even as an adult, Coleridge, who had also been a pupil at Christ's Hospital, found that Boyer's 'severities, even now, not seldom furnish the dreams by which the blind fancy would fain interpret to the mind the painful sensations of distempered sleep'.

4 I borrow this excruciating pun from Michael Leunig, *The*

Penguin Leunig (Melbourne: Penguin Books, Australia, 1974), p.104.

5 See E.V. Lucas, *The Life of Charles Lamb*, 2 vols (London: Methuen, 1905), vol.1, p.309.

6 The phrase is Johnson's, from his 'Joseph Addison', in *Lives of the Poets*, 2 vols (London: Oxford University Press, 1961), vol.1.

7 There were about 200 editions of *Divine Songs* between 1775 and 1825.

8 First published in 1804–5, it included verse by Jane and Ann Taylor, their brother Isaac, Bernard Barton, and Adelaide O'Keefe.

9 *Ulysses* was conceived as a commercial venture, to cash in on the success which Fénelon's *Telemachus* had enjoyed in England.

10 Cf. Forrest Reid, writing of Sir John Gilbert's illustrations to Shakespeare, 1856–8: 'So far from throwing a light on the text, these drawings cast a shadow: they stand, in fact, in much the same relation to it as do Lamb's Tales; they miss everything, or nearly everything that matters' (*Illustrators of the Sixties*, London: Faber & Gwyer, 1928).

11 Cf. Leslie Fiedler's Introduction to *Beyond The Looking Glass*, ed. J. Cott (London: Hart-Davis, 1974).

12 The Fenwick Notes, in *The Prose Works of Wordsworth*, ed. A.B. Grosart, 3 vols (London: Moxon, 1876), vol.III, p.22.

13 *The Enquirer: Reflections on Education, Manners and Literature* (London, 1797).

14 *Works*, vol.VI (1905), pp.252–3.

15 Coleridge referred to Mrs Barbauld as 'that pleonasm of nakedness; since, as if it were not enough to be *bare*, she was also bald'; to her brother, Dr Aikin, as an 'aching void'; and to their nephew, Arthur, as 'a void aching'. Southey wrote to Coleridge in 1804: 'Lamb should singe Mrs Barebald's [*sic*] flaxen wig with squibs, and tie crackers to her petticoats till she leapt about like a parched pea for very torture.'

16 Cf. Florence V. Barry, *A Century of Children's Books* (London: Methuen, 1922), p.153: 'It was doubtless through Godwin that, instead of following the traditions he admired, he began by "adapting" greater works, and went on to write about children from a grown-up point of view.'

17 See Chapter Six, n.13.

18 See, for example, *Letters, The Middle Years*, ed. E. de Selincourt, 2 vols (Oxford, 1937), vol.I, p.101.

19 'Judiciously' because he had a reputation for immorality, extreme rationalism, and Jacobinism, largely as a result of his *Political Justice* (1793; 2nd edn, 1795), and his *Memoirs* of Mary

Wollstonecraft (1798). His more recent writings, especially those for the stage, had earned him much contempt and abuse.

20 Cf. Tristram Shandy: 'I am convinced that there is a North-west passage to the intellectual world. . . . The whole entirely depends upon the auxiliary verbs' (Laurence Sterne, *The Life and Opinions of Tristram Shandy*, 9 vols, York, later London, 1760–7, vol.v, ch.XLII). One is reminded also of Jeremy Bentham and James Stuart Mill.

21 Cf, Locke: 'The sure and only way to get true knowledge is to form in our minds clear and settled notions of things, with names annexed to those determined ideas' (*The Conduct of the Understanding*, sect. XV).

22 Godwin has been credited with the authorship, or editorship, of *Tabart's Collection of Popular Stories for the Nursery . . .*, 4 vols (1804). On stylistic grounds, comparing them with the *Fables, Ancient and Modern*, 2 vols (London: Thomas Hodgkins [1805]), the attribution seems unlikely; and Don Locke writes:

> Because the Juvenile Library's adaptation of Jauffret's *Dramas for Children* is given as by 'The Editor of Tarbart's Popular Tales', and an advertisement at the end of the volume ascribes the French version of 'Baldwin's' (i.e. Godwin's) *Fables* to the same author, Godwin has been credited with all these works. In fact the French translation of the *Fables*, and hence presumably also the *Dramas for Children* and the Tabart anthologies, were the work of his wife. . . . (*A Fantasy of Reason: The Life and Thought of William Godwin*, London, Boston and Henley: Routledge & Kegan Paul, 1980, p.212)

23 *Fables*, vol.1.

24 *Letters, The Middle Years*, vol.1,p.427, dated 9 March 1811. After Wordsworth's refusal, Coleridge offered one of his own poems as a substitute, and a possible sequel of three volumes of a 'junior Plutarch', but neither venture appears to have seen the light of day.

25 Yet even so they touched an occasional nerve in some who had grown up in the Age of Sensibility; in 1831, Landor, for instance, confessed to Crabb Robinson: 'I pressed my temples with both hands, and tears ran down to my elbows'.

26 Godwin is here quoting R.L. Edgeworth's attempted rebuttal of Dr Johnson's famous observation that babies wish to hear stories not of babies but of giants. Edgeworth returned to this question again, in his Introduction to *The Parent's Assistant*, vol.1,p.xi:

> Dr Johnson – to recur to him, not from a spirit of contradiction, but from a fear that his authority should

establish dangerous errors – Dr Johnson says, that 'Babies
do not like to hear stories of babies like themselves; that they
require to have their imaginations raised by tales of giants
and fairies, and castles and inchantments.' The fact remains
to be proved: but supposing that they do prefer such tales, is
this a reason why they should be indulged in reading them?
It may be said that a little experience in life would soon
convince them, that fairies and giants, and enchanters, are
not to be met with in the world. But why should the mind be
filled with fantastic visions, instead of useful knowledge?
Why should so much valuable time be lost? Why should we
vitiate their taste, and spoil their appetite, by suffering them
to feed upon sweetmeats? It is to be hoped, that the magic of
Dr Johnson's name will not have power to restore the reign
of fairies.

Cf. Mrs Godwin's Preface to *Mrs Leicester's School* (1809):
'The great error of many juvenile books is their deviation from
truth . . . why add to the labour [of education] by impressing
false ideas on the mind of an infant . . .?'

27 *Letters of Charles Lamb*, ed. E.V. Lucas, 3 vols (London: J.M.
Dent and Methuen, 1935), vol. 2, p. 53: letter dated 11 March
1808.

28 Locke, *Fantasy of Reason*, p. 227.

29 'A Dissertation on Roast Pig'.

30 Cf. Coleridge's 'Lecture on Education' (May 1808):
In speaking of Education as a means of strengthening the
character, he opposed our system of 'cramming' children. . . . He censured the practice of carrying the notion of
making learning easy much too far; and especially satirised
the good books in Miss Edgeworth's style. 'I infinitely
prefer the little books of "The Seven Champions of
Christendom", "Jack the Giant Killer", etc. etc. – for at
least they make the child forget himself – to your moral tales
where a good little boy comes in and says, "Mama, I met a
poor beggar man and gave him the sixpence you gave me
yesterday. Did I do right?" – "O yes, my dear; to be sure you
did." This is not virtue, but vanity; such books and such
lessons do not teach goodness, but – if I might venture such
a word – goodyness.'

31 The saner insouciant side of Lamb is seen in his views on *The
Ancient Mariner*:
Mrs Barbauld once told me . . . that there were two faults in

it, – it was improbable, and had no moral. As for the probability, I owned that that might admit some question; but as to the want of a moral, I told her that in my own judgment the poem had too much; and that the only, or chief, fault . . . was the obtrusion of the moral sentiment so openly on the reader as a principle or cause of action in a work of such pure imagination. It ought to have had no more moral than the Arabian Night's tale of the merchant's sitting down to eat dates by the side of a well, and throwing the shells aside, and lo! a genie starts up, and says he must kill the aforesaid merchant, *because* one of the date shells had, it seems, put out the eye of the genie's son. (*Specimens of the Table-Talk of S.T. Coleridge*, 1851, p.86)

32 Lamb to Wordsworth (29 January 1807); *Works*, vol. VI (1905), p. 372.
33 *London Magazine* (January 1822); reprinted in *Essays of Elia* (1823): *Works*, vol. II, pp. 100–3.
34 *Works*, vol. V, p. 3.
35 ibid., vol. V, p. 364.
36 ibid., vol. II, pp. 65–70.
37 Cf. Wordsworth's 'Ode: Intimations of Immortality . . .', especially ll. 58–66.
38 Southey complained: 'This poor child . . . had been bred in the ways of modern philosophy.'
39 Francis, Lord Jeffrey: review of Byron, *Edinburgh Review* (February 1822).

CHAPTER NINE

'RÉPONSE SANS RÉPLIQUE'

> There is, first, the literature of *knowledge*; and, secondly, the literature of *power*. The function of the first is – to *teach*; the function of the second is – to move: the first is a rudder; the second, an oar or a sail. The first speaks to the *mere* discursive understanding; the second speaks ultimately, it may happen, to the higher understanding or reason, but always *through* affections of pleasure and sympathy.
>
> (De Quincey, 'The poetry of Pope', *North British Review*, August 1848)[1]

1

In April 1843, Wordsworth observed of Southey: 'Books were his passion,' and went on to admit, 'And wandering, I can with truth affirm, was mine.' He concludes philosophically: 'But this propensity in me was happily counteracted by inability from want of fortune to fulfil my wishes.'[2]

Southey was in the habit of confessing that, had he been born a Roman Catholic, nothing would have delighted him more than to have been a Benedictine monk, 'in a convent, furnished with an inexhaustible library'. Wordsworth, conversely, was an extravagant and incorrigible walker, up to a few weeks before his death at eighty. Yet there is a strong case for arguing that for Wordsworth, certainly in his formative years, reading was in essence not so far removed from wandering: the two activities, ostensibly so unlike, offered him the same fundamental satisfactions – not so much a way of finding enjoyment as of satisfying deep personal needs, even of affirming selfhood. For certain essential purposes, reading and wandering were interchangeable, or at least so alike as to be indistinguishable.

In order to explore this paradox, I can think of no better place to begin, or end, than *The Prelude*, but first I want to offer a characteristic sentence or two from his *Autobiographical Memoranda* of 1847:

> Of my earliest days at school I have little to say, but that they were very happy ones, chiefly because I was left at liberty, then and in the vacations, to read whatever books I liked. For example, I read all Fielding's works, Don Quixote, Gil Blas, and any part of Swift that I liked; Gulliver's Travels, and the Tale of a Tub, being both much to my taste.[3]

In other words, he was free to wander *among* books at his own will, free from supervision or prevenient care; and we can also note, in passing, that Wordsworth's list contains no 'books for children'.[4]

It is in book V of *The Prelude* that he gives this matter close and passionate attention. And of course book V is entitled 'Books': a title that has led to not a little disappointment for readers who discover that the poet gives his mind, not to his undergraduate or adult reading, but to reading in childhood and youth. It is perhaps for this reason that, of all the books of *The Prelude*, book V has received scantest attention. But it is precisely here that Wordsworth presses some of his central claims, and affirms some of his cardinal beliefs, especially in respect of education through books and its relationship with education through, or by, Nature.

Not surprisingly, as he proceeds to lay out for our inspection the literature that seems to him almost as powerful as Nature, he offers Shakespeare, Milton and Homer as pinnacles of human culture. In a surreal anxiety-dream, in which a deluge is about to overwhelm the earth, he sees this great legacy as grievously threatened by apocalyptic oblitera-

tion: his sense – and therefore, our sense – of their precious-
ness and vulnerability are thereby intensified and rendered
more urgent. But he then proceeds to offer what in painting
would be a touching little genre-scene, reminiscent of
Sidney's *Defence of Poetry*[5] and of Mark Akenside's *Pleasures
of Imagination.* Let us not forget, or fail to value, he says:

>   the low and wren-like warblings, made
> For cottagers and spinners at the wheel
> And weary travellers when they rest themselves
> By the highways and hedges: ballad-tunes,
> Food for the hungry ears of little ones. . . .[6]

Akenside's earlier picture of 'little ones' is perhaps the best
moment of his rather didactic poem:

>   by night
> The village-matron, round the blazing hearth,
> Suspends the infant-audience with her tales. . . .
> At every solemn pause the croud recoil
> Gazing each other speechless, and congeal'd
> With shivering sighs: till eager for the event,
> Around the Beldame all erect they hang,
> Each trembling heart with grateful terrors quell'd.[7]

The crucial shift between Akenside and Wordsworth – and it
is a difference of era as well as of the quality of the two minds –
is between a hedonistic, pleasurable, epicurean view of
imagination and one that goes much deeper, goes indeed to
preconscious levels: Wordsworth's claim for these 'rude'
ballads and tales is that they are 'as powers / For ever to be
hallowed – only less / For what we may become, and what we
need / Than Nature's self which is the breath of God.'[8]
    The authentic, historical truth of such scenes, of a commu-
nity of listeners, rapt, possessed, and fed by a singer or story-
teller, is confirmed time and again by one of their keenest
witnesses in England – John Clare, who had the peculiar
advantage of writing his testimony from within such a
community: Wordsworth, like Akenside, was *spectator ab*

extra. As for Wordsworth's large, and unprecedented, claim – 'only less . . . Than Nature's self' – it not only serves as a climax to the movement of the verse-paragraph, but also implicitly affirms Wordsworth's intuition that literature depends on the proto-art of folklore and draws some of its best energies thence;[9] and it also offers the high point from which he can then descend to consider those who in his own day worked to deny Nature, i.e. the nature in, and of, the child.

Current educational innovation – derived, not from the 'common-sense' of such as Johnson or the ingenuous wisdom of such as Shenstone's school-mistress, but from the ferment in psychology and morality that marked the 1790s and early 1800s – Wordsworth perceived as 'an evil which these days have laid / Upon the children of the land – a pest / That might have dried me up body and soul.'[10] Then follows one of the poem's richest and most resonant tropes:

> Oh, where had been the man, the poet where –
> Where had we been we two, belovèd friend,
> If we, in lieu of wandering as we did
> Through heights and hollows bye-spots of tales
> Rich with indigenous produce, open ground
> Of fancy, happy pastures ranged at will,[11]
> Had been attended, followed, watched, and noosed,
> Each in his several melancholy walk,
> Stringed like a poor man's heifer at its feed,
> Led through the lanes in forlorn servitude;
> Or rather like a stallèd ox shut out
> From touch of growing grass, that may not taste
> A flower till it have yielded up its sweets
> A prelibation to the mower's scythe.[12]

The metaphor 'If we . . . ranged at will' is of course making the same point as the old man of seventy-seven made in the *Autobiographical Memoranda*. It is perfectly judged: the young reader *wandered*, at will, through heights, hollows and bye-spots of tales; the metaphor is indeed so apt that there is no need to 'interpret' its parts, to tease out what its local details signify.[13] If we ourselves have been fortunate in our childhood reading, we too have wandered through such places, such 'landscapes', and we also have found them 'rich with indigenous produce'. The image of literature as 'food' ('Food for the hungry ears . . .') is thus deftly sustained. And the correspondences between such metaphorical 'wandering' – the free-ranging fancy going where it will in its reading and listening – and literally wandering over hills and valleys are so intimately and neatly dove-tailed that in the '1850' revision of the poem Wordsworth could directly substitute 'vales' for 'tales' ('Through heights and hollows and bye-spots of . . .'), descending in the event to a less richly suggestive level of meaning.

In both cases – 'vales' and 'tales' – the heights and hollows hint at a range of experiences, ministrations of both joy and fear, cheerfulness and gloom, a sense of both amenity and strenuousness, a variety of motions, of ups and downs: the vicarious experience of the page, the motion of the mind, is experienced physically, feelingly, kinaesthetically; as a journey, out and back; away from the familiar locality, into unknown territory, and then a return, a coming home: a metaphor we can surely endorse if we have ever 'lost ourselves' in a book.

And such explorations, such ventures, on the part of children, were frustrated, prevented, by those who 'attended, followed, watched, and noosed' (i.e. haltered) them, who forced each child to follow a strait and narrow path, separated from friends and companionship, but in pedagogical leading-strings; and allowed to 'feed' only after the mower had first culled the richest part of the pasture. The Norton editors offer a useful footnote to the image of the 'mower's scythe', in observing that 'Wordsworth has in mind the reduction of literature to edifying tales such as those of Thomas Day's *Sandford and Merton* (1783–9) and Maria Edgeworth's *Parents' Assistant* (1796—1801).'[14] This gloss seems entirely appropriate, for in both instances there is the strongly felt presence of a prevenient and weeding hand, clearly determined that children shall neither feed on noxious weeds nor eat too much rich or frivolous food! But the editors could have adduced a case much nearer home: namely, *A Father's Instructions to his Children: consisting of Tales, Fables, and Reflections; designed to promote The Love of Virtue, A Taste for Knowledge, and an early acquaintance with the Works of Nature. By Dr Percival, of Manchester* (1775).[15]

Up to this point in the book, Wordsworth's account of those influences that go to support and feed the young mind had dwelt on singularly *modest* elements – children listening to ballad-singers; himself and Coleridge wandering freely both in tales and vales, unattended, unwatched. This modesty is sustained in the account of his own mother that immediately, and contrastively, follows the image of the mower's scythe with its faint frisson, from the pastoral tradition, of death. It may seem odd that he introduces her through the emblem of 'the parent hen amid her brood' but it serves to exemplify two salient virtues: 'Yet doth she little more / Than move with them in tenderness and love'; and 'alike from seed of theirs / And call of her own natural appetites – / She scratches, ransacks up the earth for food / Which they partake at pleasure.'[16] It is indeed a modest emblem, and yet in its unpretentious fashion it points to a natural morality, a natural piety, that is construed as precisely *not* a denial of nature: the mother hen satisfies her own needs, which are seen as in harmony with those of her brood; and the brood 'partake *at pleasure*'.

Turning directly to his own mother, he affirms that she 'was pure / From feverish dread of error and mishap / And evil, overweeningly so called'; nor was she 'selfish with unnecessary cares'.[17] Dr Percival in his *Father's Instructions* had also offered his readers the emblem, the type, of the parent hen, but the difference of significance is instructive:

Mark the parent hen! said a father to his beloved son. With what anxious care does she call together her offspring. . . . Does not this sight suggest to you the tenderness and affection of your mother? Her watchful care protected you in the helpless period of infancy. . . . She merits your warmest gratitude, esteem and veneration.

It almost seems that Wordsworth was offering a rebuttal of Percival's 'anxious care' in his neat and searching paradox of 'selfish with unnecessary cares'.[18] But what sets the seal on the wise mother's virtue and good sense is that Wordsworth sees her 'Fetching her goodness rather from times past/ Than shaping novelties from those to come.'[19] It is a delightful and engaging image; as if she has just gone down to the bottom of the garden or to an old neighbour's house: virtue or sanity is thus domesticated and given a 'local habitation'; and, contrasting directly with the fashionable and frantic search for the latest psychological theories about child-rearing, it offers a persuasive image of continuity, rendered local by that verb 'fetching'.

In the 1850 revision, a further potent image is added: a person such as his mother 'draws for minds that are left free to trust / In the simplicities of opening life / Sweet honey out of spurned or dreaded weeds.'[20] It was precisely the aim of such as Day, Percival and the Edgeworths to keep children well away from spurned and dreaded 'weeds'. The erection around children of *cordons sanitaires* by parents and guardians, motivated by 'feverish dread of error and mishap', was a common phenomenon in Wordsworth's time,[21] for the era had witnessed not only an unprecedented flood of books on the rearing and education of children, but also some bizarre and even well-publicized experiments in infant upbringing which exemplified, in quite extreme forms, such 'feverish dread.'[22] Let two examples suffice.

My first is as pathetic as it is absurd: Thomas Williams Malkin died on 31 July 1802, at the age of six years and nine months. His father, Benjamin Heath Malkin, sometime headmaster of Bury Grammar School, was the author of *The Scenery, Antiquities and Biography of South Wales*, and a friend of Thomas Johnes of Hafod.[23] On occasions he dined with William Godwin at Horne Tooke's, and with Flaxman, Hoare and Joseph Johnson at Fuseli's: a minor character in the radical, rationalist, dissenting world of the late eighteenth century.

In November 1802, he published a memoir of his son in the *Monthly Magazine*,[24] met Blake in 1803, and published *A Father's Memoirs of His Child* in 1806.[25] The book had a frontispiece by Blake and was dedicated to Johnes. The dedicatory letter reads in part: 'We have both[26] of us felt, I hope we may say duly, the importance of the office of parent, which nature and society have entrusted to our care. We have both met with the best materials to work upon.'[27] He confesses to having hesitated to offer his memoir to the world: his doubt

> took its rise from a prevailing folly of the time. The passion for infantine and puerile exhibitions, so far from having been a motive for taking advantage of the popular caprice, had almost weighed upon my mind, to defer or abandon the project. . . . This town has of late been in a fever of precocious admiration; ready to catch at whatever might administer food to the rage for novelty and the surprising. The most approved models of just recitation, of impressive eloquence, of passionate expression, have been laid on the shelf for inarticulate lispings, or at best for a parrot-taught monotony, the effect of premature and master-ridden study. The powers of music have been called in, to inspire the fatuity of childhood. Memory has been loaded with all the lumber of misplaced erudition.[28]

He then devotes most of his dedicatory letter to introducing the poems of Blake ostensibly[29] to Johnes but in effect to a larger public, which in the event included not only Crabb Robinson but also Wordsworth and his sister Dorothy[30]

What, then, of the child? Both from the testimony of his proud parents and from the evidence of his own precocious writings – he was an incorrigible epistolarian – he emerges as a self-conscious, self-displaying, obsequious prig, as a victim of almost intolerable pressures, and as a little *monstrum eruditionis*.[31] His childish drawings were pressed on Blake for comment, and the poet uncharacteristically beat about the bush, locked in a kind of stammer, symptomatic, it seems, of embarrassment and a desire to exercise tact:

> They are all firm, determinate outline, or identical form. . . . Even the copy from Raphael's Cartoon . . . is a firm, determinate outline. . . . The map of Allestone has the same character of the firm and determinate. . . . this little boy . . . had that greatest of all blessings, a strong imagination, a clear idea, and a determinate vision of things in his own mind.[32]

Here is a characteristic example of the boy's numerous letters, written at the age of four:

> My Dearest Mother,
> I was four years old yesterday. I have got several new books; Mrs Trimmer's English Description: Mental Improvement, by Mrs Priscilla Wakefield; and a Latin Grammar, and English Prints. I think I have got a great many besides the old ones that I had before. Every day I lay up all my Maps, and Chronological Tables are all dissected. I know you love me very much, when I am a good boy, and I hope I shall be always a good boy. Benjamin [a younger brother] knows all his letters, except one or two, and I hope he will know how to read soon. Papa is going to teach me to learn Latin on Friday. That will be to-morrow.

> T.W. Malkin

His father observes:

> In the few volumes, which were set aside as exclusively his own, he seldom suffered even errors of the press, so trifling as those of punctuation, to pass without being

marked by a pencil he kept for the purpose. His books engaged his earliest attention in the morning; and it was rarely that the allurements of the breakfast-table could prevail with him to leave unfinished a story in which he was interested, or a lesson in which he was not perfect.[33]

And generalizes:

While we trace the actual progress of an almost infantine mind, through knowledge up to virtue, we at once ascertain an important fact. Wherever the physical and intellectual powers are endued with suitable vigour, it is within the province of education to impart an early taste for elegant and rational pursuits; it is within the latitude of a discriminating judgment, to abridge the mental imbecility of childhood, without quenching the natural and salutary fire of the animal spirits. To aim at those frivolous accomplishments of declamation and histrionic exhibition, which may manufacture pertness in a boy, but will never send a man into the world, is the reproach and folly of our present times. Not for such attainments do I contend; but for the timely cultivation of useful and substantial knowledge, stripped of its wilder, and as we may call them, forest shoots, by the urbanity and good temper of those who superintend its growth.[34]

How, in the event, was Malkin's pious *Memoir* received?

[*The British Critic*:] this book . . . is one of the most idle and superfluous works that we have ever seen . . . it exemplifies chiefly what is seen continually, that the partiality of parents can easily convert trifles into prodigies.

[Christopher Lake Moody, *The Monthly Review*:] we are not sure that this precocity of genius is desirable; nor that this exhibition of it is likely to do any good, unless the melancholy termination of the tale should teach parents, instead of being solicitous for premature mental im-

provement in their children, to study to give them that
vigour of constitution which is essential to their attainment of manhood. . . . Mr Malkin's ardor is not sufficiently chastised by judgment.[35]

The Malkin *Memoirs* exemplify, almost like a case-book,
Wordsworth's charge of 'feverish dread of error and mishap':
it is notable that wherever error or mishap might conceivably
lurk, the prevenient and anxious care of Thomas's parents
rushed in to prevent anything untoward, either in matters of
morality, religion (especially as it touched on the matter of
salvation), or reason;[36] and in the child's reading, his
encyclopaedic reading, no hint of frivolity, no whiff of mere
enjoyment or pleasure, is allowed. Thus, his reading included
Evenings at Home; Mrs Trimmer's *English Description*; Mrs
Wakefield's *Mental Improvement*; Latin grammar; Greek
grammar; *Illustrious Heads*; chronological tables; the Bible;
and *The Book of Quadrupeds*;[37] his own most revealing
comment is: 'geography, I find, is a very clever thing for me to
know'. He died with a geographical jig-saw puzzle, intended
for instruction rather than amusement, in his hands. One is
reminded of Edward Young's *Fifth Satire*:

> Like cats in air-pumps, to subsist we strive
> On joys too thin to keep the soul alive.

My second example is even more extraordinary: it can be
said to derive philosophically from the polymathic influences
and ambitions of the Lunar Society: and circumstantially
from the moment when, in 1795, Tom Wedgwood inherited a
fortune from his father, Josiah, and decided to disburse some
of it to philanthropic ends. He discussed the question with
William Godwin, and also with Basil Montagu, the friend of
Wordsworth and Dorothy. He slowly hatched a scheme, and
in July 1797 wrote an outline in a letter to Godwin.[38]
Essentially it derived from the theory of the Association of
Ideas, and Wedgwood argued that given the chaos of impressions and perceptions that characterized the formative years

of any normal life it was a miracle that anyone developed a coherent mind at all. 'What a host of half-formed impressions and abortive conceptions blended into a mass of confusion.'[39] An alternative, a neat, clear, controlled, co-ordinated alternative, had to be found, and once a child was reared in such an orderly fashion the result (genius!) would speak for itself. Beddoes, Godwin, Horne Tooke, Holcroft and others would provide the philosophical and psychological rationale and *modus operandi*; and who better to act as superintendents of the child–subject than Wordsworth and Coleridge?

> One, or two, superintendents of the practical part. The only persons that I know of as at all likely for this purpose, are Wordsworth and Coleridge. I never saw or had any communication with either of them. Wordsworth, I understand to have many of the requisite qualities and from what I hear of him, he has only to be convinced that this is the most promising mode of benefiting society, to engage him to come forward with alacrity. The talents of Coleridge I suppose are considerable &, like Wordsworth's, quite disengaged. I am only afraid that the former [i.e. Coleridge] may be too much a poet and religionist to suit our views.

In order that the child should not be exposed to contradictory impressions, it would be necessary for his every waking moment to be supervised, and for his very movements and environment to be rigorously controlled. In the Autumn of 1797, Tom Wedgwood was with Wordsworth at Alfoxden and put his proposal to him. Wordsworth's response was such that Wedgwood quickly became disenchanted with him;[40] early in 1798, Wordsworth wrote coolly to a friend: 'No doubt you have heard of the munificence of the Wedgwoods towards Coleridge. I hope the fruit will be good as the seed is noble.' Certainly, Coleridge persisted in his pursuit of method and system; in 1799 he wrote, to Josiah Jr, from Germany: 'I have attended the lectures on Physiology, Anatomy, and Natural History, with regularity, and have endeavoured to understand these subjects.'[41] It seems probable, as David Erdman argues, that it was a result of Wedgwood's plausible scheme that Wordsworth was provoked to ask himself 'Yes, but how was *my* mind formed? Was it shaped by relentless supervision? By a careful programming?' And his answer, considered long and hard, was *The Prelude*. To put it another way, Wordsworth was ready to begin *The Prelude*: all that was needed was the provoking irritation offered by Tom Wedgwood.

Lines 290–369 of book V comprise a portrait of a 'monster-child', such as the Malkin parents fondly set out to rear and such as might have come out of Wedgwood's behaviourist experiment. The Norton editors, on the basis of the evidence of the manuscripts, date these lines to February 1804. Muriel Jaeger's suggestion[42] that they derive from Wordsworth's reading of Malkin's *Memoirs* cannot therefore be supported; and six-and-a-half years had passed since Wedgwood had put his proposal to Wordsworth. But there is really no pressing need to affix a singular historical source for Wordsworth's portrait: the essential point is that both Malkin and Wedgwood exemplify different aspects of a general fever that gripped England at that time, of which no one who read even the newspapers could fail to be unaware. And Wordsworth had immediate, even intimate, reasons for observing such aberrations in child-rearing with keen interest:[43] whatever the dynamic roots of *The Prelude* may have been, Wordsworth's interest in the formative aspects of childhood experience did not depend on the sensational experiments, the fervent arguments, the plague of anxieties of the time; but in so far as Wordsworth construed his own early life as profoundly normative, as in an important sense exemplary, the perversions, the monsters, clearly offered him a timely, and poetically effective, range of contrasts.

So from the 'benign' and 'hopeful' heart of his own mother, he turns to the 'child, no child, / But a dwarf man'. I have already used the term 'portrait' to speak of this paragraph, but 'caricature' would be a more appropriate term; indeed, there is a sharpness, a grotesque touch, an element of savagery, even, such as characterized English caricature before the relative moderation and amenity of the 1830s (such as we find in the work of John Doyle) became fashionable; and many of the graphic details of Wordsworth's portrayal of the child support this view: certainly, most of the sharply telling effects have the vividly emblematic quality of such works as Gillray's and Rowlandson's. Wordsworth uses the conflating and incongruous devices of caricature: 'child' and 'man' are superimposed, telescoped, to produce 'dwarf'; his gifts 'bubble o'er'; he is a 'garnished dish'; fully panoplied; his brain is over-run by a 'rank growth of propositions' – one can almost see them, as in a satirical cartoon; and he carries a globe and sceptre, transformed, as in the metamorphoses of caricature, into telescope, crucible and map.[44] And, of course, like Wedgwood's intended victim, the child is a prisoner: his path is 'choked with grammars' and,

> ever as a thought of purer birth
> Rises to lead him toward a better clime,
> Some intermeddler still is on the watch
> To drive him back, and pound him, like a stray,
> Within the pinfold of his own conceit.[45]

an image that directly echoes lines 238–45.
Like little Malkin, this monster child

> must live
> Knowing that he grows wiser every day
> Or else not live at all, and seeing too
> Each little drop of wisdom as it falls
> Into the dimpling cistern of his heart.[46]

The child perceives wisdom atomistically, as explicit, and incremental; in other words, in Wordworth's world, it is not wisdom at all. But worst of all, the child, incarcerated in a mad forcing-house,[47] is cut off from Nature, which is here figured as a benign old woman: the child has no play-things, and has no consciousness of the earth as a benign playground:

Meanwhile old Grandame Earth is grieved to find
The playthings which her love designed for him
Unthought of – in their woodland beds the flowers
Weep, and the river-sides are all forlorn.[48]

As with the figure of the Mower, we are once more close to intimations of death; in this instance, the death of the spirit, the death of nature in the child; indeed, as we shall see, the death of the child. As for books in such a child's life, it is clear that apart from grammars, he is busily acquiring 'useful knowledge' – 'names of districts, cities, towns': for 'in learning and in books / He is a prodigy'. So artificial is the child, so very much a product of a denaturalized, enclosed, factitious environment, that the moment he is exposed to 'the air of common sense', the 'corps / Slips from us into powder'. It is a bizarre and disturbing image – of a corpse, long dead, being exhumed, and disintegrating on its first contact with the air.

We have already been offered, through the progression of contrasts that gives book V its articulation, various intimations of an alternative, older, sanity and wisdom, and Wordsworth now plunges us into one of his most enthusiastic and ostensibly fantastic exclamations:

Oh, give us once again the wishing-cap
Of Fortunatus, and the invisible coat
Of Jack the Giant-killer, Robin Hood,
And Sabra in the forest with St George![49]

This is an emphatic reversion to a more primal world – that of the chap-book romance: a world that many progressive educational innovators of Wordsworth's time would have dismissed as over-run with dreaded weeds: the whole thrust of the Enlightenment's view of the culture of childhood, was that it would be far saner, far more rational, far more intellectually effective if such nonsense as romance were expelled from the child's world.[50]

Here, however, romance takes its place alongside the

mother 'fetching her goodness rather from times past' and offers a vivid manifesto of that reaction against the rationalistic, the 'enlightened', and the 'useful' that was to characterize conservative thought for the next forty years and to continue to erupt sporadically ever since.[51] One might adduce here not only Walter Scott, but that tradition which, with hindsight, we can now characterize as Wordsworthian, represented most persuasively by Dickens and Ruskin. An account of the persisting enthusiasm for chap-book romances throughout the eighteenth century has already been given in Chapter Two.

Meanwhile, the specific gift that they confer on the child, in Wordsworth's argument, is this:

> The child whose love is here, at least doth reap
> One precious gain – that he forgets himself.[52]

To be absorbed, self-forgetfully, in a 'virtual' reality outside oneself, to be possessed or captivated by such a phenomenon – this is in itself a good. To attempt to justify such a claim on any prior grounds would be to fall prey to a kind of reductivism: one either recognizes the truth of the claim, or one does not. But Wordsworth already had his reinforcing article of faith available, for the paragraph that follows – lines 370–88 – dates from 1798–9. The vexation, impatience, and scorn of these lines, directed at the rationalizing folly of educational philosophers and psychologists, may well, indeed, have been provoked by Wedgwood or the Edgeworths, but the main rhetorical effect, apart from paradoxically diminishing the rationalists by building them up, is to lead us to a central affirmation –

> A wiser spirit is at work for us,
> A better eye than theirs, most prodigal
> Of blessings, and most studious of our good,
> Even in what seem our most unfruitful hours[.][53]

If it is *seemingly* unfruitful for a child to lose himself in old romances, it is equally so to stand at evening imitating the hooting of owls – and this is where Wordsworth springs his trap. Through the Boy of Winander he leads us into an awestruck recognition of the numinous power of the time and place, a power that Wordsworth sees as *preconsciously* affecting the child deeply; a silent meditation over the grave of the owl-teasing boy, now returned to nature; and a celebration of the benign, unpretentious sanity of the boy's erstwhile schoolmistress: a transformation of Shenstone's quaint antiquarianism into a compelling centre of benign energy and happiness: here his lines gather to themselves the rhythms and counterpoint, the bustle and liveliness of a crowd of exuberant children at play – the play of

> real children, not too wise,
> Too learned, or too good, but wanton, fresh,
> And bandied up and down by love and hate;
> Fierce, moody, patient, venturous, modest, shy,
> Mad at their sports like withered leaves in winds[.][54]

And the paragraph ends with a kind of prayer, a prayer that such natural energies shall survive:

> May books and nature be their early joy,
> And knowledge, rightly honored with that name –
> Knowledge not purchased with the loss of power![55]

lines that might serve as an epigraph for many of Dickens's chapters on children in school; but which would have been greeted by the members of the Society for the Diffusion of Useful Knowledge with an uncomprehending shake of the head.

Wordsworth's next paragraph contains a more problematical claim; akin in some respects to the observation that Keats offered in his letter to George and Tom Keats in December 1818: 'the excellence of every Art is its intensity, capable of making all disagreeables evaporate, from their being in close relationship with Beauty and Truth. . . .'[56] When a drowned man is pulled out of the lake – 'ghastly face, a spectre shape' – the nine-year old boy is not afraid: he feels 'no vulgar fear' ('no soul-debasing fear' in the 1850 text); and the reason adduced for this tranquil freedom from fear, horror or terror is that he had already witnessed such sights – his 'inner eye' had already seen them 'among the shining streams / Of fairy-land, the forests of romance'. The horrible spectacle is alchemically neutralized by the prior experience, the virtual experience, of such dreadful sights in fantasies and romances. So that his experience of fictive dread makes available to him 'a spirit' that 'hallowed' what he actually saw 'With decoration and ideal grace, / A dignity, a smoothness, like the words [1850: works] / of Grecian art and purest poesy.'[57] The Norton editors invite us here to compare Coleridge's celebrated letter of October 1797, in which he claims that from his early reading of fairy-tales and the *Thousand and One Nights* his mind had 'been habituated *to the Vast* – & I never regarded *my senses* in any way as the criteria of my belief',[58] but I am not convinced that these instances are usefully comparable. There is, even allowing for the idiosyncracies of Coleridge's epistolary manner and the curious leaps of his mind, something emphatically nebulous, cosmic and metaphysical in his term 'the Vast', with its characteristic capitalization: he is asking the word to do an undue amount of his work for him. Wordsworth, rather, is claiming that the virtual, fictive, imagined, contemplation of the dead or 'such sights' has a beneficially transforming effect on one's response to the actuality, whenever one should subsequently encounter it. Whether or not one is inclined to accept this claim – and it has become something of a truism in English-teaching circles – it nevertheless serves well as a preface to the next three paragraphs.

These celebrate the way in which books can create a sense of kinship, of community; of the ways in which we can recognize our own more private impulses and aspirations in the words on the page. These linked paragraphs begin in a mood of exhilaration that clearly belonged back in Wordsworth's early years, and yet is here communicated as still vivid, fresh and powerful. The immediacy of these retrieved moments is comparable to the best of Tolstoy's *Childhood, Boyhood and Youth*, to Gosse's *Father and Son*, and to the early pages of George Tyrrell's extraordinary *Autobiography*. But what was it that produced so intense a mood of exhilaration, indeed of exaltation? It was his devouring of the *Thousand and One Nights*.

The *Arabian Nights*, as we tend to call them, came to him in truncated form, in 'a little yellow canvas-covered book', and he was told that this book contained only a small selection of the tales: this announcement 'was in truth to me / A promise scarcely earthly'. He and a friend 'religiously' saved their pennies in order to buy all of the tales, but they never succeeded in saving enough. The books are transformed: from yellow, to 'That golden store of books' – there is an almost Arabian hint of untold wealth here – and his 'devouring' of them competes with his passion for fishing:

> I . . . have read, devouring as I read,
> Defrauding the day's glory – desperate –
> Till with a sudden bound of smart reproach
> Such as an idler deals with in his shame,
> I to my sport betook myself again.[59]

Suffice it to say that here Wordsworth offers us a totally convincing sense of a paranormal state, a state of almost intolerable excitement, of possession, of irresistible temptation, indeed of a kind of gluttony, shot through with a strong element of guilt or shame that to succumb, to be possessed in such a way, would be morally reprehensible. Certainly, in its high-pitched emotional intensity, its sense of the extraordinary, this episode constitutes one of the high points of book V, indeed of the whole poem.

His next paragraph is more measured, reflective and philosophical, but constitutes a searching defence of such fantasies as the *Thousand and One Nights* and of the child's possession of, and by, them. It is, centrally, a legitimation of the non-didactic imagination, of the teller of tales who has no moralizing designs on his audience: a defence of fiction in

itself, of 'fictive music', to borrow a term from Wallace
Stevens. And as in the case of the hooting child assimilating
'unawares' the 'solemn imagery' of the evening hillside, so,
here, the process, the educating process, is essentially *pre-
conscious*: Wordsworth offers it, without apology or strenuous claim, as the operation of 'a gracious spirit' mediated by
tellers of tales:

> invisibly
> It comes, directing those to works of love
> Who care not, know not, think not, what they do.[60]

or, in the 1850 version:

> invisibly
> It comes, to works of unreproved delight,
> And tendency benign, directing those
> Who care not, know not, think not what they do.

No more direct confrontation with those of a didactic
persuasion could be imagined, for the defence here is of a deep
insouciance, a trust, a freedom from good intentions: the
defence is of insouciance, and is itself insouciant. And again
Wordsworth brings us back to one of his basic recurrent
images – that of sustenance:

> Dumb yearnings, hidden appetites, are ours,
> And they must have their food.[61]

('They must' is italicized in the 1850 version.)

This again is an uncompromising riposte to the rational
educators of the English enlightenment. It implicitly recognizes an epistemological limit: the yearnings are 'dumb': the
appetites are 'hidden'. It is as if he is throwing down the
gauntlet of the unknowable to the Wedgwoods and
Edgeworths, with their reductive pursuit of a psychological
omniscience. Indeed it is for such psychologists that he
reserves his most extreme abuse, for at line 549 they are
characterized as less than human, indeed as simian.

The context is an interesting one: Wordsworth presses his

claim for fictions, tales, fantasies, romances, beyond the years of childhood and into the perturbations and tensions of adolescence, a time when the individual often loses childhood's uncritical sense of community, and discovers a disconcerting sense of isolation, of unrelatedness, of disconnectedness.

Christopher Wordsworth, treating of the *Lyrical Ballads*, wrote that Wordsworth 'seemed to take a pleasure in running counter to conventional usages, and in defying received opinions'; some of his poems 'seemed like wanton affronts to the judgement of the world, and might be resented by many as indicating a temper which would hurl defiance against public opinion with wayward wilfulness, petulant pride, and random recklessness.'[62]

Now this could be read, out of context, as a reasonably accurate characterization of the antinomian adolescent: and just as Wordsworth's defence of insouciance is itself insouciant, so his representation of the complex uncertainties and tensions of adolescence is characterized by an almost adolescent passion! But the passion is not merely a matter of prickly contrariness; more usefully, more positively, it is an affirmation of kinship, of secret sympathy, of community: a sense of deep community between the adolescent reader and the tellers of tales, the creators of fiction, those who provide an 'alternative' world within which the adolescent can continue to live even while the actual world is less than amenable to his living needs, desires and aspirations. It is not that Wordsworth is denying the root-meaning of the word 'adolescent' – to grow up, to become adult – but rather that he is claiming that in the midst of tension –

> Unwilling to forego, confess, submit,
> Uneasy and unsettled . . .
> . . . not yet tamed
> And humbled down

– the adolescent can find deep affinity and companionship, strength and consolation, from those

who make our wish our power, our thought a deed,
An empire, a possession.[63]

One of the abiding questions for any culture such as ours,
whose epistemology is rooted in the empirical sciences, in the
claims of rationality, in the light of consciousness, is to
concede an appropriate status to the claims of fantasy, of
fictions, both literary and existential. Wordsworth's claim is
that fictions are not to be endorsed on exclusively rational
grounds, indeed that the endorsement must transcend the
rational, or go beneath it. The 'ape philosophy'[64] dismisses
the tellers of tales as 'Imposters, drivellers, dotards': Wordsworth's answer is not a dialectically rational answer, but
rather a presentation of an epiphany: the 'forgers of lawless
tales' are apostrophized as

> Ye whom time
> And seasons serve – all faculties – to whom
> Earth crouches, th' elements are potter's clay,
> Space like a heaven filled up with northern lights,
> Here, nowhere, there, and everywhere at once.[65]

Such an appeal is implicitly confessional; as Stanley Cavell
has remarked, 'In confessing you do not explain or justify, but
describe how it is with you. And confession, unlike dogma, is
not to be believed but tested, and accepted or rejected.'[66]
What is involved at such moments in *The Prelude* is our
recognizing – or, conversely, our failing to recognize – what
Wittgenstein has called 'forms of life'. Here, as elsewhere, the
'success' of the poem depends not on an intellectual assent to
propositions, psychological or philosophical, but on an
existential or phenomenological recognition of 'what happened'. And Wordsworth could have said to those who failed
to 'recognize' his forms of life what Eliot put into Harry's
mouth in *The Family Reunion*:

> people to whom nothing has ever happened
> Cannot understand the unimportance of events.[67]

The Prelude is emphatically and essentially the utterance of someone to whom something has happened: and to recognize the truth of the report necessarily involves the reader who does so recognize in a reaching out, an affirmation of a bond, a kinship. In this sense, the poem *is* philosophical, for to affirm that bond, to accept kinship, involves also our assent to certain views of the nature of learning, of growth, of education in its radical, inner, sense: it is to insist that there are indeed roots, and continuities, and gifts; and that there is also a converse (even if 'clever') rootlessness, a mechanistic fallacy, with which many of the rational educationists of the late eighteenth century were infatuated.

As for the 'forms of life' that Wordsworth offers his readers, and how we respond to them, the poet realized that it is through sharing such forms with others, through recognizing others' forms in ourselves, that a sense of community depends; and he recognized his community as with those who created fictions:

> oh, then we feel, we feel,
> We know, when we have friends.[68]

Or, in the words of Stanley Cavell, putting the matter more 'philosophically':

> We learn and teach words in certain contexts, and then we are expected, and expect others, to be able to project them into further contexts. Nothing insures that this projection will take place (in particular, not the grasping of universals nor the grasping of books of rules), just as nothing insures that we will make, and understand, the same projections. That on the whole we do is a matter of our sharing routes of interest and feeling, modes of response, senses of humor and of significance and of fulfilment, of what is outrageous, of what is similar to what else, what a rebuke, what forgiveness, of when an utterance is an assertion, when an appeal, when an explanation – all the whirl of organism Wittgenstein calls

'forms of life'. Human speech and activity, sanity and community, rest upon nothing more, but nothing less, than this.[69]

Book V has seventy-five more lines to run, yet I confess that most of the remainder reads to me like an anti-climax. Certainly there is a fascinating paragraph on his adolescent discovery of poetry, but he is moving into a phase of his life where critical consciousness, the gift of maturation, slowly supplants the preconscious – 'words themselves / Move us with conscious pleasure' – and my purpose in this chapter – co-extensive with book V! – has been to consider Wordsworth's view of education, of formative influences, in the child's pre-conscious, pre-conceptualizing years. But it would be churlish not to recognize the distinctive and powerful fusion that occurs in lines 619–29, where the sense of something-more-to-be-known in the mysterious forces of Nature is also found to be aroused by literature; I use the word 'fusion' in order to stress that what Wordsworth achieves here is more than interaction: the teasing, suggestive, growth-inducing invitations of Nature, and of literature, become inextricably intertwined. Both offer 'flashes', 'a glory scarce their own': in a word, epiphanies, perceived momentarily, as by a flash of lightning; and it is perfectly appropriate that, with the exception of eight structurally convenient, rather prosy lines by way of coda, the fifth book should end by affirming a vision both of a nature and of a literature that are, like grace, inherently unavailable to the exclusively rational, positivist, or analytical mind.

One last word. In a memorable essay,[70] Lionel Trilling observed that he found in book V a kind of excess, a gratuitous anger or indignation, an intemperateness that he found not altogether pleasing or decorous. What Trilling seems to me to be overlooking here is that, whilst the poem has a truth, a power, that continues to tell even when the poem is taken out of context, book V depends, for some of its intentions and tactics, on its moment in time and on Wordsworth's urgent conviction that there was 'something rotten in the state' of English society and, in particular, of its formative agencies. The most emphatic recognition of the timeliness, appropriateness, and justice of book V is, I think, to be found in the vivacious *Lectures on Poetry* of Francis Hastings Doyle, sometime Professor of Poetry at Oxford:

> It is pleasant to see how genius and common sense unite, and arm him as it were with a two-handed sword, to strike down the champions of a plan for educating – hardly boys and girls – little lay figures rather, able to eat and drink and talk, certainly to talk. A plan that came into fashion some sixty or seventy years ago, and, even now, is not as much discredited as one could wish. You of a younger generation can hardly realise the intense hatred with which all right-hearted children of my time regarded Harry and Lucy, and those other little prigs, gathering buttercups – I beg their pardon, ranunculos – something or other, under the eye of an omniscient tutor, in 'Evenings at home'. I can only say, that having been robbed, at one period of my life, of the 'Arabian Nights', and 'Robinson Crusoe', and fastened down to these quasi-scientific dogmas in exchange, I have been imbued with an unjust prejudice against many respectable plants ever since. Papilionaceous flowers, in particular, I have always regarded as personal enemies. The true answer to all the nonsense talked about useful knowledge is now obvious enough . . . but there can be no doubt, I think, that the earliest form and the most effective form of this unanswerable answer, this *'réponse sans réplique'*, is to be assigned – I had almost said, is to be scored – to Wordsworth in *The Prelude*.[71]

NOTES AND REFERENCES

1 Reprinted in *De Quincey as Critic*, ed. John E. Jordan (London and Boston: Routledge & Kegan Paul, 1973), p. 269.

2 Christopher Wordsworth, *Memoirs of William Wordsworth* (1851), vol. 2, p. 32.

3 ibid., vol. 1, p. 10.

4 Cf. Dickens's list of his own early reading: 'Roderick Random, Tom Jones, The Vicar of Wakefield, Don Quixote, Gil Blas, Robinson Crusoe'. See Harry Stone, *Dickens and the Invisible World* (London and Basingstoke: Macmillan, 1980), ch. 3.

5 'A tale which holdeth children from play, and old men from the chimney corner' (*A Defence of Poetry*, ed. J. van Dorsten, London: Oxford University Press, 1975, p. 40). Cf. George Cruickshank's illustration of the Grimms' *Kinder- und Hausmärchen*, translated by Edgar Taylor and 'a circle of relatives' as *German Popular Stories*, 2 vols (London: vol. I, C. Baldwyn, 1823; vol. II, James Robins & Co., 1826).

6 *The Prelude, 1799, 1805, 1850*, ed. Jonathan Wordsworth, M.H. Abrams and Stephen Gill (New York: Norton, 1979), bk V, ll. 28–12. I quote from the 1805 text, unless otherwise stated.

7 *Pleasures of Imagination*. The quotation is from the 1754 edition, bk I, ll. 255–70. Akenside's poem disappoints because, as Morton Paley has remarked, 'he does exactly what he says he will not do, and writes a didactic poem in discursive language' (*Energy and Imagination*, London: Oxford University Press, 1970, p. 227).

8 *The Prelude*, bk V, ll. 220–2.

9 Cf. J.L. Lowes: 'to attempt to trace the prints of the *Arabian Nights*, and the *Seven Champions* . . . and "Tom Hickathrift" in "The Rime of the Ancient Mariner", and "Christabel", and "Kubla Khan" were like seeking the sun and rain of vanished yesterdays in the limbs and foliage of the oak. But the rain and the sun are there' (*The Road to Xanadu*, London: Constable & Co., 1927, p. 460). R.P. Blackmur: 'The mind uses what it must. I would suppose that in the voices of the children which reverberate through the *Four Quartets* lie more than echoes of Grimm's [*sic*] tales of *The Juniper Tree* and of *The Singing Bone*. They were present in *Ash Wednesday* and they are present here' (*Language as Gesture*, London: Allen & Unwin, 1954, p. 194). D.W. Harding: 'It is not surprising . . . that variants of the Cinderella story as well as the psychologically allied story of the foundling princess, should be prominent among the basic themes of Jane Austen's novels' (Introduction to *Persuasion*, Harmondsworth: Penguin Books, 1965). Seamus Heaney on Dorothy Wordsworth's entry in her *Journal* for 29 April 1802: she describes herself and her brother lying under a blanket of fallen leaves: 'It did go through me with a kind of pang of

connection. . . . . Maybe it connects with the child's fear of rustlings and hedges – dead leaves – or maybe the fear that somehow hung around the memory of the story of *The Babes in the Wood*.' Roman Jakobson on Afanas'ev's *Russian Fairy Tales*: 'Without it . . . there would have been less richness of protean imagery in the poetry of Esenin, who, after long searchings in the hungry years of the civil war, procured a copy. . . .' (*Russian Fairy Tales*, London: Sheldon Press, 1976, p.637).

10 *The Prelude*, bk V, ll. 227–9.

11 Catherine Sinclair, in the Preface to *Holiday House* (1839), wrote that she had 'endeavoured to paint that species of noisy, frolicsome, mischievous children which is now almost extinct, wishing to preserve a sort of fabulous remembrance of days long past, when young people were like wild horses on the prairies, rather than like well-broken hacks on the road.'

12 *The Prelude*, bk V, ll. 232–45.

13 For an excellent account of the kinds of metaphors present in *The Prelude*, see H. Lindenberger, *On Wordsworth's Prelude* (Princeton: Princeton University Press, 1963), ch. 3.

14 *The Prelude*, p. 164, n. 7.

15 Thomas Percival was an active member of the Manchester Literary and Philosophical Society, and a friend of Diderot, Hume and Voltaire.

16 *The Prelude*, bk V, ll. 250–1, 253–6.

17 ibid., ll. 276–8, 280.

18 Percival's *Instructions*, p. 112, offers the following remark: ' "To rear the tender thought; / To teach the young idea how to shoot . . ." is a pleasing, though anxious, task.' The image of the mother-hen also occurs in John Gay: 'The hen, who from the chilly air / With pious wings protects her care, / And ev'ry fowl that flies at large / Instructs me in a parent's charge' (Introduction, *Fables*, Glasgow, 1752: a copy of this edition was in Wordsworth's library).

19 *The Prelude*, bk V, ll. 267–8.

20 ibid. (1850 text), ll. 276–8.

21 See, for example, Keats's letters for a wry running commentary on Dilke's tiresome anxiety over his son's education; Dilke was significantly characterized by Keats as a 'Godwin perfectibity Man'. Cf. *The Prelude*, bk XIII, ll. 315–26; and Keats's letter to the George Keatses of February–May 1819 (*Letters*, ed. R. Gittings, London: Oxford University Press, 1963, p. 233).

22 The newspapers of the period frequently contained reports of child-prodigies being displayed for public admiration. Cf. *The Journals of Claire Clairmont*, ed. M.K. Stocking (Cambridge,

Mass.: Harvard University Press, 1968), pp. 18–19, for examples of forced precociousness in the children of the Godwin household.

23 On Johnes and Hafod, see *Landscape in Britain, c. 1750–1850* (London: Tate Gallery, 1973).

24 *The Monthly Magazine and British Register*, vol. xiv (1 November 1802), p. 329.

25 In the same year, 1806, Benjamin Tabart published *The Juvenile Plutarch: containing Accounts of the Lives of Celebrated Children, and of the Infancy of Persons who have been Illustrious for their Virtues and Talents* – a two-volume edition of the one-volume version published in 1801 by R. Phillips (both have been attributed to J.F. Savill). Vol. ii included not only Pope and Milton but also Thomas Williams Malkin.

26 Johnes was a friend of Sir James Edward Smith, founder of the Linnean Society, who especially admired Johnes's young daughter on account of her precocious botanical and entomological studies.

27 B. Malkin, *A Father's Memoirs of His Child* (London: Longman, Hurst, Rees & Orme, 1806), p.v. Allowing for differences of motive, it is interesting to compare the last sentence with Henry James's 'how far Osmond's desire to be effective was capable of going – to the point of playing theoretic tricks on the delicate organism of his daughter' (*The Portrait of a Lady*, 1881).

28 Malkin, ibid., pp. x–xi.

29 'Ostensibly' because he had already presented a copy of *Songs of Innocence* to Johnes in 1805.

30 It is clear from the textual evidence of Dorothy's notebooks that she derived her copies of the Blake poems from Malkin's text.

31 Cf. Anon., *The First Lines of Education according to Philosophical Principles* (London, 1811); 'It is infinitely better for a child to be healthy and stout, than a *monstrum eruditionis*.'

32 *William Blake's Writings*, ed. G.E. Bentley, Jr, 2 vols (Oxford: Clarendon Press, 1978), vol. ii, pp. 818–19; Malkin, op. cit., p. 34.

33 The corrective or censoring red pencil was also a salient feature of the Edgeworth household.

34 Malkin's concern for urbanity and elegance marks him off from Mrs Trimmer, whose priorities were almost exclusively moral/religious.

35 *The British Critic* (September 1806), p. 339; and, for Moody, *The Monthly Review* (October 1806), p. 216. For an enthusiastic response, see *The Annual Review*, vol. v, pp. 379–81. Beckford possessed a copy of Malkin's *Memoirs* and annotated it thus:

'Surely the receiver and disseminator of such trash is as bad as the thief who seems to have stolen them from the walls of Bedlam.'

36 The following passage is representative:

His mother had been conversing with him on the happiness and advantage of a virtuous life, as connected with the prospect of a world to come. Thomas, after having interchanged many remarks on the subject, with a strong expression of interest, and in a high tone of animation, exclaimed, 'Do you know, Mama, that what we have been talking of makes me almost wish not to live long, that I may have the pleasure of mounting!' He spoke this with unusual energy, and a countenance strongly lighted up with a marked emphasis in the conclusion, raising his hand above his head, and following it with uplifted eyes. He seemed for the moment to be raised to a high pitch of enthusiasm.

37 J. Aikin and A.L. Barbauld, *Evenings at Home*, 6 vols (London: J. Johnson, 1792–6); S. Trimmer, *A Description of a Set of Prints for English History; contained in a set of easy lessons*, 2 vols (London: John Marshall, [1792]); P. Wakefield, *Mental Improvement: or, The beauties and wonders of nature and art. In a series of instructive conversations* (1794); the *Book of Quadrupeds* could be one of many; the *Illustrious Heads* I have failed to identify, but it seems probable that it was a collection of portraits with texts of exemplary lives. Cf. Lamb's letter to Coleridge (23 October 1802), quoted on p.247.

38 The complete text of the letter is given by David Erdman, who first recognized its significance, in his essay, 'Coleridge, Wordsworth, and the Wedgwood Fund', *Bulletin of the New York Public Library*, vol.60 (1956). The original manuscript is in the Abinger Collection.

Erdman's argument – that Wedgwood unwittingly provoked Wordsworth to reflect as never before on how it is that we grow as persons and minds, and thus sowed the seeds for *The Prelude* – seems to me entirely convincing: of the same cohering order as Trilling's connecting Keats's response to Godwinian rationalism and his insights into Negative Capability.

39 The utilitarians were all keen to anatomize the processes of early learning and the formation of mind. Cf. James Mill:

It appears to us that few biographers have the same opinions which we have formed respecting the importance of the early part of life. When a man has risen to great intellectual or moral eminence, the process by which his mind was formed is one of the most instructive circumstances which can be unveiled to mankind.

Mill argued for the importance of 'the most minute information' (A. Bain, *James Mill, A Biography*, 1882, p. 57), and John
Bowring wrote: 'It were well if anecdotes of childhood were most
diligently collected; and if the seemingly unimportant events of
early life were more thoughtfully watched and studied, both by
parents and observers' (*Memoirs*, p. 17). Carlyle argued that 'it is
the duty of all men . . . to note-down with accuracy the
characteristic circumstances of their Education, what furthered,
what hindered, what in any way modified it' (*Sartor Resartus*,
bk 2, ch. 2).

40 By 1798, according to Coleridge, Wedgwood 'expressed a very
indifferent opinion' of Wordsworth. See M. Moorman, *Wordsworth, The Early Years* (Oxford: Clarendon Press, 1957), p. 337.

41 Letter of 21 May 1799. It is worth noting that Coleridge, despite
marginal reservations, had been captivated by the Edgeworths'
Practical Education, and that on meeting Tom Wedgwood for
the first time he wrote of him: 'He possesses the *finest*, the *subtlest*
mind and taste I have ever yet met with'.

42 Muriel Jaeger, *Before Victoria* (London: Chatto & Windus,
1956), ch. 5.

43 In September 1795, William and Dorothy became foster-
parents to two-year-old Basil, the son of their friend Basil
Montagu, whom Wordsworth described as 'very generous but
. . . the arrantest Mar-plan that ever lived'. It was Basil junior
who inspired Wordsworth's 'Anecdote for Fathers'.

44 Cruikshank uses a similar set of images in his satire on 'The Age
of Intellect': see the cameo of the child and grandmother
discussing the evacuation of eggs in *Scraps and Sketches* (May
1828), reproduced in R.A. Vogler, *Graphic Works of George
Cruikshank* (New York: Dover Books, 1979).

45 *The Prelude*, bk V (1850 text), ll. 332–6.

46 ibid., ll. 341–5.

47 Both Carlyle, in *Sartor Resartus*, and Dickens, in *Dombey and
Son* and elsewhere, use this image of the institution as a kind of
'hot-house' in which the child-plant is brought on too fast by
force-feeding in an artificially controlled and *enclosed* environment. Tom Wedgwood specified: 'The child must never go out
of doors or leave his own apartment'. He himself seems to have
had a life-long neurotic need for such artificial enclosure; in
December 1799 Josiah described him as living in a sealed room,
with double-glazing and double doors, in a temperature maintained at a constant 70°F. He also spent time as a patient in Dr
Beddoes' Pneumatic Institute in Bristol, a short-lived experiment in the treatment of respiratory diseases, to which Tom had
donated £10,000. For a wry comment on hot-houses and

untimely death, see Bewick, *Memoir* (1860), p. 29.

48 *The Prelude*, bk V, ll. 343–6.

49 ibid., ll. 364–7. On this paragraph, Francis Hastings Doyle had this to say:

> This passage, touched as it is with a flavour of wholesome bitterness, is eminently interesting and eminently wise. It is moreover, so far as I know, the first distinct protest against those Aikens's and Edgeworth's, who, deceived by their own fluent plausibilities, set themselves to the unpromising task of reaping corn fit to make bread, and gathering ripe fruit, in the early spring. The great aspiring faculties of wonder and reverence, together with the great creative faculty of the imagination, are apt to sicken and wither away, unless cultivated at the proper season. . . . But this sort of knowledge we owe, in no small degree, to Wordsworth, and to the men whom Wordsworth influenced. (*Lectures on Poetry*, second series, 1877, p. 33)

50 For a single-minded pursuit of this goal, see *Practical Education*, chs XII and XIII.

51 Carlyle, Scott, Dickens and Ruskin are the best-known representatives of this 'conservatism', but see the example of Henry Cole, founder of what is now the Victoria and Albert Museum: 'The Making of *The Home Treasury*', in *Children's Literature*, ed. F. Butler (New Haven and London: Yale University Press, 1980), pp. 35–52.

52 *The Prelude*, bk V, ll. 368–9.

53 ibid., ll. 385–8.

54 ibid., ll. 436–40.

55 ibid., ll. 447–9.

56 *Letters*, p. 42.

57 *The Prelude*, bk V, ll. 479–81.

58 Letter endorsed 16 October 1797.

59 *The Prelude*, bk V, ll. 508–15.

60 ibid., ll. 517–19; (1850 text), ll. 492–5.

61 ibid., ll. 530–1; (1850 text), ll. 506–7.

62 Wordsworth, *Memoirs*, vol. 1, p. 125. Cf. *The Prelude*, bk V (1799 text), ll. 411–17; Jean Paul Richter, *Flegeljahre* (1804); and Maria Edgeworth, 'Forester', in *Moral Tales*.

63 *The Prelude*, bk V, ll. 543–6, 552–3.

64 By 'philosophy' Wordsworth intends 'experimental philosophy' – what would now be defined as empirical and specifically behaviourist.

65 *The Prelude*, bk V, ll. 553–7.

66 Stanley Cavell, 'The availability of Wittgenstein's later philosophy', in *Wittgenstein, The Philosophical Investigations*, ed. G. Pitcher (New York: Doubleday, 1966), p. 183.
67 *The Family Reunion* (London: Faber & Faber, 1939), p. 28.
68 *The Prelude*, bk V, ll. 546–7.
69 Cavell, op.cit., p. 160.
70 'Wordsworth and the rabbis', in *The Opposing Self* (London: Secker & Warburg, 1955).
71 Doyle, op.cit., p. 31.

AFTERWORD

This brief survey of books for eighteenth-century children, and of certain related questions, has been ruthlessly selective: I am aware of having left out many texts that could be said to merit attention, but I have tried to confine the discussion to texts that are currently available, either because they have never been out of print or because they have been reprinted in recent years.

As for the underground tradition of romance and fantasy, I have contented myself with charting the enthusiasms of a variety of remarkable readers through the century. I have offered virtually no interpretation of any of the tales. A larger question nevertheless insists on an airing: why all this fuss over approval or disapproval of little stories enjoyed by young and/or unsophisticated readers? Tales of anthropomorphic cats, of a hypersomniac girl in a tangle of brambles, of 'so many dragons, so many giants, so many unheard-of adventures . . . so many and such monstrous absurdities'! A tale, for example, of twin brothers, separated at birth by melodramatic calamity, that left one of them to be reared in the wild by bears! Harvey Darton has written of this story, *Valentine and Orson*, that it was 'translated very early from the French, and probably printed and published by [Wynkyn] de Worde'; that 'dated versions appeared in 1637, 1649, 1664, 1667, 1680 (two), 1682, 1685, 1688, 1694, 1696'; and that 'eighteenth century . . . chapbook editions . . . have been conjecturally dated 1710, 1750, 1790'.[1] He observes that it was 'one of the most popular of all the Romances', and then he offers his extraordinary judgement that it is 'intricate and dull as a story'. Intricate some versions may be, but dull?

The brothers are twins, as alike genetically as may be, and

their separation at birth is simply the result of an arbitrary
accident, of mere chance, with no rhyme or reason to it. They
go, or are taken, their several ways, and duly grow up. Or do
they? Valentine acquires all the fine graces and talents of the
courtly ideal, while Orson becomes a bear-man, a man-bear.
From another point of view – and both are present in the tale –
Valentine becomes a cissy, while Orson preserves all the
'natural' virtue of the 'noble savage'. The relationship
between them when they finally meet up with each other – and
we, the readers, need them so to meet – is extremely tense, and
incorporates our realization that when they fight a duel, each
is attacking what is, in effect, a latent and as yet unrealized part
of his own self. As with Quixote and Sancho Panza, there is a
richly suggestive balancing, a nervous equilibrium. Neither
part or party is complete without the other: each then has to
learn to value that part of the self which he sees so vividly
incorporated in the other, but which has hitherto been denied
in himself. At the same time there is unavoidable conflict
between Culture and Nature. Part of the truth of the tale, and
it is never a dull truth, is that we only become whole when the
respective claims of Valentine and Orson are properly
recognized. Or, to borrow a phrase from Geoffrey Hartman,
'Apollo retrieves his garland by hobnobbing with hobgoblin'.
The final wisdom of the tale is that it is the wild man who has
to be acknowledged and allowed to enter into the heritage of
human civilization.[2]

Underlying all the old tale's drama of the quest for
'wholeness' are two other even deeper questions, left quietly
implicit: who would I 'be' if I hadn't been 'me'? What is it that
is distinctively human about us? And undeniably the tale
embodies G.K. Chesterton's 'three great paradoxes by which
we live':

Fairy tales are the only true accounts that man has ever
given of his destiny. 'Jack the Giant-Killer' is the
embodiment of the first . . . the paradox of courage: the
paradox which says, 'You must defy the thing that is

terrifying; unless you are frightened you are not brave.'
'Cinderella' is the second. . . . Humility which says,
'Look for the best in the thing, ignorant of its merit. . . .'
And 'Beauty and the Beast' is the third: the paradox of
Faith – the absolutely necessary and wildly unreasonable
maxim which says . . . 'You must love the thing first and
make it lovable afterwards.'[3]

The distinctive virtue of *Valentine and Orson*, a story whose
meanings are always implicit, tucked away deep down in the
narrative, is that it can bring us to 'know feelingly' such
things, long before we can *think* them, let alone articulate our
thoughts. For the tale is the purest manifestation of the fact
that 'art' offers its gifts to us below and before thought: pre-
conceptually, pre-critically, pre-consciously. All we have to
do is to allow ourselves to be possessed and so disappear into
this other 'reality' which is never mediated as philosophy, or
as morality, or as political theory, but rather as 'virtual'
experience.

It is, then, one of the ironies of our cultural history that
almost as soon as the 'fairy-tale' was rehabilitated and allowed
into more lives, as soon as it emerged from the hedgerows or
from below stairs, the itch to 'understand' battened on it, and
determined readers began to search for positivist and reductive explanations of meaning. In the nineteenth century many
of these efforts to reduce fiction to something other than itself
came to rest on natural phenomena – sunrise and sunset, the
seasons, and especially winter–death and spring–rebirth.
More recently, since Freud, we have allowed ourselves to be
infatuated by psychoanalytic explanation; in extreme cases, as
in Fromm's notorious reading[4] of *Red Riding Hood*, every
element of the tale is drained dry, and forced to yield up its
'meaning', to give up its ghost – the little girl's hood, for
example, signifies menstruation. And of course, it is simply
not true: we know that Fromm is perversely wrong, because
before he offered his 'explanation', we did not 'know' it. But
every time that someone says something true about such a

tale, we recognize it as true, simply because we already 'knew' it before they said it.[5]

As adults we come to know that as we return to these tales, and switch off all the intellectual fads of the past two hundred years, we journey both back and forwards, into another place; and on our return, when we have 'come out', we know that we have been somewhere else; out, into, back to, a deeper, less 'knowing', more protean place, not unlike that state of being that William James tried to give an account and a legitimation of in his remarkable lecture, 'On a Certain Blindness in Human Beings'.[6]

But one question remains. Do the vicarious experiences of cruelty, of terror, of rejection, of the monstrous, cause emotional damage to the sensitive child? Of all the eighteenth-century objections to fantasy, this is the one that has persisted most tenaciously into our own time. One of the wisest readers of these tales, W.H. Auden, concluded:

> As to fears, there are, I think, well-authenticated cases of children being dangerously terrified by some fairy story. Often, however, this arises from the child having heard the story only once. Familiarity with the story by repetition turns the pain of fear into the pleasure of a fear faced and mastered.[7]

Auden's recognition and acceptance of the paradoxical satisfactions of 'a fear faced and mastered' is, I suggest, unlikely to have satisfied any such extreme rationalist as Edgeworth or Day, let alone Godwin. And the last hundred years have seen sporadic outbreaks of 'the dream of reason' committed to a mental or moral hygiene in the name of a more rational society. When the hard-line students of child-behaviour of post-revolutionary Russia ushered in yet another dawn of reason one of their first targets was the fairy-tale. Kornei Chukovsky has charted this particular phase of social-realist positivism in vivid, and sometimes hilarious detail. He had no difficulty in identifying his enemies in the struggle for the child's soul, for their theory of knowledge was so conspicuously philistine. But the itch to deny the child's right to a rich and fructifying fantasy-life, the itch to force the child to 'be sensible', to be 'realistic', to 'grow up', is a disease that many otherwise well-meaning adults are prone to. The fact that we *mean* well is no justification, for in so doing we deny essential meanings;

> Even after Michael was interviewed about his toy robot, he wrote this: 'Thunder Tom is King of the Robots. One day there was a robot battle. . . .'
> 'This is O.K.,' Mrs Howard said when she heard Michael's story. 'But why don't you write the truth about your robot?'
> She asked Michael questions and listened to his answers. Soon he'd launched into a detailed account of how he'd won Thunder Tom by getting good grades.[9]

Such a teacherly intervention in the 1970s may serve to recall Wordsworth's words:

> the tutors of our youth,
> The guides, the wardens of our faculties,
> And stewards of our labour, watchful men
> And skilful in the usury of time,
> Sages who in their prescience would control
> All accidents, and to the very road
> Which they have fashioned would confine us down,
> Like engines; when will they be taught
> That in the unreasoning progress of the world
> A wiser spirit is at work for us,
> A better eye than theirs, most prodigal
> Of blessings, and most studious of our good,
> Even in what seem our most unfruitful hours?[10]

From the same context – a liberal and well-meaning American primary school in which children are being encouraged to pay special attention to the craft of writing – one draws evidence of the significant collocation of an attitude to language that derives ultimately from John Locke and of an implicit view of fantasy as something inherently trivial, merely 'personal', even regressive: if indeed the protean world of wonders is by now reduced to the banality of 'gum-drop land' then we are entitled to talk of deprivation: 'the hungry sheep look up and are not fed'!

The teacher

> believes when children write about their dog's hurt foot, or their baby sister, they will revise more than if they write make-believe stories about gum-drop land. These are her reasons:
>
> 1 When children have something *real* [*sic*] to write about, they have a standard of measurement (truth) [*sic*] which motivates them to find the precise word, to achieve the right tone.
> 2 When children know and care about their subject, they want to communicate it.
> 3 Real experience [*sic*] can fit onto half a page . . . stories often take pages to develop. Shorter pieces are more revisable.[11]

The Edgeworthian, empiricist, view of what can be said to constitute 'reality' clearly persists; but, fortunately for the deeper health of young readers and listeners, the Wordworthian view will always have the energy and the will to challenge it, and to appeal to the larger, more resonant, possibility. Hazlitt's prophecy has proved to be prescient: 'Society, by degrees, is constructed into a machine that carries us safely and insipidly from one end of life to the other, in a very comfortable prose style',[12] and the continuing influence of those who 'prose' makes it all the more necesary that we should take it upon ourselves to work as 'custodians of the real world which, in our more perceptive moments, we know to be the magic one'.[13]

If, meanwhile, we feel uneasy in our unempirical belief, we can take consolation and strength from a distinguished neuro-physiologist:

> There is surely a deep biological reason for the importance of fiction: that it states and considers alternative

possible realities – allowing escape from the prison of current fact . . . it is only by considering what might be that we can change effectively what is, or predict what is likely to be. Fiction has the immense biological significance of allowing behaviour to follow plans removed from, though related sometimes in subtle ways to, worldly events.[14]

In a bleak exile, Ovid, the elegant and urbane, witty and hyper-sophisticated Roman poet, slowly acquires a grasp of the language of the primitive people into whose barbaric world he has been thrust; in David Malouf's retelling of the story, Ovid's deeper self is slowly and painfully reborn, and he himself experiences the profound mystery of metamorphosis. The primary agent of his transformation is an old illiterate peasant, with whom the poet is lodged:

> Listening to the old man now, telling his stories in our little yard, I know what the different voices signify: they are the north wind, they are wolves, they are giants, they are the ghosts of warriors, they are a shinbone, a severed head, they are the bottom of the sea. The old man's stories are fabulous beyond anything I have retold from the Greeks; but savage, a form of extravagant play that explains nothing, but speaks straight out of the nightmare landscape of this place and my dream journeys across it. Our civilized fables that account so elegantly for what we see and know seem so feeble beside these elaborate and absurd jokes the old man mutters over. They are like winter here. They fill the world. They make the head buzz, they numb the blood. They seem absolutely true and yet they explain nothing. I begin to see briefly, in snatches, how this old man, my friend, might see the world. It is astonishing. Bare, cruel, terrible, comic. And yet daily he seems nobler and more gentle than any Roman I have known.[15]

NOTES AND REFERENCES

1 F.J. Harvey Darton, *Children's Books in England*, 2nd edn (Cambridge: Cambridge University Press, 1958), p.83.

2 And that heritage, now modified by his 'entry', will then contain that which he has restored to it. Civilization will be enlarged by its recognition of what he has to offer, and by its acceptance of it.

3 See Chapter Two, n.25.

4 E. Fromm, *The Forgotten Language: An Introduction to the Understanding of Dreams, Fairy Tales, and Myths* (New York: Holt, Rinehart & Winston, 1976); typical of Fromm's positivism is his claim that 'Most of the symbolism in this tale can be understood without difficulty'.

5 Cf. De Quincey:
> It is the grandeur of all truth . . . that it is never absolutely novel to the meanest of minds: it exists eternally by way of germ or latent principle in the lowest as in the highest, needing to be developed, but never to be planted. (*North British Review*, August 1848)

6 A classic critique of the ways in which empiricist ways of knowing fail to recognize valuable forms of life.

7 'Grimm and Andersen', in *Forewords and Afterwards* (London: Faber & Faber, 1973), p.200. Auden's essay offers one of the few attempts to characterize the elements of artful perversity that separate Andersen from the true folk-tradition with which he is usually identified.

8 Kornei Chukovsky, *Two to Five* (Berkeley: University of California Press, 1968), ch.5.

9 Lucy M. Calkins, 'The Craft of Writing', *Teacher Magazine* (October 1980).

10 *The Prelude*, bk V, ll.376ff.

11 L.M. Calkins, 'Writing', *The Principal* (June 1980).

12 Hazlitt, 'On Poetry in General', in *Lectures on the English Poets* (1818).

13 William Golding, 'Custodians of the real', *The Listener* (14 November 1974), p.646. Cf. Octave Mannoni, *Clefs pour l'Imaginaire* (Paris: Seuil, 1969).

14 R.L. Gregory in *New Society* (23 May 1974).

15 David Malouf, *An Imaginary Life* (London: Picador, 1981), p. 58. Cf. *The Prelude*, bk XII, ll.161ff. and 264ff.

INDEX

Ginger, John, 93
Godwin, Mrs Mary Jane, 244–6, 258, 265n, 266n
Godwin, William, xvii, 46, 244–57, 264n
Golding, William, 307n
Goldsmith, Oliver, 93–7, 180, 242
Gomme, Sir George, 31
Goody Two-Shoes: see History of Little Goody Two-Shoes
Gosse, Edmund, 286
Governess, The, 89–93, 125, 195–6, 206n, 243
Graves, Richard, 48
Graves, Robert, 261
Gray, Thomas, 176
Grey, Jill, 89, 112n
Grimm, Jacob and Wilhelm, xv, xvi, 293nn, 307n
Grose, Francis, 17, 18
Grub Street Journal, 89
Gulliver's Travels, 29, 136, 189, 269
Guy of Warwick, 34, 38, 46, 66n, 87, 88

Hack, Maria, 197
Hadley, George, 24
Hall, Mrs S.C., 134
Hamlet, 95
Hanway, Jonas, 226
Harding, D.W., 293n
Harrington, 130, 138
Harry and Lucy, 124, 127, 139–40, 154, 202, 292
Hartley, Cecil, 101
Hartley, David, 123, 210
Hartmann, Geoffrey, 301
Harwood, Dr Edward, 43
Hawkesworth, John, 8
Hazlitt, William, 8, 44, 63, 206, 242, 305
Heaney, Seamus, 60n, 293n
Helen, 132, 167–70
Helvétius, Claude-Adrien, 3, 132
Herder, Johann Gottfried von, xiv
Hervey, John, 213
Hewitt, M., 227

Hickathrift, 31, 34, 38, 41, 48, 49, 57, 59, 60, 68n, 69n, 87, 89, 293n
Histoires ou Contes du temps passé, 13, 44, 45, 68n, 196
History of Genesis, 33
History of Little Goody Two-Shoes, The, 36, 50, 57, 58, 93–9, 158, 248
History of the Robins, The: see Fabulous Histories
Hogarth, William, 158
Holiday House, 294n
Holloway, John, 215
'Holy Thursday', 223–6
Homer, 15, 67n, 86, 243, 256, 269
Hooke, Robert, 54, 70n
Horace, 35
Horae Lyricae, 75, 215
Hughes, Mary, 137–8
Hughes, Ted, 66n
Hunt, Leigh, 158, 159, 262
Hunt, Thornton, 262–3
Hunter, John, 212
Hurd, Richard, xv, 176
Hymns in Prose for Children, 208, 215–20, 229, 235–7

Infant's Friend, The, 249
Instructions for the Education of a Daughter, 89
Island in the Moon, An, 208–14

Jack the Giant-Killer, 32, 41, 42, 43, 48, 49, 54, 56, 57, 58, 60, 63, 88, 199, 266n, 282, 301
Jacobite's Journal, 87
Jakobson, Roman, 294n
James, William, 303
Jarrell, Randall, 244
Jeffrey, Francis, Lord, 263
Jemima Placid, 99
Job, Book of, 93, 209
John Woodvil, 254, 261
Johnes, Thomas, 275
'Johnny Armstrong', 60, 95
Johnson, Joseph, 97, 210, 214, 229, 275

INDEX

Johnson, Samuel, 11, 17, 36, 42,
44, 47, 55, 72, 73, 110, 126,
175, 188, 197, 215, 265n, 271
Joseph Andrews, 88
Joyce, Jeremiah, 127, 129, 214
Juvenile Plutarch, The, 295n

Keats, John, 20n, 166, 284, 294n,
296n
Keir, James, 120, 145–6, 149–50,
157, 166
Kendrew, James, 28
Kenrick, William, 114
Kingsley, Charles, 226
Knox, Vicesimus, 4, 177, 204,
221
'Kubla Khan', 293n

La Fontaine, 116
Lackington, Joseph, 178
Lamb, Charles, xv, xvii, 92, 158,
181, 239n, 241–4, 245, 247–8,
254–63, 264n, 266n
Lamb, Mary, 243, 244, 257
Landor, W.S., 265n
Lansdowne, Lady, 148
Les Veillées du Château, 103
*Lessons for Children from Two to
Three Years Old*, 101, 122,
133–4
Letters for Literary Ladies, 160
*Life and Opinions of Tristram
Shandy*, 1, 38, 208, 265n
Life of Chaucer, 252
Linnaeus, 103
Litchfield, R.B., 171n
Little Jack, 126
Little Pretty Pocket Book, A,
81–6, 228
'livrets de colportage', 64n
Livy, 86
Lloyd, R., 176
Locke, Don, 265n
Locke, John, xvi, 1–11, 73, 79, 81,
108, 110, 117, 118, 123, 128,
132, 145, 148, 178, 213, 251,
265n, 304
Lofft, Capel, 11

Looking Glass, The or *History of a
Young Artist*, 126
Looking Glass for the Mind, 103
Lovechild, Mrs, 249
Love's Labour's Lost, 5
Lowes, J.L., 293n
Lucas, E.V., 241, 258
Lunar Society, 120, 126, 139, 145,
278

Macbeth, 95, 180
MacDonald, George, 206n
Malkin, Benjamin Heath, 274–8,
280, 295n
Malkin, Thomas Williams, 274–8,
280, 281, 295n, 296n
Malouf, David, 306
Mansfield Park, 110
Marcet, Mrs, 127, 129, 214
Marriage of Heaven and Hell, 228
Martin, John, 260
*Memoirs of Richard Lovell
Edgeworth*, 123, 141n, 148, 154
Memoirs of Thomas Bewick, 136,
142n, 298
Mental Improvement, 276n, 296n
Metamorphoses, 16
Metamorphoses, The, 137–8
Midsummer Night's Dream, A,
17
Midwife, The, 93
Mill, James, 296n
Mill, J.S., 63
Milnes, Esther, 154, 159
Milton, John, 32, 60, 269
Molyneux, William, 1
Montagu, Basil, 278
Montaigne, Michel de, 149
Montgomery, James, 239n
Monthly Magazine, 275
Monthly Review, 277
Moody, Christopher Lake, 277
Moral Tales, 160–1
More, Hannah, 98, 145
Morgan, Edwin, 60
Morgann, Maurice, xv, 135, 174,
177, 178–82, 234
'Mr Barlow', 172n